THE CURIOUS DREAMER'S
PRACTICAL GUIDE
TO
DREAM
INTERPRETATION

**A Step-by-Step Approach to Understand
Your Dreams and Improve Your Life**

NANCY WAGAMAN

ISBN: 978-0-9985459-1-2 (print)
ISBN: 978-0-9985459-0-5 (ebook)
Library of Congress Control Number: 2017903278
Printed in the U.S.A.
www.TheCuriousDreamer.com
10 9 8 7 6 5 4 3 2 1

To the hero in every one of us
who is brave enough to take the plunge
and look within.

Contents

CONTENTS

About This Book

If you want to understand the meaning of your dreams, *The Curious Dreamer's Practical Guide to Dream Interpretation* was written for you. As your personal dream coach in a book, this guide walks you step-by-step through interpreting your dreams and using them to improve your life. This practical approach to dream interpretation is rooted in applied psychology and intuition and is based on my experience of what works well in getting to the heart of dream meaning. I'm pleased to share the dream interpretation process, tips, and analysis tools I developed during years of professional dream work. I encourage you to explore the book and experiment with the various techniques as you customize your own dream interpretation experience.

The Practical Goal of Dream Interpretation

The practical goal of dream interpretation, as I see it, is to find the value in each dream so you can then apply it to improve yourself and your life. A dream's value may be profound and life changing, or as simple as the realization that eating sweets too close to bedtime can trigger nightmares. Whatever you learn from a dream you can use in a positive way. So, as you read, keep this objective ever in the forefront of your mind:

Find the value in your dreams.

How to Read This Book

Each part of this book forms the foundation for the next part, so be sure to read the parts in order from the beginning. Jumping right into interpreting dreams before learning the essentials about dreams would be like studying Advanced French before you've studied Beginning French. This book contains five main parts, followed by a quick reference and a glossary:

Part I: The Keys to Dream Interpretation (p. 1)

Essentials you need to know before interpreting dreams, which will form a foundation for all of your dream work.

Part II: How to Interpret Dreams (p. 69)
The step-by-step process for interpreting dreams—including clear, detailed instructions.

Part III: Dream Analysis Toolkit (p. 101)
A wide variety of techniques for exploring your dream's meaning as deeply as you choose.

Part IV: Dream Action Toolkit (p. 215)
A powerful set of techniques for following up on your dream—to resolve issues that came up in your dream and to use what you learned for personal growth, transformation, and healing.

Part V: Dreams Interpreted (p. 277)
Examples of dreams submitted to me for professional interpretation, along with my interpretations, feedback from the clients, and explanations of relevant dream analysis techniques for each dream.

Quick Reference (p. 299)
A condensed form of the dream interpretation process to guide you through the steps at a glance.

Glossary (p. 303)
Definitions of key terms as they are used in this book.

Style and Usage Notes
This book's casual, conversational style is intended to make it easy to read and understand.

Because this is intended as a reference book, you may notice some topics are covered more than once, each in a different way. For example, intuition is discussed as a part of "A Model of Consciousness" (p. 10) and again in greater depth in the chapter titled "Intuition: Your Dream Translator" (p. 33).

When writing in first-person singular in this book, I usually refer to one gender (for example, either "she" or "he") instead of referring to both every time ("he or she"). Here are some examples of this usage: "Dream meaning is specific to each dreamer and his situation," and "Every dreamer is the ultimate authority on the meaning of her own dreams."

For the purposes of this book, "real life" to refers to a person's waking life—although what happens in the dream state is technically also part of real life, in that it's one aspect of the dreamer's personal experience.

PART I

THE KEYS TO DREAM INTERPRETATION

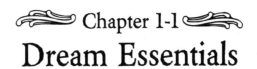

Chapter 1-1
Dream Essentials

In This Chapter:

Dreams can be sources of powerful, life-transforming information if you pay attention to their meanings. They provide glimpses of yourself and your life that you might not otherwise see: your deepest desires, untapped potential, self-defeating patterns, and opportunities for greater happiness. Locked within your dreams are empowering insights, waiting to be discovered like your own personal buried treasure.

Because dream meanings are individual to each person, you must look within yourself to find true dream meaning. Although you may look to external sources for ideas about possible meanings, ultimately you must look inward and rely on your own intuition to confirm dream meaning. This book shows you how.

Introduction to Dream Interpretation

Dream interpretation begins with a subjective dream—a story. Then, in some mysterious way, you extract some meaning or message from the dream. "Something happens" and you suddenly understand the dream's meaning. But how?

Taking the Mystery Out of Dream Interpretation

The process of translating dream symbolism into meaning remains mysterious to many of us. Often it's not even clear where to start when interpreting a dream, especially when the dream doesn't seem to make any sense. In this book I attempt to take the mystery out of the dream interpretation process by suggesting a practical approach, clearly presented with step-by-step instructions. However, before starting to use it, you'll need to learn some essentials about dreams and dream interpretation. Here's how I suggest you use this book to learn this practical approach most effectively:

1. Learn the dream fundamentals in "Part I: The Keys to Dream Interpretation" (p. 1). Key topics including the human consciousness, the roles of analysis and intuition, how to recognize the true meaning of a dream, dream types and what they reveal, which dreams to ignore, and how to enhance dream recall.
2. Follow the step-by-step dream interpretation process in "Part II: How to Interpret Dreams" (p. 69) (summarized in "Quick Reference," p. 299), and then choose from the techniques in "Part III: Dream Analysis Toolkit" (p. 101) and "Part IV: Dream Action Toolkit" (p. 215) to customize your interpretation and follow-up process.
3. Plunge as deeply into your dream meaning as you wish. The framework presented here enables you to identify a dream's basic meaning or to explore every juicy bit of symbolism.
4. All the while, keep this goal in mind: Find the value in each dream and use it to improve yourself and your life.

Lay the Foundation First

What you'll learn in this first chapter will lay the foundation for all of your dream interpretation work later. Learning to interpret dreams is a bit like learning a new language, for which you first need to learn the pronunciation of each letter, the meanings of common words, and the grammar rules before you can speak the language well. Likewise, before you can speak the language of dreams well, you need to understand how dreams tend to speak, how to recognize certain clues in dreams, how to get the most from your dream interpretation, and pitfalls to avoid. So, in this chapter I share insights about dreams that I wish I'd understood when I started interpreting my own dreams as a young person. I share these with you in the hope that you can hit the ground running instead of having to learn the hard way.

What Are Dreams?

There is no single agreed-upon answer about what dreams are or why we have them. Dreams have been described as desires fulfilled, deepest fears played out, playtime for the subconscious mind, a cleaning out of residues from the previous day, stories created by the dreamer to occupy sleep time, random firings at brain synapses, or explorations of nonphysical levels of existence, among other descriptions. Dreams may happen for a reason, or may not. Dream researchers continue to make intriguing discoveries about dreaming and about the brain during dreaming. However, although research has been nibbling away at the mysteries, much about dreams still remains beyond the reaches of science.

Clues from the Content of Dreams

The content of dreams suggests a lot about them, even if it doesn't explain exactly why they occur. During dreams, the subconscious mind often seems to create its own version of a story from the dreamer's waking life or mind. Sometimes a dream is a close-up snapshot of a recent real-life situation, and other times a dream may revisit a long-lost memory or feeling, possibly pointing to some unfinished business from the past. Occasionally, a dream may chase you through the night, threatening you with your worst fear. So, the thread of similarity that runs through many dreams is that they often seem to be related to something that's on your subconscious mind at the time of the dream.

Some dreams convey a clear sense of urgency or importance. Occasionally a dream practically hits you over the head to get your attention. An epic story line, larger-than-life character, or overwhelming emotion might grab you and refuse to let go. Other times, you might awaken from a dream with a strong sense that you need to pay attention to it. So, dreams also often contain cues conveying the relative importance of their subject matter.

Dreamers often report strong emotions during dreams—emotions interpreted as positive, such as courage or pride—or emotions interpreted as negative, such as fear, anger, or frustration. You may notice that you sometimes experience emotions even more deeply during the dream state than while awake. So, these strong dream emotions may indicate a subject matter that is particularly important to you or that you care about deeply—a situation or topic that triggers a big emotional response within you.

Dreams often portray either something desired or pleasant—or something feared, disliked, or unpleasant. In other words, dreams tend to devote a lot of their content to creating desired experiences, such as positive relationships and having fun—and to undesired experiences, such as missing an exam or forgetting to wear clothes outside the house. So, the nature of dream content may suggest that one role of dreams is to help us figure out how to create more desired and fewer undesired experiences in our waking lives.

A Practical Focus

While science continues to explore questions about the nature of dreams and why we dream, we dreamers are still pondering the meanings of the images that dance across our minds each night. I suggest a practical focus: rather than spending time wondering why you had a particular dream or where it came from, I suggest that your time is better spent finding the value in each dream. If you can find a way to make sense of your dreams so that you can use them in a positive and productive way, why wouldn't you?

Finding the Value in Dreams

I propose an ultimate goal of dream interpretation as "finding the value in each dream," rather than analyzing just for the sake of analysis. Finding value in a dream means gleaning some useful meaning from each dream that can help you improve your life or your state of being. For example, dreams can point the way out of old patterns and into new opportunity. They can reveal solutions to problems in your personal relationships. Dreams can also suggest changes in your way of thinking that make life a much more pleasant experience. Virtually every dream offers some value, even if it's simply the realization that you really don't like spiders or that you currently are craving ice cream.

If you pay attention to your dreams, they can help you:

- Better understand yourself and your needs.
- Get answers to important questions.
- Clarify life purpose and direction.
- Discover creative ideas and visions.
- Help resolve issues from the past.
- Resolve fears and move ahead.
- Identify important health conditions.
- Learn how to reduce stress in your life.

Here's an example of focusing on the value of a dream rather than analyzing just for the sake of analysis. After dreaming about a purple giraffe, you realize that the giraffe represents your sister-in-law. The fact that she showed up in your dream as a giraffe provides an interesting insight into how your subconscious mind works. However, this way of thinking about your sister-in-law is not particularly helpful in improving your relationship with her. If you ask yourself, "What is the value here?" and "How can I use this dream in a positive way?", you may begin to see the true value in the dream. Perhaps the dream is highlighting the way you judge your sister-in-law as too eccentric—the exact judgment that is holding you back from enjoying your relationship with her. If you can release your judgment of her and instead celebrate her gifts and uniqueness, you can create a much more positive experience for yourself (and perhaps also for her) whenever you two interact.

Dreams Are a Window into Your Subconscious Mind

Because dreams provide a connection into your subconscious mind, they offer otherwise rare insights into your subconscious dynamics. A dream can convey feelings, thoughts, ideas, desires, and other psychological factors that may lie buried when you're awake.

You may be surprised to discover what your dreams reveal about what's going on within your subconscious mind. Subconscious factors such as beliefs, judgments, fears, and biases have great influence on your conscious mind. These factors can negatively influence your thoughts, behaviors, emotions, and interactions with others—without your awareness. The subconscious mind can be a tough nut to crack (it is subconscious, after all), and so it is especially convenient that your dreams provide a nightly portal directly into your subconscious mind.

In fact, dream interpretation is one of the only ways to get a clear picture of what's going on in your subconscious mind. When operating without your awareness, the dynamics of your subconscious mind can stealthily sabotage you and defeat even your greatest determination to create what you want in your life.

Dreams Tell You About You

Your dreams are *all you*. They are *your* experiences and are witnessed by *you*. In a sense, they present a pure form of information from your subconscious mind—the hidden part of you that sees and remembers all the details of your daily life, and then plays them back in its own dream language. The subconscious mind is not necessarily an ultimate authority, but it does provide a unique and often useful perspective on your life, thoughts, and feelings—offering a great counterpart to your conscious perceptions.

According to an ancient proverb, "A dream uninterpreted is like a letter unopened." Think of dreaming as like receiving nightly emails from your subconscious mind providing another perspective on what's going on within your consciousness. Dreams give you an opportunity to learn more about yourself—your desires, motivations, what's holding you back, and much more—and you can use what you learn to transform your life into a more pleasant and rewarding experience.

Dreams Often Represent Real Life

Your journey through a dream often parallels your journey through a part of your waking life—where the characters, events, and feelings in the dream echo the characters, events, and feelings in your waking life. Although the dream elements can represent something beyond their face value, your feelings during the dream are almost always similar to your actual feelings about the real-life situation to which the dream refers. Therefore, your feelings during a dream offer a huge clue to your dream's meaning. (For more about using dream feelings to uncover dream meaning, see "Chapter 3-4: TOOL: Emotion Analysis," p. 114.)

Dream Meaning Is Personal

The meaning of a particular dream depends on the individual dreamer and his situation, perspective, biases, and many other factors. Just as in waking life, your preconceptions help shape your reactions to the events you experience during dreams. In dreams, preconceptions also seem to influence which symbols the subconscious mind chooses to portray elements of real life. For example, if two people witnessed the same car crash, one of them might have a dream afterward in which the cars appear as toy cars crashing into each other on a miniature track, while the other person might dream about two airplanes crashing into each other. Your subconscious mind chooses which symbols to use in telling its dream stories, and your subconscious mind's choices of symbols can be influenced by many factors, including:

- Your personality, perceptions, preconceptions, and experiences of a particular symbol. For example, you may associate bread primarily with your mother because it brings to mind the sandwiches she used to make, while a baker might associate bread primarily with his work.
- The content and context of the particular dream. A symbol could have one meaning in your current dream and a completely different meaning in a future dream. For example, your subconscious mind might use a daisy to symbolize summer because that's the season when daisies bloom, but a few years later it might use a daisy to symbolize love because your boyfriend just gave you a bunch of daisies in real life.

- Your current thoughts and feelings. Your experiences from earlier in the day and your current thoughts can influence your dreams and the way your subconscious mind selects symbols to tell its dream story.

A Dream Can Have More Than One Meaning

A particular dream may contain multiple layers of meaning. The subconscious mind can do an amazing job of creating dreams, and it's sometimes very clever in the way it weaves a dream together. Sometimes several issues or concerns are sort of "stacked together" in a dream, layer upon layer, where one symbol represents two or more aspects of a dreamer's waking life.

One example of a dream with multiple layers of meaning is a dream about trying to walk to work with an injured foot. This dream could represent an actual foot problem the dreamer had in real life at the time, but may also represent the dreamer's difficulty in "moving forward" in his career—since feet play a key role in moving the body forward physically.

Another example is a married woman dreaming that she in a relationship again with her first boyfriend. As described by a client, this dream seemed to express the following multiple layers of meaning that reflected the dynamics within her subconscious mind at the time of the dream:

- The importance of being close to someone and enjoying that kind of close friendship, mutual encouragement, and sharing. Her relationship with her first boyfriend was the first time she experienced those feelings, and so they are strongly associated with him in her subconscious mind.
- A particular need to feel close to someone at the time of the dream, perhaps because of a challenging situation she was dealing with then.
- An appreciation of the positive aspects of her first boyfriend, such as his sense of humor and kindness.
- An acknowledgment that her husband has many positive aspects in common with her first boyfriend, such as a sense of humor and kindness.

Dreams Are Real Experiences Themselves

If you wake up from a dream and say to yourself, "It wasn't real," you are partially correct. Although the dream wasn't "real" in terms of happening on the physical level of your existence, it was real in the sense that it did happen, on some level of your awareness. You experienced it, and your experience of it was real.

Dreams are real experiences—as real as waking experiences—but they occur on non-physical levels. It's possible that the subconscious mind doesn't see much difference between waking and dreaming experiences. Both waking and dream experiences engage the mind, trigger reactions, elicit emotions, and occupy your time and energy. For example, encountering a grizzly bear in a dream would likely trigger a similar reaction within you as if you encountered one in real life. In a way, we are just as alive in our dreams as when we are awake. So, in that way, dreams are like a world in which you can experience things you couldn't—or wouldn't want to—experience in waking life. Whether the dream world is real or not, your experiences of it are real.

A Model of Consciousness

In order to understand dreams, it's helpful to first understand the context in which they occur. In other words, every dream is a product of the vibrant, active environment within you at the time of the dream. In this section, I present a model of that inner environment, based on my observations of how it seems to function. In keeping with the practical approach of this book, this is intended as a working model to facilitate dream interpretation and other inner processes.

Your Consciousness Is Your Nonphysical Self

Your **consciousness** can be described as the collective aspects of your nonphysical self, such as the mental and emotional aspects. In other words, your consciousness is the total of your nonphysical being, including all the different aspects of your inner experience.

Conscious Mind and Subconscious Mind

A basic Model of Consciousness divides the consciousness into two parts: a conscious part (of which you are aware) and a subconscious part (of which you are not aware), as shown in Figure A. The conscious part can be referred to as the **conscious mind**, which includes all aspects of your consciousness of which you are aware. Likewise, the **subconscious mind** refers to aspects of your consciousness of which you are not aware. (Note that the word "mind" in this case is used in a broader sense to refer to all levels of consciousness, not just the mental level.)

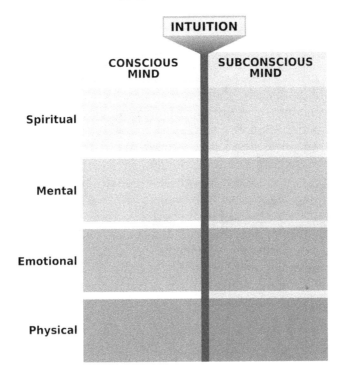

Fig. A. Model of Consciousness

In the model shown in Figure A, the conscious mind and subconscious mind are both involved in the physical, emotional, mental, and spiritual levels—or you might say that all four of those levels extend throughout both the conscious mind and subconscious mind.

The "I" in Your Consciousness

There is an aspect of you who is the "I" in "I am," the one who is reading this right now. Your "I" is the one who is speaking when you say the words, "I exist." You might think of your "I" as the one who is in charge within you.

Your "I" exists independently from the emotional, mental, subconscious, and spiritual levels within you, yet it can reside in any of those levels in any given moment. As you go through your daily life, your "I" shifts between those levels. Your "I" acts like a channel selector on a TV, tuning to different "channels" within your consciousness (physical, emotional, mental, or spiritual). In other words, in any particular moment, your "inner TV" is tuned to some "channel" within your consciousness—meaning your awareness is focused within that "channel." For example, when your channel selector is tuned to the "Emotion Channel"—meaning when your "I" is focused within the emotional level of your conscious-ness—you are feeling or expressing emotion. When your channel selector is tuned to the "Mental Channel"—meaning when your "I" is focused within your mental level—you are engaged in mental activity, such as logical thought or analysis.

Your "I" can shift from one level of the conscious mind to another at will, or even unintentionally—such as when you shift from (mental) analy-sis of a problem into experiencing (emotional) frustration. Your "I" can also straddle more than one level simultaneously. In the TV analogy, it's like receiving two different channels at once, blended together. For example, during a bubble bath you might be focusing simultaneously on both (physical) warmth and (emotional) nurturing—or when eating spa-ghetti you might be focusing simultaneously on (physical) taste and (mental) analysis of what ingredients the sauce might contain.

Consider the example in Figure B, which illustrates how your focus can shift dynamically among different areas within your consciousness:

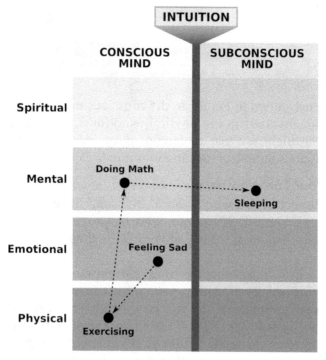

Fig. B. Model of Consciousness: Example

In Figure B, first your "I" is focused primarily within your conscious emotional level when you're feeling sad because you missed a concert you wanted to attend, then it shifts focus to your conscious physical level while exercising, then it's focused within your conscious mental level while working on math problems, and then finally it's focused within your subconscious mental level when you're asleep and you're dreaming about solving math problems (shown as "Sleeping" on the right-hand side of Figure B).

Another example in Figure C shows a different sequence of focus points. First, your "I" is focused within your conscious emotional level when you're feeling afraid of a big spider in your room, then it shifts focus to your mental level while you're learning to speak Italian, then it's focused within your physical level while you're doing laundry, and then it's focused within your subconscious emotional level when you're having a scary nightmare.

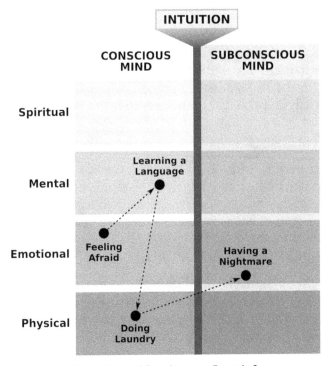

Fig. C. Model of Consciousness: Example 2

The level in which your "I" is focused—the level within which your "I" is operating—affects the way you experience things. In other words, you might experience a particular situation completely differently depending on the level within which your "I" is focused. Consider an example in which you are introduced to a new woman at work. If you are operating primarily from your physical level, you might primarily notice her (physical) warm, firm handshake and come away with a good impression of her. If you're engaging primarily from your mental level you might focus on a (mental) grammar mistake she makes and therefore judge her as inferior. If you are primarily focused in your emotional level, the (emotional) adoration in her eyes when she talks about her children might elicit the feeling within you that she is a caring person. If operating primarily from your spiritual level, you might notice the (spiritual) sense of benevolence that emanates from her and how uplifted you feel in her presence. The actual situation contains cues occuring on all four levels, but your state of mind and choice of focus determines which cues you notice—and which you choose to view as important—thereby influencing your experience of the situation and reaction to it.

The "I" aspect of your consciousness is where your personal power lies. From the perspective of your "I," you can observe and even master the levels of your consciousness. From within your "I" you can become a neutral observer, thus breaking free of mental and emotional preconceptions and other limitations. You will discover the power of your "I" more fully as you work with the techniques in the toolkits later in this book (see "Part III: Dream Analysis Toolkit," p. 101, and "Part IV: Dream Action Toolkit," p. 215).

Waking and Sleeping

While you're awake, your "I" is usually focused somewhere within the physical, emotional, mental, or spiritual levels of the conscious mind, and while you're asleep your "I" tends to be focused somewhere within those four levels of your subconscious mind. As you recall a dream after you wake up, you bring the dream from the subconscious mind into the conscious mind and store it in conscious memory.

Conscious and Subconscious Influences

You may already be aware of some ways that dynamics within your conscious mind can influence other parts of your consciousness, such as when you consciously decide to love yourself instead of judge yourself, or you decide to persevere through a scary situation regardless of your fear. Likewise, dynamics within your subconscious mind can affect other areas of your consciousness, often without your conscious awareness of their effects. For example, perhaps you've experienced a situation in which you immediately liked or disliked a person as soon as you saw them—or perhaps you've resisted trying a new kind of vegetable—without really knowing why. Chances are that your conscious mind was being influenced by dynamics within your subconscious mind. Maybe the new person was wearing orange, your least favorite color—and maybe trying a new vegetable subconsciously reminded you of your mother trying to get you to eat mushy, overcooked broccoli. One reason that dreams are such valuable resources is the insight they provide into subconscious dynamics that may be affecting or even limiting you without you realizing it.

Intuition

I think of intuition as a channel that delivers truth, resulting in a direct knowing that is independent of rational thought. Revisiting the TV analogy, intuition is like a TV channel that broadcasts intuitive insights within your consciousness—and like on your real TV, you may not receive a particular intuitive "broadcast" unless your inner TV is tuned to the "Intuition Channel" and you're paying attention to it. However, in some cases intuitive insights are so strong they seem to override all the channels, creating "Aha" moments that you can't possibly miss.

Another way to think about intuition is like a river of truth flowing through your consciousness, where the river's continual evaporation of water humidifying the air is like intuition's truth permeating your consciousness. You may not always be aware of the river's humidity in the air, but you can feel it if you pay attention to it. Likewise, you can sense intuitive insights by paying attention to them—by attuning to them. In the case of the river, you can access its water by going directly to the river and standing in it, just as you can learn to tune into your intuition by focusing into it directly (more in "Intuition: The Key to Recognizing Dream Meaning," p. 33).

A Context for Dream Interpretation

This section presents the heart of the dream interpretation process, including the dream interpretation model on which this book is based. In this section, I'll explain the key components of my dream interpretation model, how each is important, how each contributes to the dream interpretation process, and how they work together to make it more effective. These components are the nuts and bolts of the dream interpretation process presented in "Part II: How to Interpret Dreams" (p. 69). A solid understanding of them will help you along your way when you begin the process of interpreting your dreams.

The Dream Team: Dream Analysis and Intuition

Dream interpretation is more of an art than a science. You can analyze a dream and generate theories about what it might mean, but theories alone can prove ultimately fruitless without intuition to recognize which of those theoretical meanings rings true. Dream analysis and intuition are both valuable parts of the dream interpretation process, and they work hand-in-hand in the approach that I present in this book.

Intuition is the ultimate mechanism behind understanding dream meaning—experiencing that flash of recognition, the sudden sense of knowing that pervades all of your being. When you awaken from a dream, you may know immediately—intuitively—what it means, when your intuition automatically comes forward with the dream's meaning and no further interpretation is needed. But intuition may not always be as forthcoming, and it can be drowned out by the other factors in your head—such as your hopes, fears, and ego. This is where logical dream analysis can help.

When you aren't sure what a particular dream means, using analysis techniques to explore a dream can help trigger a moment of intuitive recognition. The process of analysis essentially parades a series of possible meanings past your "inner intuitive eye," each time asking it, "Is this the meaning?" and prompting your intuition to respond.

Intuition plays a dual role in dream interpretation. Dreams often have a much deeper—and sometimes completely different—meaning than the obvious one. Intuition is not only important for confirming the meaning and message of a dream as a whole, but it also plays a key role in translating specific symbols from the language of your subconscious mind into the language of your conscious mind. Because intuition is such a key part of the dream interpretation process, a full chapter of this book is dedicated to the topic (see "Chapter 1-3: Intuition: Your Dream Translator," p. 33). You can also benefit from developing your own ability to access your intuition, for use in both dream interpretation and in your daily life (see "Tips for Developing Dream Intuition," p. 39).

Dream Interpretation vs. Dream Analysis

The terms "dream interpretation" and "dream analysis" are often used interchangeably. However, for the purposes of this book I am choosing to define these two terms more specifically, in a way that further clarifies the process of understanding dreams. My definitions are not an attempt to redefine any standard definition—but instead, to form a construct that facilitates the process of extracting meaning from dreams. On other words, I'm defining these terms in a way that helps us figure out what our dreams mean.

Dream interpretation can occur in many ways, and in many modes within the consciousness. You might interpret a dream based solely on intuition, or you might focus on it mentally and analyze it systematically, or you might follow the emotion of the dream until it reveals the dream's meaning. Figure D depicts this model of dream interpretation, showing how dream interpretation can involve one or more modes of activity within the consciousness.

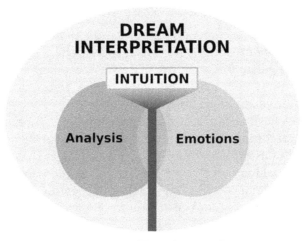

Fig. D. Model of Dream Interpretation

I think of **dream analysis** as an active mental process (driven by the mental level, as opposed to the emotional or subconscious level)—as a systematic examination of a dream, such as a logical assessment of its symbolism and structure—which may involve placing the dream into various frameworks, examining hierarchies of its symbolism, or deconstructing it in order to understand it better. I consider dream analysis to be a mental process, using the mind as a tool in the overall dream interpretation process, applying the mind to examine a dream for clues to its meaning.

I think of **dream interpretation** as the broader idea of assigning meaning to a dream or its parts—including dream analysis (an active mental process) as well as subjective assessment and non-mental elements such as intuition and emotions. This broader way of defining dream interpretation means that it can be active, passive, or both. This definition leaves plenty of room for anything that may happen during the process of discovering a dream's meaning—mental or non-mental. This is important because there's one non-mental aspect that's the ultimate key to dream interpretation: intuition. Your intuition is what tells you when you have arrived at the true meaning of your dream. (Read more about the key role of intuition in dream interpretation in "Intuition: The Key to Recognizing Dream Meaning," p. 33.)

So, I think of dream analysis as an active mental process, and I think of dream interpretation as an active or passive process (or both) occurring anywhere in a person's consciousness—mental, emotional, subconscious, or anywhere else.

In some cases, dream interpretation may not involve all of the types of processes just discussed. For example, sometimes you might wake up already knowing intuitively what a dream means. In that case, no dream analysis or any other method of interpretation is necessary, unless you want to dig into the dream for more details about its meaning. However, this kind of immediate knowing doesn't always happen, and so you may need to spend some time exploring your dream before arriving at that moment of intuitive understanding.

In this model, all techniques for understanding a dream—including dream analysis techniques—are applied *in service to your intuition.* In other words, the goal of using analysis techniques is to trigger that flash of intuitive recognition telling you that you've arrived at the true meaning. The dream analysis techniques in this book help you examine the dream, turn it around in your mind, and look at it in different ways—all in the hope of coming across a meaning that your intuition will recognize as the correct one.

Understanding dream meaning—*knowing* that you've arrived at the true meaning of a particular dream—can only be accomplished through intuition. You can analyze a dream all day, but you won't know its meaning for sure until your intuition confirms that you've discovered its true meaning.

Finding the True Meaning

The question that dream interpretation asks is, "What does my dream mean?" In other words, when you set out to interpret a dream, you seek to understand the true meaning that your subconscious mind wove into the dream as it was created. You want to understand the one true meaning of the dream. You aren't looking for what your friend thinks the dream means or what a dream dictionary says it means. You're looking for what it means to *you.* So, in this book the "true meaning" of a dream refers to the accurate translation of what your subconscious mind was portraying in the dream. As you consider different meanings for a particular dream, the true meaning is usually the one that resonates with you, the one that rings true according to your intuition, the one that your subconscious mind recognizes that it created.

When searching for true dream meaning, one huge clue is that dreams are very often portraying something from your real life or something that's been on your mind. So, as you review your dream, it makes sense to look for parallels between the dream and your current life and feelings. For example, you may notice that a particular feeling you had during the dream is the same feeling you experienced recently in real life (such as feeling abandoned, betrayed, acknowledged, or valued), which may lead you to discover that the dream is retelling the story of that particular situation from your real life.

The primary challenge in dream interpretation is that the subconscious mind often uses symbols to tell its stories—symbols whose meanings may not be obvious to you. Therefore, you may not immediately know how to interpret them. In that case, you have the opportunity to explore further using various dream analysis techniques—such as the ones in "Part III: Dream Analysis Toolkit" (p. 101)—to help translate the language of the subconscious mind into a meaning that you recognize. During this exploration you may come up with some guesses about meaning, or you may consult a dream dictionary that gives you some ideas about possible meanings. However, the goal of this exploration process is the flash of recognition that occurs when you come upon the true meaning, and you feel a "resonance" as if that meaning "lines up" with your entire being. (For more on recognizing dream meaning, see "Chapter 1-3: Intuition: Your Dream Translator," p. 33.)

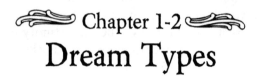

Chapter 1-2
Dream Types

In This Chapter:

Dream types are categories of dreams based on their nature, content, and structure. Different dreams portray meaning in different ways—such as clarifying a real-life situation, rehearsing an upcoming real-life event, or delivering a message regarding your life direction. When interpreting your dream, determining its dream type can help you understand its meaning. Once you identify what type of dream it is, you better understand its context—which can reveal more clues about the dream and its theme, symbols, and message.

Common Dream Types

This chapter describes the dream type categories I've created based on my observations of the different kinds of dreams that tend to occur. They are intended as an aid to dream interpretation rather than as a definitive categorization of dreams. You might choose to categorize your dreams in a completely different way. I encourage you to use whatever approach works best for you.

In my experience, the Clarification Dream is by far the most common, whereas the Premonition Dream and Interaction Dream happen much more rarely.

Keep in mind that a particular dream can fit into more than one dream type category. For example, a Clarification Dream can also be a Timeline Dream if it contains a series of events that parallels a real-life series of events.

Clarification Dream

A Clarification Dream clarifies something about yourself or your life, often providing insight into your experience of a current or past situation in your waking life. This type of dream presents your subconscious mind's version of an aspect of yourself or your life—sometimes in an exaggerated manner. In my experience, this is by far the most common type of dream.

A Clarification Dream often conveys what you subconsciously feel or think about a particular aspect of your life, or how strongly you feel about it, even when you might not be aware of those thoughts and feelings in a waking state. Key elements in this type of dream can take on a different appearance than they have in real life. For example, one person from your real life might appear as a different person in a dream, but still have similar characteristics or something else in common with the real-life person— such as your current spouse being represented in a dream by your former relationship partner, where both were creative and eccentric in real life.

Clarification Dreams can clarify a number of different aspects of your life. For example, they can:

- Reveal your current feelings about the past, present, or future.
- Expose your beliefs and judgments about yourself, and other self-defeating aspects of your inner dialogue (the negative or positive "tapes" you play in your head).
- Show how far you've come in your life or in a project.
- Clarify your thoughts and feelings about a person, relationship, group, or other external influence.
- Convey your purpose(s), joys, desires, fears, or expectations.

Example A:
You dreamed that you were home alone, sleeping in your bed, when you heard someone trying to force open the front door. You heard footsteps coming down the hall towards your room, and then a man dressed in black entered your room and came toward you. You knew he meant to harm you, and you felt terrified and helpless.

This dream may convey your feelings of vulnerability and fear of others invading your space, either literally (physically) or figuratively (emotionally or mentally). The house may represent you—your physical body, mind, emotions, or life experience, or some other aspect. If so, then the intrusion into the house could represent your perception of someone intruding into your personal space in real life—such as to gain power, manipulate you, or take something from you. This dream may be pointing to a real-life situation of your personal boundaries being violated by someone, or your fear of that.

Example B:

In real life, you have been happily married for 15 years. You dreamed that you were attending a dance with your old high school sweetheart and someone else came up and asked your sweetheart to dance. Your sweetheart told the person, "Thanks for asking, but I only want to dance with my partner," meaning you.

Your high school sweetheart in this dream may represent your current spouse, and the person asking him or her to dance may represent a recent social situation in which your spouse demonstrated loyalty and you felt secure in your relationship. This dream seems to portray how happy you are with your spouse and his or her loyalty to you, and it seems to convey your feeling of trust and security in the relationship.

Symbolism Dream

A Symbolism Dream prominently features one or more key symbols around which the dream is centered, and that the dreamer experiences as having great significance. These key dream elements almost always represent something other than themselves and carry a deeper meaning. An example of a Symbolism Dream might be a dream about traveling down a road, and at the road's end was a huge white rose in the sky. You might conclude this is a Symbolism Dream because of the very prominent rose symbol.

Example A:

You dreamed that you lost your keys.

The keys may be a symbol of your identity or sense of self, from which you feel separated. Perhaps you feel lost, or you are struggling with your own identity—who you are, what your values are, how you project yourself to others, or something else. If you felt during the dream that your keys had been stolen, then the dream could represent a feeling of someone—or others in general—overriding or threatening your identity somehow in your life.

Example B:
You dreamed that your car was stolen.

The car could be a symbol of your personal security, freedom, or ability to make progress—which perhaps you feel or fear being threatened in your life. In a dream, a car being taken from you can represent a feeling of others impeding your progress, or otherwise "taking from you" without your permission.

Timeline Dream

A Timeline Dream portrays a sequence of events or other time-related aspects of your life, beginning at a certain point in your life and ending at a later point. A Timeline Dream usually portrays a series of events from the past, but can also include current and (anticipated, expected, or predicted) future events. The events or elements in your dream may be unfamiliar to you (not literal) but represent actual circumstances in your life. A timeline dream often also functions as a Clarification Dream (see "Clarification Dream," p. 21), so pay attention to the details.

Example A:
You dreamed that as you walked across a neighbor's backyard deck someone handed you a large piece of paper, then you walked back to your house and the mailman delivered you a letter announcing you had won the lottery. Then suddenly you were in a large parking lot and someone handed you the keys to one of the cars.

This dream could represent the portion of your life when you graduated college (represented by receiving the paper as you walk across the deck), got a job (your new income represented by winning the lottery), and bought a car (represented by receiving keys to a car). Most likely this dream contains elements that will help clarify your thoughts and feelings about that portion of your life.

Example B:
You dreamed that you were sitting in your backyard when a group of birds landed in the yard and stayed a while. Then you were on a riverboat that arrived at a river port. You disembarked into the nearby city and noticed a bank there, and you thought maybe you'd go in to see what kind of money they had.

This dream could represent the portion of your life when your relatives came to visit (represented by the birds landing in your yard), then you got a new job (represented by the boat arriving at a new place) that offered benefits requiring you to make a decision about stock choices (represented by the bank offering "different kinds" of money). Again, this dream most likely contains some detailed elements that will help clarify your thoughts and feelings about that portion of your life.

Rehearsal Dream

A Rehearsal Dream involves a run-through of an actual event you're expecting in the future. This type of dream allows the subconscious mind to prepare in advance for an important, pleasant, or potentially traumatic event. Depending on your emotions about the event, during the dream your subconscious mind may choose to run through either the best-case scenario and the pleasure you expect the event to bring, or the worst-case scenario and the potential unpleasantness of which you're afraid. In the worst-case scenario, because the dream tells you what your fears are, you have a chance to work through them before the event if you choose to do so.

Example A:

In real life, you are scheduled to give a speech next week. You dreamed that as you arrived at the podium to give your speech, you tripped over an electrical cord, and when you opened your mouth to speak, nothing came out.

In this dream, your subconscious mind may be portraying its worst fears about giving the speech, exploring how you would feel if those fears actually came true. Now that you've identified your fears, you have the opportunity to address them, perhaps by practicing your speech in front of others ahead of time and by watching where you step as you approach the podium.

Example B:

In real life, your spouse is away on a business trip in Europe and is expected to return tomorrow. You dreamed that your spouse came home, gave you a big hug, presented you with a wonderful ring purchased in Spain, and then you two had a lovely evening.

In this dream, your subconscious mind may be anticipating the pleasant aspects of your spouse's return. Your feelings during the dream may also reveal some important information about your subconscious perception of your relationship. For example, your feeling upon seeing your spouse again may reflect your deep feelings about the relationship, and the ring may represent your perception of your spouse's thoughtfulness, generosity of self, or the value he or she brings to the relationship.

Transformative Dream

A Transformative Dream is a dream during which actual transformation took place within you while you were in the dream state. In other words, while you were dreaming something within your consciousness shifted into a healthier, more integrated state—and the transformation took place before the dream ended. So, a Transformative Dream is a dream during which inner healing took place. Examples of transformations that may occur during this type of dream include:

• You accept a change that has occurred in your life.
• You reach closure with something or someone from your past.
• You release a judgment or let go of a grudge.
• You recognize and release a limiting belief.

In some Transformative Dreams you are the only character, such as a dream in which you bought yourself ten dozen roses—which prompted you to realize that you are worthy of appreciation and to release your judgment of yourself as "unworthy." Other Transformative Dreams may include additional characters or external factors—people you know, society, the environment, or the world. For example, consider a dream in which you were falling from a great height and a large group of people gathered below to catch you, leading you to release your limiting belief that "the world is not a supportive place."

Example A:
In real life, your best friend in middle school betrayed you by telling a secret she promised to keep. She never apologized and her betrayal ended your friendship. In your dream last night, this friend approached you and apologized for betraying you. You immediately forgave her during the dream and felt a huge relief, leaving you with only feelings of happiness about your friendship and about all the good times you shared in the past.

In this dream, your subconscious mind may have been revisiting this betrayal from the past because something reminded you of it recently or because the memory of it happened to surface during the dream state. Your subconscious mind may have constructed this dream situation to create an opportunity for you to release your judgment of your friend. Perhaps a part of you decided that you had held on to that judgment long enough and it was time to let go of the past.

Example B:
You dreamed that a dark cloud was following you around wherever you went, repeatedly striking you with lightening. You noticed during the dream that each

lightening bolt was shaped like the word "failure." Finally, you got fed up and the next time the lightening struck, you grabbed the lightening bolt and pulled on it, straightening the word "failure" into a straight line like you were pulling a bent wire out straight. As the shape of the word "failure" disappeared, you felt a positive shift within you and a feeling of empowerment.

The dark cloud in this dream may have represented your judgment of yourself that triggered you to attack yourself periodically in real life by calling yourself a failure (represented by the lightening bolts that were shaped like the word "failure"). During the dream you decided that enough was enough, and you released the judgment (through the dream action of straightening out the bolt so the word "failure" disappeared). Upon awakening from this dream, you realize that in real life you've been judging yourself as a "failure," and that the inner shift you felt during the dream was because you had released that judgment during the dream state (through the dream action of "erasing" the word "failure"). You now feel lighter and you no longer judge yourself as a failure. You feel much more positive about yourself and more optimistic about the possibilities in your future.

Message Dream

A Message Dream contains information from a source outside of yourself, often with an indication that you or someone else needs to know something or that some action may be needed. It can be similar to other types of dreams, except the content is influenced by a source external to your own consciousness. The nature of the message could be to:

- Clarify a situation in your life.
- Indicate that you are on-track or off-track somehow in your life.
- Answer a question you've had on your mind.
- Solve a problem you've been pondering.
- Supply a creative idea.
- Warn you about what could happen if you don't take action or make a change.
- Provide perspective about your life, such as how things are actually better than you realized.

It's not always obvious whether a dream message comes from an outside source or from within your own consciousness. You may know intuitively, but it can often be challenging to differentiate your own intuition from your wishes, hopes, expectations, imaginings, or fears. I suggest that even more important than the source of a message is its value to you.

Consider whether the message feels accurate, appropriate, useful, and constructive, and make sure that it works toward improving your life for the greatest good of all involved. In other words, focus on the value in the message.

In my experience, Message Dreams are much rarer than dreams that portray the dreamer's own wish fulfillment, fears, or other mental and emotional factors.

Example A:

In real life, you are considering taking a new job with either the Shamrock Construction Company or with another company. You dreamed that you were at work, where you looked out the window and saw a large patch of clover. In the middle of the patch was a giant golden clover that brought you a feeling of well-being, joy, and security. You sensed intuitively that the vision in the dream came from a source outside yourself, carrying a message.

The message in this dream may be a positive indication about the job at Shamrock Construction Company (represented by the golden shamrock) and may indicate that the job is worth at least seriously considering. According to your intuition, this is a message from an outside source, perhaps spiritual guidance. However, this dream might merely portray the fulfillment of your wish for a great new job, rather than a message from an outside source. You would be wise to base your job decision on real-life, verifiable facts while keeping this possible dream message in mind.

Example B:

In real life, you are a musician writing a new piece of music, and you have become stuck while working on one particular part of it. In your dream, you were playing a piano and you heard yourself playing a musical phrase that fits perfectly into the gap in the piece you are writing. You had the intuitive sense that the inspiration came from somewhere other than yourself.

According to your intuition, this dream may be providing inspiration from an external source. The musical information specifically applies to your current challenge with your musical composition and apparently is intended as a possible solution. Again, because it can be very challenging to know intuitively the source of dream information, a better question is whether the information is valuable and can be used productively to improve your life—in this case, your music project.

Premonition or ESP Dream

A Premonition Dream predicts actual future events. This type of dream seems to be rare. Therefore, if you have a dream that you think predicts the future, I suggest that there's a very good chance it does not. The only sure way to identify a Premonition Dream is to wait and see if it comes true in real life. You could also try these other methods of exploring a dream's predictive qualities:

- If you receive any specific information during the dream, you can confirm it with a verifiable source. For example, if you dream of your sister becoming ill, you can check with her about how she's feeling.
- Consult your own intuition or inner knowing. However, proceed with caution, since it can be very tricky to distinguish between your intuition and other factors within your consciousness such as fears, expectations, or hopes.
- Consult an intuitive professional. See tips for choosing wisely in "Working With a Dream Interpretation Professional" (p. 42).

Some people claim to have experienced other ESP types of dreams, including:

- Shared dream, in which two or more people encounter each other in their dreams, dreaming the same dream at exactly the same time.
- Clairvoyant dream, in which the dreamer sees in real-time something that really exists or is happening elsewhere, without any independent knowledge of it.
- Telepathic dream, in which the dreamer receives a message from another living person.

Like Premonition Dreams, these all seem to be rare, and these dream types aren't particularly useful in the dream interpretation process. If you suspect you have had one of these kinds of dreams, I suggest exploring it for other possible meanings (fears, expectations, hopes, and other feelings) first, before coming to any conclusions.

Example A:

In real life, it is winter and your brother is planning to leave for a business trip to Minneapolis in two days. You dreamed that your brother's plane crash-landed due to ice on the runway and your brother survived but sustained some injuries.

This dream could be a premonition that your brother's plane will have problems. However, use caution because this dream could merely be a Clarification Dream highlighting your personal fears about your brother's trip, or even your general concern about your brother's well-being. To verify whether this dream is an actual prediction you can use your intuition, or you might decide to consult with an intuitive professional (but choose wisely, as described in "Working With a Dream Interpretation

Professional," p. 42). You might also decide to tell your brother about the dream and your sense about the dream, and let him decide what to do with the information.

Example B:

You dreamed that you were driving down a street lined with houses, and suddenly a certain house drew your attention. The house was yellow, red, and green, and on it was a large house number of 734. Upon awakening you realize that yellow, red, and green are the colors on your state lottery tickets.

This dream could be a prediction that 7-3-4 will be winning numbers for your lottery. However, it very well may *not* be a prediction—instead, it could simply represent a wish to win the lottery, or a desire to leave your job, among many other possibilities. And even if the dream were predictive, it does not indicate which day or which lottery game. The only sure way to verify whether this as an actual prediction is to watch the lottery results for after-the-fact verification.

Interaction Dream

An Interaction Dream involves contact with another person—sometimes a loved one who has passed on, sometimes an individual who is still living, or other possibilities. If the person is someone you know, (in my experience) that person will likely appear as himself or herself—realistic, not symbolic—rather than looking like another person. If the person is someone who has passed on, sometimes dreamers report that in the dream the person appeared younger than the age at which she died.

The content of Interaction Dreams can vary, but often some particular feeling or sense is conveyed from the "dream visitor" to the dreamer, such as a feeling that all is well with the visitor. In fact, in the majority of dreams I've seen that seemed to be an interaction with a loved one who has passed on, the visitor emanated a profound feeling of peace, well-being, love, and goodwill. If a deceased person you knew in real life expresses negativity such as anger, hurt, or blame in a dream—in my opinion, this could cast doubt on the idea that this was an interaction with the real person you knew.

During an Interaction Dream, sometimes unfinished business is resolved or the dreamer's questions are answered in the dream state. For example, actions that occurred in the past with this person can be reversed or balanced, such as when someone who harmed you in the past comes back in your dream state and offers you a kind action. As with other dream types whose sources are tricky to identify for sure, I suggest gleaning from the dream any value you can use in a beneficial way, rather than dwelling on the question of whether the interaction was real. The questions of "How is this dream useful to me?" and "What can I learn from it?" are much more worthy of your time than "Was I really interacting with that particular person?"—especially when you may never be able to answer the latter question with any certainty.

Example A:

In your dream, the boy who bullied you in high school approached you, expressed his deep regret, and offered you a gift that had great meaning and value for you. You accepted his apology, took the gift, and shook hands with him. You sensed that the person in the dream was the real person, and you now feel at peace concerning your history with him.

According to your intuition, the person in the dream was really the person he appeared to be. You may have interacted with the real person on a subconscious level, and he may have no memory of the interaction. A key to knowing if the person is really who he appears to be is your recognition of the person's "essence" or soul, as well as his appearance. This kind of recognition can be tricky unless your intuition is extremely well developed, because a person in a dream is very often a mock-up of that person rather than the actual person. This dream could have been a "reversal of fortune" or a case in which unfinished business from the past was resolved. To determine whether this was an actual interaction and not just a mock-up of your own subconscious creation, use your intuition. However, because this dream seems to have brought you closure regarding an issue from the past, consider if it really matters whether the interaction was real or imagined.

Example B:

In your dream, your aunt (who died two months ago in real life) appeared and told you that she was doing well and was very happy, and that she was with your grandmother (who died several years ago). You immediately recognized her "essence" and knew intuitively that it was actually her appearing in your dream. She conveyed to you a strong feeling of peace, well-being, and love.

Because your intuition tells you that the person you saw was actually your aunt, this dream may have been an actual interaction with her. You sensed that her intention was to let you know that she is okay, and that she and your grandmother are together. To determine whether this was an actual interaction and not just a mock-up of your own creation, use your intuition, or you might choose to get input from an intuitive expert (if so, choose wisely as discussed in "Working With a Dream Interpretation Professional," p. 42).

Toxic Dream

A Toxic Dream is triggered by a toxic state, in which you are physically, mentally, or emotionally overloaded during sleep. Toxic Dreams are usually very realistic and upsetting dreams. They can be terrible nightmares. Often, having a Toxic Dream simply indicates that you were in a toxic state at the time of the dream, more than providing any useful meaning to interpret. These dreams can result from a number of factors occurring the day or evening before, including:

- Eating refined carbohydrates (such as sweets or white flour), processed or junk food, additives, or preservatives.
- Eating too much, especially close to bedtime.
- Ingesting drugs, alcohol, caffeine, tobacco, or other substances that are psychoactive or that stress or overload the body.
- Taking certain prescription medications, or changing your dose (consult your doctor if you suspect this is an issue).
- Eating foods to which you have a sensitivity or allergy (common culprits are wheat, gluten, dairy, soy, nuts, eggs, and corn).
- Encountering environmental toxins (such as from mold, new carpet, cleaning chemicals, or exhaust fumes).
- Being stressed (the biochemical results of stress can overload the body, as external toxins can).
- Being emotionally toxic, such as going to bed angry or hateful.
- Not getting enough rest (sleep deprivation can deny the body its critical nighttime detoxing, leaving more toxins in the body).
- Being ill or otherwise not feeling well.

Often Toxic Dreams are nightmares that play upon your subconscious fears. For tips on dealing with problem dreams like this, see "Chapter 3-25: TOOL: Dealing with Nightmares" (p. 206).

Example A:

You ate a large piece of pie just before going to bed, and you dreamed that a monster was coming after you and inflicted serious physical harm on you.

This dream may point to a subconscious fear of being victimized, but the main significance is the physical state of overload while the body was going through its sleep cycle. To avoid this situation, you might avoid carbohydrate-intense foods and avoid eating so close to bedtime.

Example B:

You have been very stressed the last three days and haven't slept well for the last week. You dreamed that you seriously injured yourself in a household accident, but that when you picked up the phone and dialed 911 you kept getting the wrong number and couldn't get through.

This dream may indicate a feeling of helplessness, possibly due to an underlying feeling that your life is out of control due to your recent stressful situation. On a physical level, your body may have been overwhelmed by stress-related biochemicals and an over-stimulated condition, creating an extra challenge during the sleep cycle. To avoid this situation, you might apply some stress management techniques such as delegating or re-organizing your tasks to reduce your stress load, free-form writing to get out your frustrations (more in "Chapter 3-23: TOOL: Free-Form Writing," p. 198), or meditation and visualization.

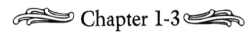

Chapter 1-3
Intuition: Your Dream Translator

In This Chapter:

If you're like many people, when you have a dream you wonder what meaning it carries, and also perhaps why you had the dream in the first place. Here is how you're going to discover the answers to those questions: **your intuition is going to tell you.** Your intuition is your own personal translator of the language of dream symbolism.

Intuition: The Key to Recognizing Dream Meaning

There is no interpretation process that can walk you through a few standard steps and automatically arrive at a formulaic meaning of your dream. Dream interpretation is not linear and logical like a math problem. Rather, it is subjective and non-linear—more like interpreting a painting or a piece of music. Sometimes it involves muddling around in your dream for a while, trying different ways of looking at it, until you reach a moment of enlightenment when your intuition confirms the dream's meaning. That is why your intuition is so important in recognizing the true dream meaning.

How to Recognize Your Dream's Meaning

Intuition is key in understanding dream meaning because it is the part of you that recognizes the truth. It's through your intuition that you recognize the true meaning of a dream.

Each dream could potentially have many different possible meanings. The logical mind can analyze a dream and suggest a variety of potential meanings. However, the challenge is recognizing the true meaning when you see it. Perhaps you'll come across the true meaning while you're reviewing your dream, when you're trying different analysis techniques, while you're discussing the dream with a friend, or at some other point. You could use every approach there is and still not know which meaning is correct, until you recognize it intuitively.

Only *you* can definitively recognize the true meaning of your dream. I use the word "recognize" because identifying dream meaning doesn't involve rational knowing. You already know the meaning of the dream, at least subconsciously, since the dream originally took place in your own subconscious mind. Dream interpretation simply involves using the conscious mind to explore different possible meanings until one resonates with what you already know—when your intuition tells you, "Yes! That's what the dream means." This recognition of dream meaning is what I call *dream intuition.* In practice, dream intuition is the use of intuition in the dream interpretation process.

Before learning to apply intuition in the process of dream interpretation, you may find it helpful to understand intuition itself, how it tends to work, how it can be obscured, and how it feels and does not feel—all of which will be discussed in the next few sections.

About Intuition

Intuition can be defined as knowing, independent of any rational process or sensory cues. So, by definition, intuition occurs separately from and outside of the rational thought process. Some people describe intuition as insight, which we might think of as "sight into our inner wisdom" or "viewing the truth."

Everyone has intuition. We've all experienced intuition, whether or not we recognized it at the time. You probably can think of at least one experience when you had a sudden realization, an instant when you suddenly just *knew* something—independent of any knowledge you already had or any sensory cues. Intuition is within you all the time, although you may not always be aware of it.

You may find it helpful to think of intuition as a channel through which truth flows, as shown previously in the Model of Consciousness depicted in Figure A in "Conscious Mind and Subconscious Mind" (p. 11). In that model, we saw how your "I" can focus within different levels of your consciousness (such as physical, emotional, or mental) at different times, where your "I" is sort of like the channel selector on a television.

With practice, you can learn to focus on your "intuition channel" whenever you like. Furthermore, while you are focused within your intuition, you can "aim" your intuition at different topics—kind of like using the "on demand" feature of a television network to watch whatever show you want. In other words, once you've learned to focus within your intuition, you can direct your intuition to a particular topic to explore the truth about it—such as identifying your judgments that keep you from moving forward in a relationship, discovering irrational beliefs underlying a particular fear, or understanding the dream you had last night.

One reason I think of intuition as a channel is that different kinds of information seem to flow through it. You might receive an intuitive hunch to turn right instead of left. You might get an intuitive sense that the reason you're feeling down today is because you judged yourself as "not good enough" when you were getting dressed this morning. You might get an intuitive sense about another person you just met being friendly or dangerous. Some people claim to have received inner warnings, such as a strong sense that they should not get on a plane that later ended up crashing. Others say they've gotten an intuitive sense when a particular family member was ill or in trouble. So, if intuition includes such different kinds of information—and if that information comes from different sources both inside and outside yourself—then intuition seems to work more like a channel through which information flows than a finite source of information within a person. This is why I talk about intuition as channel through which we can connect to the truth.

How Intuition Can Be Obscured

Although intuition tends to be continuously active, it may not always be clear and obvious to you. The greatest challenge with intuition is that it can easily be confused with or drowned out by other factors within your consciousness—thoughts, fears, hopes, judgments, memories, imaginings, daydreams, and so on. With all that other activity in your mind, you may not be able to discern intuition—which tends to show up as quiet and neutral, rather than demanding your attention.

Intuition can be obscured when you mistake one of those other mental or emotional factors as being your intuition and focus on it instead. When a particular idea enters your consciousness, you may not be able to tell whether it's an intuitive insight or another factor you're mistaking for intuitive truth. This isn't to say that those other factors don't have value, because they can have. However, they are not intuition and they should not be taken as such. Discerning intuition from other factors is a skill that can be developed through practice, which will be discussed in more detail later.

Intuition can also be obscured when those other mental and emotional factors distract you from it, especially when they show up strongly. For example, you might experience a fear so strong that you can't see past it. When your mind is full of other factors, they can obscure your intuition, whether they are strong or not. When there's a lot going on in your mind—such as worries, hopes, beliefs, and imaginings—recognizing your intuition can feel like searching for one softball in a barrel full of baseballs, racquet balls, and tennis balls. However, practicing meditation and becoming more skilled at working through mental and emotional issues can help you learn to switch into that quiet state of mind in which you can clearly access your intuition.

How Intuition Feels

Each person may experience intuition in his or her own way. Intuition may also show up differently for the same person in different kinds of situations. From my experience and descriptions I've heard from others, intuition often shows up as a very quiet, peaceful sense of knowing. It can feel like a small, quiet instinct or just an instant realization. It can also feel like a thought that suddenly comes into your mind but is not a part of a logical thought process. Sometimes it shows up as a thought like "What if this were true? Wouldn't that be interesting?" and then you find out that it *is* true and that was your intuition speaking.

Intuition often shows up suddenly and quietly, emerging subtly from somewhere in the depths of your consciousness, rather than jumping up and down screaming for attention.

Intuition tends to be neutral, rather than positive or negative—although you may have an instantaneous positive or negative reaction to what your intuition tells you.

How Dream Intuition Feels

Dream intuition is an intuitive realization—or a series of intuitive realizations—during dream interpretation. As you consider different possible meanings of your dream, pay attention to which meaning resonates with you intuitively. When you come upon the true meaning, you will likely have an "Aha!" moment in which your intuition tells you that you've found the true meaning. You might experience this intuitive knowing as a sudden:

• Flash of recognition.
• Sense that everything within you is in alignment.
• Feeling of peace and completion.
• Feeling of knowing or release in your stomach or "gut," or all over.

36

• All-over feeling of well-being, or that all is right with the world.

I suggest paying attention to your experience of intuition during dream interpretation—how it feels when an intuitive realization suddenly shows up in your head, and you "just know." Notice what that inner experience feels like, so that next time you interpret a dream and come across a meaning that triggers that same feeling, you'll pay attention to it.

How Intuition Does Not Feel

Below are some tips to help you avoid the pitfall of mistaking as intuition the other factors in your consciousness—such as emotions, rational thoughts, ego, and subconscious dynamics. Learning more about what the other factors feel like can help you recognize them when they show up and help you learn to discern them from intuition.

Intuition Is Not Emotion

Intuition does not originate in your emotions, although you may react emotionally after an intuitive insight. Emotions such as the following are often mistaken as intuition:

• Fear that a certain dream meaning is correct.
• Hope that a certain dream meaning is correct.
• Feeling of dread in the pit of the stomach.
• Nervousness such as "butterflies in the stomach."
• Excitement about a possible dream meaning.

If you are having a strong emotion and wondering if it's your intuition talking, get to the bottom of that emotion and determine what triggered it. Perhaps the emotion was triggered by something you thought or imagined. Consider what was going on in your consciousness right before the emotion began.

When the subject matter is a very emotional topic for you—such as the safety of your family—that emotion may obscure your intuition. In these cases, sometimes it helps to distance yourself from it or take a break for a while, or talk it over with someone you trust who can help work through the emotion.

Intuition Is Not Logic

Intuition is not a thought process, although an intuitive insight or hunch may suddenly show up during a logical thought process, although independent of it. Some of the mental factors that can be mistaken as intuition are:

• A belief that a certain dream meaning is correct.
• A desire for a certain dream meaning to be correct.

- Your ego wanting to be "right" because it thinks it "knows."
- An assumption that a certain dream meaning is correct because it makes the most sense.

When intuition tells you something, you suddenly have a deep sense of knowing—which feels different from thinking you know, assuming you know, or wanting to know so badly that you convince yourself you know. If you are hooked on the idea that "I have to be right," or you have an ego attachment to being right or "knowing," that may actually block you from connecting with your intuition. You'll need to set aside your mentalizing and your ego in order to tap into your intuition.

Intuition Is Not Imagination

The imagination is very powerful, and it can be especially active when we want to know or understand something. When we don't have complete information about something, the imagination often fills in the gaps. Its activity can be mistaken as intuition, as in the following examples:

- Imagining that you know intuitively when you don't.
- Imagining that a dream is literally true when it's not.
- Imagining that a dream is a prediction when it's not.

Intuition Is Not Physical

You may have physical sensations that accompany your intuitive knowing, such as a "gut feeling"—although intuition often shows up simply as a sudden, strong sense of knowing, without any particular physical sensations. Sometimes certain physical sensations can be mistaken as intuition—perhaps body sensations that were triggered by the intuitive realization, or by thoughts or emotions that are unrelated to any intuitive activity. The following examples include some physical dynamics that might be mistaken for intuition:

- Tension in the gut or other body part.
- A "glowing" feeling in a particular area of the body.
- Twitches or the jitters.
- Indigestion and hunger pangs.

So, a physical sensation alone tends not to be as reliable an indicator of intuition as the sudden inner sense of knowing.

Intuition Does Not Have Personality

Your personal intuition will not show up as a loud voice or boisterous vision. Instead, intuition tends to be a quiet, still "knowing." Intuition does not insist or force a certain action or opinion on you. It does not try to scare you, control you, or order you to do things. It is neutral; it just *is*. If you are experiencing something in your head that exhibits noticeable personality traits like the ones just described, the source is most likely not your intuition.

Pay Attention to First Hunches

Sometimes your first hunch about the meaning of a dream is actually based in intuition and is correct. For example, you may wake up knowing immediately that the dream you just had was about your stress at work or about a recent reunion with an old friend. If you have that familiar recognition of intuitive knowing, then perhaps you've already discovered the true meaning of the dream. However, you may still want to consider other meanings to make sure you've got it right—especially since other factors such as fear or desire can be mistaken as intuition. Once you have a clear intuitive "knowing" about your dream's meaning, then you might choose to analyze its details further for deeper insight, including any aspects that point to beneficial changes in your life or mind. For example, in a dream about stress at work, perhaps the dream depicts the underlying cause of the stress, such as a habit, an activity, or a co-worker who triggers your stress response. The dream might also highlight self-defeating beliefs that contribute to your stress, such as "If I don't say yes to everything, people won't like me" or "I don't deserve to take breaks and relax."

Tips for Developing Dream Intuition

Because of the personal nature of your dreams and how they relate to what's going on in your life, you as the dreamer are in the best position to interpret your own dreams based on your own intuition. Although we all have intuition within us, practice and experience can help develop it to the point where we can intuitively interpret the details of our dreams quickly.

As you practice dream interpretation, you are improving your ability to discern your intuition from the other factors in your consciousness. You are also learning to understand a new language—the language of dream symbolism—as discussed in other sections of this book. Both of these skills improve with practice.

Here are some guidelines and tips for using and developing your dream intuition:

• Developing your intuition in general can help you interpret your dreams more quickly and accurately. Meditation and intuition exercises are helpful for developing your intuitive skills. You can find intuition development exercises online and in many intuition books.

39

- The more time you spend with your dreams, the more likely that your dream intuition will develop. Think about your dreams, talk about them with others, explore possible meanings and see which resonate for you. As you work with more of your dreams, you'll start to see patterns of intuitive recognition, and you'll recognize your intuitive knowing more easily when it shows up.

- You may be more attuned to your dream intuition immediately after you wake up, while you are still close to the dream.

- Keep an open mind when considering your dreams. Approach your interpretation with the belief that you already know on some level what a dream means, and set out to discover that meaning. Let go of any attachment to the outcome of the dream interpretation, and set aside any hope or fear that the dream needs to mean a certain thing. Create a neutral space within yourself in which to explore the dream. One helpful approach when considering different possible meanings is to ask yourself, "What if the dream means this..." rather than telling yourself, "I think the dream means this...."

- Don't jump to any conclusions about a dream's meaning. Remember that dreams are very often not about what they appear to be about on the surface and, therefore, discovering true meaning can require a process that takes time. Because the subconscious mind tends to speak using the language of symbols and imagery in dreams, some degree of translation is usually required. For example, a person in a dream can represent another person, a quality you'd like more of, or something else. An animal can represent a quality, a person, a responsibility, or something else. So, give your intuition the time and space to explore the dream, allowing the process to unfold as you consider the various clues to meaning.

- Remember that intuition is always consistent within itself—intuition's truth is truth, and truth doesn't change over time unless the actual answer changes over time. Each dream is a distinct entity that only happens once (except for recurring dreams) and, therefore, a dream's meaning is current only at the time of the dream and does not change over time. So, if according to your intuition the buffalo in your dream represented your supervisor at work, then your intuition will say the same thing every time you ask it whom the buffalo represented in that dream. If you at first you think your intuition tells you the buffalo represented your supervisor, but five minutes later it tells you the buffalo represented your spouse, then it probably wasn't your intuition you were hearing both of those times. You may have mistaken something else—such as an assumption or a fear—as intuition.

Intuition Practice and Tracking

As you pay attention to how you experience your own intuitive knowing, you can begin to recognize the difference between your intuition and other internal dynamics such as emotions, thoughts, and imaginings. Each internal factor feels different, once you learn to discern among them, although the differences can be very subtle.

One way to practice recognizing your own intuition is to create an intuition notebook in which you track your insights that you believe come from your intuition. For each insight you experience, describe what the inner experience felt like, how you felt mentally, emotionally, and physically, what you were thinking or talking about just before the intuition showed up, circumstances such as what you were doing and where you were, and so on. Then check your insight against reality (as is feasible) and note how accurate each insight turned out to be, and whether it was intuition or perhaps just your fear, imagination, desire, or some other factor. Tracking these details gives you a chance to practice your intuition and to practice discerning your intuition from other inner factors, and it may point out certain situations in which your intuition tends to be more active or more available to you. For example, some people notice that intuitive insights tend to come forward very often when they are taking a shower, are relaxed, or are engaged in an easy activity that leaves the consciousness free to roam—such as doing housework or going for a walk.

If Your Intuition Still Isn't Clear

To hone your intuitive skills further, keep practicing. Learning to discern intuition from other factors in your consciousness (such as fear, hope, and desire) is a process. It can take years to develop the ability to tap into your intuition at will, quickly and accurately. However, as you practice you should notice improvements over time. You might want to practice your intuitive skills further by tracking and evaluating your intuitive insights as described in "Intuition Practice and Tracking" (p. 41)—or through intuition exercises, many of which can be found online and in books.

Put yourself in situations where your intuition tends to be clearer—for example, when you're relaxed, near water, in nature, engaged in a monotonous activity, or when you center yourself spiritually through prayer or spiritual meditation.

To confirm or supplement your own intuition, you can consult with an intuitive dream professional who can help interpret your dreams or guide you through your own interpretation process. See tips for choosing wisely in "Working With a Dream Interpretation Professional" (p. 42).

Working With a Dream Interpretation Professional

Developing your own intuition is a worthwhile effort, and it can benefit you in all areas of your life. However, as you are honing your intuitive skills you may encounter dreams that puzzle you, the meanings of which you can't unravel regardless of what you try. In those cases, you might decide to consult an intuitive dream interpretation professional. If you do, it is important to choose wisely and look for a qualified professional who meets criteria such as these:

- Credentials such as an advanced degree in psychology.
- Extensive dream interpretation experience based in psychology and intuition.
- A focus on your personal growth rather than just information.
- Positive feedback from clients.
- The willingness to say "I don't know" when he doesn't know or when his intuition is unclear.

The results you experience when working with an intuitive dream professional will vary depending on the person you choose, the information you provide, and the questions you ask. Keep in mind that the results may differ from what you expect, and the dream meanings suggested may not be the ones you were prepared to hear. When considering the professional's interpretation, you may find it beneficial to keep an open mind while still paying attention to your own intuition. Here are some other tips for a positive experience with a dream professional:

- Write a dream description that you can provide to the professional. Include any feelings you had during the dream, specific symbols or anything else that stood out, and any real-life situations or events that may be related to the dream.
- Express any expectations to the professional ahead of time, and ask specific questions about anything in the dream that you want to understand better.
- Be sure to arrange for a long enough dream interpretation to address the dream and all your questions about it, especially if your dream was long or included several parts.

To get an idea of the kind of information and insights a professional dream interpretation can provide, see the dream samples in "Part V: Dreams Interpreted" (p. 277) and the more extensive collection of samples on my professional dream services site, MyDreamVisions.com.

Chapter 1-4
Dreams of Special Note

In This Chapter:

Sometimes a particular dream, by its nature, requires us to pay special attention to it or view it differently than a typical dream. For example, recurring dreams are often very important to interpret because they may be pointing to a pressing matter that needs your attention. On the other hand, a nightmare may or may not be worthy of interpretation, depending on what triggered it in the first place. Then there are certain other kinds of dreams that offer no useful information and would be a waste of your time to interpret. This chapter presents several kinds of dreams that you may want to handle differently than usual when you encounter them.

Recurring Dreams

A recurring dream is a dream that occurs on more than one occasion, each time repeating the same or similar content. Recurring dreams may be the subconscious mind's attempt to deal with an issue that is weighing heavily on the dreamer's mind. These kinds of dreams may reflect something that has happened in the dreamer's real life—such abandonment or betrayal—or something that persists or repeats within the dreamer's mind—such as a fear or a desire.

Possible Dynamics Behind Recurring Dreams

Although we may not be able to say exactly why people have recurring dreams, I've noticed certain patterns of inner dynamics that have seemed to emerge among cases of recurring dreams. These dynamics are not mutually exclusive, and more than one of the following could be involved in a certain series of recurring dreams.

Important or Urgent Matters

Some recurring dreams contain subject matter relating to something that was important or urgent to the dreamer at the time of the dream, such as feeling afraid about missing a mortgage payment, or feeling worried about a child who is about to go off to school for the first time.

Challenging Life Events

A recurring dream may reflect a life event that is challenging to accept, understand, or cope with, perhaps because it's a lot for the subconscious mind to process. Examples include a traumatic event, a betrayal, a significant life change, or something else the subconscious mind strives to make sense of and recover from.

Unresolved Issues or Unfinished Business

Unresolved issues or other unfinished business also tend to show up in recurring dreams. In these cases, an inner process or outer action may be necessary to resolve the situation before the dream stops recurring. If the dream keeps recurring, it could mean you haven't addressed the underlying issue yet—such as by releasing a grudge, repaying a debt, or forgiving yourself for a past action.

A Message the Dreamer Hasn't Gotten Yet

Some recurring dreams seem to be trying to deliver a message and tend to keep repeating until the dreamer receives the message. The message might come in the form of a warning, such as a dream portraying the dreamer losing everything she loves if she continues her gambling habit. A message could also show up in the form of a direction indicator, such as a dream showing how much richer the dreamer's life experience would be if she stopped gambling and put that energy toward meaningful pursuits.

Recurring Real-Life Event

A dream might also recur if each instance of the dream is triggered by a real-life recurring event, such as a scorpion nightmare that recurs each time you encounter a certain scary person in real life, or a dream about being abandoned at sea every time a certain real-life friend lets you down.

Recreating a Pleasant Experience

If the recurring dream is pleasant, it may simply be repeating due to its enjoyable content, or perhaps it reflects a desire for more of that kind of experience in your waking life.

Recurring Theme Across Different Dreams

A recurring theme may appear across a series of dreams, even if the details of each dream differ. Consider an example in which you dreamed that you drove off a bridge, two nights later you dreamed that you jumped off of a tall building, and then the following week you dreamed that you slipped off the edge of a cliff. In this case the recurring theme would be falling, even though the circumstances were different in each dream. So, in analyzing this series of dreams, you might start by exploring the feelings you had while falling, since falling was the common element across all the dreams. Perhaps when you were falling you felt helpless, out of control, and afraid. So, then you might consider what situation in real life has triggered these same kinds of feelings in the past, which may prompt you to recognize the real-life issue these dreams were portraying.

How to Interpret Recurring Dreams

I suggest interpreting recurring dreams the same way you would any other dream, except pay special attention to the aspects of the dream that are the same in each dream. In other words, focus on what is similar across all the dreams, such as flying or losing an item. The repeated aspect probably points to whatever pressing matter is on your subconscious mind. So, chances are that exploring the pattern across the dreams will help you recognize a parallel, persistent issue or recurring pattern in your real life.

Nightmares

Most people have nightmares at least occasionally. When you experience a nightmare, you might want to consider possible underlying factors such as these:

- Some nightmares are Toxic Dreams (see more about this dream type in "Toxic Dream," p. 31), which are typically very realistic and upsetting dreams that occur in response to certain kinds of foods, drugs, or toxins, or in times of physical, mental, or emotional stress.
- Nightmares may occur when the subconscious mind plays out subconscious fears or rehearses worst-case scenarios during the dream state. It's possible in these cases that the subconscious mind is trying to prepare in order to avoid or to better handle a scary situation in real life.

- Experiencing a traumatic event in real life—or in a TV show, movie, book, video game, or other alternate reality—can also trigger a nightmare.
- A nightmare can also occur when a person has abandoned responsibility for himself or his own well-being. In other words, engaging in activities such as overeating sweets or consuming a large amount of alcohol can be ways of abandoning responsibility for yourself that open the door for nightmares to occur (read more in "Toxic Dream," p. 31).
- Allowing a "negative cloud" to perpetuate within your consciousness can also lead to nightmares. Dark emotions and negative inner influences often indicate a matter within yourself that needs your attention, which you can address using techniques such as the ones in "Part IV: Dream Action Toolkit" (p. 215).

Nightmares can be interpreted using the same techniques as other dreams—looking for parallels with situations in the dreamer's real life, but paying special attention to possible links to subconscious fears and recent traumatic experiences (either real or virtual, such as watching a movie). However, if a nightmare was a Toxic Dream, it may simply have been triggered by your toxic state at the time of the dream, and therefore it may offer no useful meaning to interpret.

To read about techniques for dealing with nightmares, see "Chapter 3-25: TOOL: Dealing with Nightmares" (p. 206).

Dreams to Ignore

Occasionally you may have a dream that is not worth your time to interpret. The following kinds of dreams—in my experience—tend to be of little or no value to interpret, and can actually be counterproductive to interpret because they focus your energy in a negative direction—such as dwelling on your fears or distracting you with random messages. However, you are the dreamer, so you are in charge. Use your best judgment and follow your intuition when deciding whether a particular dream might offer any value through an interpretation process.

Hypnagogic Dreams Often Contain No Useful Meaning

Hypnagogic dreams are dreams that tend to occur just after you have fallen asleep. These dreams often seem very realistic and vivid. In this kind of dream, you may hear voices talking to you, or you may see words or numbers. Sometimes a hypnagogic dream contains something that feels very important or urgent during the dream, but turns out to be nonsense when you awake. As you drift off to sleep, you may dream that you are continuing to do things that you were doing earlier in the day, such as dreaming that you're knitting after you spent all evening working on your knitting project.

Hypnagogic dreams often don't offer any useful meaning that can be applied in your daily life, perhaps due to the shallow sleep state in which they occur. As with any dream, you can look for any value the dream may contain, but I suggest not spending much time interpreting these kinds of dreams.

Toxic Dreams Are Often the Toxic State Speaking

Toxic Dreams typically occur when you are in a physically, mentally, or emotionally toxic state—or when you are physically, mentally, or emotionally overloaded during sleep (for more details, see "Toxic Dream," p. 31). In my experience, the content of many Toxic Dreams seems to be primarily triggered by the toxic state, and they often don't contain any valuable content for interpretation. That's not to say that Toxic Dreams can't contain valuable content. However, if you have a dream that you know was triggered by one or more Toxic Dream factors (as listed in "Toxic Dream," p. 31), you might choose to be very skeptical about its value, and not take it very seriously.

To read about tips for dealing with Toxic Dreams and other nightmares, see "Chapter 3-25: TOOL: Dealing with Nightmares" (p. 206).

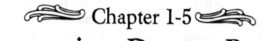

Chapter 1-5
Improving Dream Recall

In This Chapter:

When it comes to dreams, you can only interpret what you can remember. The approaches in this chapter can help you improve the chances of transporting each dream from the depths of your subconscious mind into the light of your conscious mind so you can explore its meaning. This chapter begins with tips for remembering your dreams in general, and then provides suggestions for enhancing your recall of a specific dream you've just experienced. (You may notice that some topics and techniques are visited twice in this chapter: first as they apply to improving general dream recall, and then as they apply to help you recall a fresh dream just after you've woken up from it.)

How to Improve Your Dream Recall

Sometimes people only remember bits and pieces of a dream once they wake up, or perhaps they only remember a dream occasionally. Some say they never remember dreams at all. Whether you usually remember your dreams or not, you can improve your dream recall. In general, the more you focus on dreams and dreaming—the more attention and energy you give them—the better the chance that your dream recall will improve.

"Recall" literally means to "call back," which is very appropriate when we think about dream recall. Recalling a dream involves "calling the dream back to you"—pulling it out of your subconscious mind where it originated, into your conscious mind so that you can access it when you are awake. There are many ways to prompt, trigger, and coax dream memories out of the subconscious mind into the conscious mind. I've included some of my favorites here, and you might even come up with your own techniques by experimenting with what works best for you.

(If you're trying to recall a specific dream you've already had, see "Tips for Recalling a Dream You Just Had," p. 56.)

Stop Telling Yourself You Can't Remember

If your subconscious mind is the one who created the dream, then your memory of the dream remains somewhere within your consciousness, even if it's trapped in your subconscious mind. Each time you say, "I never dream," or "I don't remember my dreams," these statements act as affirmations that reinforce a pattern of not remembering—virtually ensuring that your dreams stay locked away in your subconscious mind. Consider replacing these kinds of statements with a positive intention, such as "I intend to remember the dreams that are beneficial for me to remember." If you're discussing dreams with others, consider replacing "I don't remember my dreams" with something like "In the past I tended not to remember my dreams, but I intend to improve my dream recall." (Read more about setting intentions in "Chapter 4-7: TOOL: Setting Intentions," p. 234.)

Wake Up Quietly

If possible, wake up in the morning with a minimum of external disturbances that bring you out of your sleep state too quickly. The more quietly and naturally you wake up, the better your dream recall will likely be.

Waking up without a wake-up alarm can facilitate dream recall, although that's not always practical. If you need to wake up by a certain time, try to use something that awakens you gently with soft music or with a sound that gets progressively louder until you turn it off. Your wake-up device should be easy to turn off, because it's important not to move around much physically before you review your dream in your head. Ideally, you'll be able to review the dream from beginning to end before you open your eyes.

If you sleep in an environment that's often noisy in the mornings, you might opt for some earplugs if you can do so safely. If people around you often wake you up before it's time for you to wake up, consider creating a "do not disturb" rule or some other "no interruptions" arrangement such as a sign on your door. If you encounter too many disturbances to concentrate in the morning, review the dream in your mind before opening your eyes, write as much of a description as you can, and then come back to it later.

Plan to Interpret

Schedule time to review your dreams immediately after you wake up, while you are still sleepy, while the dream is still fresh. Try to arrange things so you won't distract yourself during this time, because a clear mental space provides room for you to recreate the entire dream experience, including story, visuals, and emotions. Distractions can also interfere with your intuition and thought continuity. So, eliminate potential distractions ahead of time: complete some of your morning tasks the night before, and save your other morning tasks for after your dream work. That means not looking at your to-do list or getting up to make coffee before you review your dream, or you risk forgetting the details of your dream.

If you can't create time for dream work when you first wake up, review the dream before opening your eyes, write a few keywords to help you remember the dream, and then wait until later to write a full description when you have time. If you don't have much time in the mornings, you might quickly review the sequence of dream scenes before opening your eyes, and then use the time while you're showering or getting ready for work to review your dream by replaying it in your head to help you remember it later.

Keep Your Dream Journal Handy

Keep a dream journal and pen next to your bed where you can easily reach them when you wake up, without getting out of bed. A dream journal not only gives you a ready place to write about your dreams, but it also reinforces your focus on remembering your dreams. Each time you see it before you go to bed, it reminds you that you want to remember your dreams. Keeping your dream journal within arm's reach allows you to pick it up and begin writing without having to search for it or get out of bed, which can bring you out of your sleepy state when dream recall is best. (Read more about dream journaling in "Dream Journaling," p. 60.)

Get into the Habit of Writing Dream Descriptions

Each morning, write what you can remember about your dreams the previous night, even if you don't go ahead and interpret them right then. The process of writing out your dream descriptions can help you remember the dreams and can actually trigger additional memories about the dream as you revisualize each part. Also, getting into this habit can help train your mind to remember your dreams in the future.

Stay in the Same Location to Write

You can enhance your dream recall by staying in the location where you had your dream (typically in your bed) to write your dream description. Changing your environment can take you out of that twilight state in which dream recall tends to be the most clear and complete.

Set a Pre-Sleep Intention

Each time you close your eyes to go to sleep—whether at night or before a daytime nap—set an intention to remember your dreams. To set an intention, think or say to yourself something like "I intend to remember the dreams that are beneficial for me to remember" or "I intend to remember my dreams that are for the highest good to remember." (For more about intentions, see "Chapter 4-7: TOOL: Setting Intentions," p. 234.) The reason you may not want to set an intention to remember all of your dreams is that some dreams are not beneficial to remember, because remembering them can reintroduce issues that have already been resolved or can recreate the negativity from a nightmare.

Pray at Bedtime

If you are spiritually inclined (or even if you are not), you may get positive results from saying a bedtime prayer or doing a spiritual meditation. A spiritual focus at bedtime can elevate your consciousness and lead to a different quality of dreams. Just as working through anger before going to sleep shifts your consciousness into a more positive state, focusing on your spiritual level (see Figure A in "Conscious Mind and Subconscious Mind," p. 11) before sleeping can lead to dreams that are more uplifting, provide greater clarity, or are more beneficial in other ways. In your prayer, you might ask that the Divine presence (or whatever name with which you feel comfortable) be with you throughout the night, and ask for assistance with remembering the dreams that are beneficial for you to remember. You can find more ideas to deepen your spiritual connection in "Chapter 4-16: TOOL: Deepening Your Spirituality" (p. 272), many of which you can use at bedtime.

Focus on Your Dreams and Dreaming

Paying attention to the dreams you do remember can help you remember more about your dreams in the future. Spending time on dream-related activities such as the following can help bring the idea of remembering your dreams to the forefront of your mind:

- Remembering and writing about your dreams.
- Interpreting your dreams.
- Talking with others about your dreams.
- Setting intentions for dreaming and dream recall (see "Set a Pre-Sleep Intention," p. 51).
- Reading your dream journal.
- Free-form writing about dreaming (see "Free-Form Writing to Improve Dream Recall," below).

Be Consistent

Setting up a consistent routine can also encourage dream recall. This includes setting a pre-sleep intention (see "Chapter 4-7: TOOL: Setting Intentions," p. 234.) and making sure your dream interpretation supplies—journal, pen, and anything else you need—are handy each night when you go to bed. Your pre-sleep intention can be anything you like, such as "I intend to sleep well and awake refreshed" or "I intend to rest peacefully and awake in the morning with greater clarity." You might also add a specific "dream intention" to your bedtime ritual, such as "I intend to remember my dreams that are beneficial for me to remember." In the morning, be sure you pay attention to the dreams you remember. Even if you don't write a full description and interpretation, I suggest at least jotting a few notes in your dream journal. Engaging in this kind of dream-related routine consistently over a period of days and weeks will likely improve your dream recall.

Free-Form Writing to Improve Dream Recall

Free-form writing involves writing whatever is present in your mind, whatever you are thinking or feeling in the moment, whatever words come forward. This technique can be a wonderful way to tap into your subconscious mind—the domain of dreams—and provide clues about issues related to your dreaming and recall processes.

The steps below show how to adapt the free-form writing technique to help enhance dream recall in general, and to release mental and emotional obstacles that interfere with remembering dreams.

1. Sit down with pen and plenty of paper. (Do not use your dream journal, since you'll be getting rid of these pages when you're done.)
2. Start writing everything that comes to mind about remembering (or not remembering) your dreams. If nothing comes to mind, write "I am going to keep on writing" and keep writing. If you get stuck, ask yourself questions such as: "If I knew why I haven't been remembering my dreams, it would be because..." or "When I think about

remembering my dreams, I feel..." or "The reasons I want to remember my dreams are...." Don't worry about handwriting or spelling because no one will ever see this except you.

3. Keep writing until you have a definite feeling that there is nothing left to be said. Write any important realizations you want to remember on a separate paper, perhaps in your dream journal. These might include realizations like "I need to simplify my morning process to allow time to focus on my dreams" or "I'd like to wake up more gently than with a loud alarm clock" or "I used to be afraid of what my dreams were saying, but now I intend to use them to improve my life."

4. Tear up or shred the original pages you wrote, to show your subconscious mind that you are releasing everything you wrote, along with all the related mental and emotional residues. (It's not the actual tearing up that releases things; instead, tearing up the paper triggers your mind to release what the words on the paper represent within your mind.) Do not reread the pages, so that you don't reintroduce into your mind what you just released.

For more about free-form writing, see "Chapter 3-23: TOOL: Free-Form Writing" (p. 198).

Release Your Inner Blocks to Dreaming and Recall

Negative beliefs and judgments about dreams can block your access to your own dreams, interfere with remembering them, or cause inner resistance to the dream interpretation process. To remove these inner blocks, you must first become aware of them before you can release them. One simple way to do this is to write down all of your negative self-talk, judgments, and limiting beliefs about dreaming, and then tear up the paper to demonstrate to your mind that you are releasing it (see the technique in the previous section, "Free-Form Writing to Improve Dream Recall," p. 52). Again, it's not the actual tearing up of the paper that releases things. Instead, tearing up the paper triggers your mind to release what the words on the paper represent within your mind.

You might write limiting beliefs and judgments such as "I can't remember dreams," "I could never be disciplined enough to write down my dreams," "My dreams are just a bunch of nonsense," "I'm a horrible dreamer," or "I'm a failure at dream interpretation." Keep writing until you feel there's no more to write, and then tear up or shred the paper.

Stay Non-Toxic

The same factors that trigger Toxic Dreams may also interfere with dream recall (read more about those factors in "Toxic Dream," p. 31). For example, if you have a hangover from too much alcohol or sugar the night before, your brain may not be working very well when you're trying to remember what you dreamed. These kinds of factors may also dampen or distort your emotional state and hinder your ability to recall your dream emotions, which can be key in determining dream meaning. Avoiding toxins, stress, and other detrimental factors can help ensure that your body, mind, and emotions are functioning optimally, both in terms of the dream process and in general.

Put Energy Toward Dreams and Dreaming

Focusing on dreams and dream interpretation can keep dreams at the forefront of your mind and improve the chances that you will remember your dreams. The possibilities are endless, and you can have fun coming up with your own dream-related activities. The following sections describe some activities you can use to focus your energy on dreams and dream interpretation.

Repeat Your Intentions

Repeat your pre-sleep dream intention periodically throughout the day, write it and stick it on your bathroom mirror or somewhere you'll see it often, set it to music so that you can sing it to yourself, or find other creative ways to repeat your intention throughout the day.

Create an Ideal Imagined Situation

Write a paragraph that describes your ideal dream interpretation experience. Start with "I am..." and write from your personal perspective as if you're already having that ideal experience. For example, you might write: "I am awakening peacefully in a quiet environment and I am easily remembering what I dreamed last night. I feel focused as I replay the dream in my mind and then write a description of it in my dream journal. I am enjoying the dream journal that I've customized to express my creativity and enthusiasm about dreams. As I explore my dream, my intuition is in fine form and I am easily sensing the dream's true meaning. I am feeling uplifted and content as I apply what I've learned from my dream to improve my life and my state of mind."

Have Fun with Your Dream Journal

Enjoy exploring the different kinds of dream journals available on the internet or in stores. You don't even need to buy one—just browsing is enough to focus your energy on the topic of dreams. Decorate the pages of your own dream journal with stickers, or use ink-stamps to decorate or highlight parts your dream journal. Find colored pencils, markers, or pens that write in different colors to use while writing in your dream descriptions—or use them to decorate your dream journal pages.

Inspire Yourself to Dream

Find things that inspire you and put them in your dream journal. Some inspiring ideas include:

- Pictures of cozy beds or rooms in which you'd like to sleep.
- Pictures that convey settings or feelings you'd like to dream about.
- Questions you'd like answered.
- Aspects of yourself you'd like to know better or you'd like to develop (such as creativity or mental ability).
- Quotes, stories, poems, or lyrics about dreams or dreaming.
- People (such as celebrities or authors).
- Color schemes you find inspiring or peaceful.
- Pictures that evoke feelings like peace or restfulness.
- Favorite memories.
- Goals or life dreams.
- Imaginings or "castles in the air."

Discuss Your Dreams

Talk about your dreams with a supportive friend or family member who is interested in discussing dreams. Make it clear that your focus will not be on guessing the meanings of each other's dreams, which can be counterproductive because you (the dreamer) are the only one who can recognize the meaning of your dream. Instead, focus on using the process of talking about dreams as a way to celebrate them and learn about them. You may even find that you recall more details of your dream as you are describing it to another person.

Read About Dreams

Search for articles about dreams and the latest dream research. You can find a lot of information on the internet. I highly recommend focusing on articles from credible sources, such as universities, therapists, and other dream psychology experts.

Meditate

Some people, including myself, have found that meditating regularly can help in accessing the "inner dream world," perhaps because practicing meditation helps a person learn to navigate more easily between levels of consciousness—for example, between a conscious, waking state and an inwardly-focused meditative state.

Create a Dream Touchstone

Choose a physical object that reminds you about dreams and dream interpretation. Place it near where you sleep, such as on your nightstand. Select an object that you can touch and feel—one that you can pick up each night and feel in your hand, to engage your kinesthetic sense as well as your visual sense. It should be an object that will refresh your enthusiasm about dreaming and remind you to pay attention to your dreams whenever you see it. Some possibilities include a stone engraved with the word "Dream," a figurine with a dream theme, or a pendant or charm that says "Dream." You could also be creative and make a special "dream" item that inspires you.

Tips for Recalling a Dream You Just Had

This section provides tips for remembering a particular dream you've just had. For best results, I suggest you use these tips first thing when you wake up from your dream.

Begin Immediately After You Awaken

In order to remember a dream, its details must somehow cross over from your subconscious mind—where the dream occurred—into your conscious mind so you can recall it later. Usually, your best opportunity to retrieve dream details from your subconscious mind is just as you are waking up, when you are still in a sleepy, semi-awake state. Being in that twilight state is like having one foot in the subconscious mind and the other foot in the conscious mind. This puts you in a great position to pull dream details from your subconscious into your conscious memory, where you can remember them when you are fully conscious. If you wait until you're fully conscious to try to remember a dream, the details may remain inaccessible in the subconscious mind.

Replay the Dream

Immediately when you wake up from the dream, before opening your eyes, replay the entire dream sequence in your mind—even if it's the middle of the night. This will help you remember more of the dream and recall greater detail after you become fully awake. While playing back your dream in your mind, assign a keyword or phrase to each main event in the dream sequence (such as "flood, rescue, hospital, home") to help you recall the whole dream after you've opened your eyes. For best recall, review your dream in your mind immediately after awakening, and before opening your eyes or moving around physically (see more details in "1. Review Your Dream," p. 74).

Write a Description of Your Dream

Writing your dream description can actually help you recall more details of your dream. While writing a description, you are again immersing yourself in the world of that dream, which may help trigger more memories about it. For example, focusing on the details of a particular scene may lead you to remember the color of the walls, whether the door was open or closed, or a character whom you had forgotten was in the room. (Read more about this process in "2. Record Your Dream Description," p. 75).

If You Can't Remember the Whole Dream

Don't worry if you can't recall every detail of a dream—or even whole parts of the dream story. Dreamers often recall the most significant aspects of a dream, or at least a key detail that prompts them to remember more of the dream. Certainly, remembering all the rich detail of a dream can provide additional context for the dream's meaning. However, remembering just a bit of a dream may be enough to interpret the dream in a useful way, even if much of the dream was forgotten during your transition from sleeping to waking.

In fact, sometimes merely the feeling you have when you wake up from a dream can be enough to go on. For example, if you wake from a dream feeling abandoned, the dream may have been exploring a real-life feeling or fear of abandonment, which you can then explore and potentially work through.

Any shred of the dream you remember can be a point of emergence, acting as a doorway through which dream details can emerge from your subconscious memory into your conscious mind. A glimpse of a character, scene, object, color, word, or mood may be all you need to start the flow of more dream details from subconscious mind to conscious mind.

If all you can remember is a small part of your dream and you don't know how to interpret it, here are some suggestions:

- Start with the emotion that went along with the dream detail you remember, since your emotions during a dream are often the very same as your emotions about what that aspect of your dream represents in real life (see more about how to do this in "Chapter 3-4: TOOL: Emotion Analysis," p. 114).
- Try using free-form writing to help prompt you to remember more of your dream (described in the next section, "Free-Form Writing to Recall a Particular Dream," p. 58).
- Dialogue with the aspect of your dream you do recall, and see where the process leads (see more in "Chapter 3-15: TOOL: Dialogue with Your Dream Symbol," p. 160).

- Explore what you do remember using some of the other dream techniques in "Part III: Dream Analysis Toolkit" (p. 101).

Free-Form Writing to Recall a Particular Dream

You can apply the free-form writing technique to help improve your recall of a specific dream you just had, rather than to improve dream recall in general (as discussed in "Free-Form Writing to Improve Dream Recall," p. 52). This technique's free flow of expression can open the door to your subconscious mind and allow additional details about your dream to emerge. Whether you remember your entire dream or just a small portion, this technique can help bring forward additional memories and insights to help you better understand the dream's meaning:

1. Sit down with pen and paper. (Do not use your dream journal, since you'll be getting rid of these pages when you're done.)
2. If you haven't already, replay your dream in your mind from beginning to end, just as you remember it.
3. Start writing everything that comes to mind—thoughts, feelings during the dream, what stood out, your mood, and anything else about the dream experience.
4. Keep writing until you have a definite feeling that there is nothing left to be said. If nothing comes to mind, write whatever words are in your mind—"I wish I could write something," "Blah, blah, blah," or whatever pops into your head—and keep writing. If you get stuck, ask yourself questions to get going again (such as "if I had something to say about this dream, it would be..." or "What makes me most curious about this dream is..." or "When I woke up from this dream, I felt..."). Don't worry about handwriting or spelling.
5. Note in your dream journal any memories or realizations that came forward about your dream, and follow-up items.
6. (Optional) Tear up or shred the pages on which you wrote, especially if you expressed a lot of emotion or worked through issues during the process.

For more about free-form writing, see "Chapter 3-23: TOOL: Free-Form Writing" (p. 198).

Recreate Your Sleep Situation

If are having trouble remembering your dream, try lying down in the same position as when you woke up from the dream—and in the same location, if possible. Sometimes creating this physical memory of your position can trigger flashes of the dream from when you were last in that position. The point here is not to go to sleep, but to recreate the physical circumstances in which you experienced the dream. If you don't remember what position you were in during the dream, try your usual sleep position.

Lie down, relax, and close your eyes. Images or glimpses of the dream may flash into your mind, and flashes of feelings from the dream may come forward. If they do, relax and just observe them as if you are watching a movie, rather than trying to analyze them. Before opening your eyes, review what you saw and felt. Then open your eyes and write what you recalled in your dream journal.

If no dream memories come forward, try recreating your other usual sleeping positions and see if they trigger any glimpses of your dream.

Pay Attention Next Time You Fall Asleep

As you drift off to sleep, you are re-entering the realm of the subconscious mind, in which the details of all your dreams reside. Sometimes dropping off to sleep opens the door to memories of whatever you were dreaming the last time you were asleep. So, if you can't remember your dream from last night, pay attention the next time you get ready to sleep—whether it's an afternoon nap or the following night. Snapshots from your most recent dream may pop into your mind just as you are lying down or just as you are drifting off to sleep.

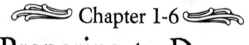# Chapter 1-6

Preparing to Dream

In This Chapter:

Before you begin interpreting your dreams, you might want to get some practical matters in order to make sure you're prepared for the dream interpretation process. You'll need a dream journal and an understanding of how to use it; you'll need to know when the best time is to interpret a dream and how long to keep your interpretation; and you can benefit from learning how to prepare for good quality sleep.

Dream Journaling

Dream journaling is the process of writing descriptions of your dreams, notes during your interpretation and follow-up process, and other dream-related writings such as personal insights and intentions. Dream journaling is an effective tool for organizing your dream work by keeping everything dream-related together in one place, and it can also enhance the dream interpretation process itself.

The Benefits of Dream Journaling

If you want to get the most from your dreams, then dream journaling is key. Writing a description of a dream when you first wake up can greatly enhance your dream interpretation process. For one thing, you'll recall more about your dream by recording it while it's still fresh, since your memory of a dream tends to fade as you transition from sleeping to awake. Also, the process of writing about your dream can often trigger memories of more dream details as you revisit the various scenes of the dream.

Writing your dream description also preserves your memory of a dream in a more permanent format. Once your dream is written down, you can come back to it later to review and interpret it. As you read the description again, often whole scenes will reappear in your mind with vivid details.

A physical, recorded dream description can help you get more from your interpretation process. Recording your dream using words and pictures provides the fullest possible record of your dream for you to interpret later. The more you remember and preserve about your dream, the more you can interpret.

A written dream description is easier to work with than the fleeting memory of a dream. The whole story of your dream is right there in front of you, so you can review it, analyze it, and jot down notes alongside it as new details of the dream or insights about meaning come forward. Your interpretation process would be much more limited if you were simply interpreting based on your mental recollection of the dream.

What You'll Need for Dream Journaling

A dream journal can be anything from a plain spiral notebook to a fancy blank journal. You could even use loose sheets of paper stapled together or kept in a loose-leaf binder. The particular physical format is not nearly as important as the writing itself. The idea here is to choose a format that will work well for your process of describing, annotating, and drawing pictures of your dreams.

You'll also need a writing implement to keep with your dream journal. I recommend using a pen that works well when writing quickly. When dream details are overflowing from your mind onto the page, you won't want anything that slows you down.

Dream journaling supplies can be as basic or elaborate as you like. A huge variety of blank journals are available for purchase, as well as many styles and sizes of notebooks. You might decide to keep a flashlight handy to avoid turning on the light in the middle of the night, or you could even buy a lighted pen for writing in the dark. Some people enjoy decorating the covers of their dream journals with drawings or craft materials, using colored pencils or markers during the dream interpretation process, or other creative approaches.

The Case for Journaling on Paper

I highly recommend journaling on paper rather than on an electronic device such as a computer, tablet device, or smartphone—for several reasons.

First, you ideally need to start writing your dream description immediately after you wake up, while dream details are still fresh, before you transition from a sleepy state into an awake state, and while you are still in the same place where you had the dream (usually your bed). Therefore, your dream journal always needs to be where you can easily reach it from where you are sleeping without having to sit up or get out of bed. That isn't always possible when using an electronic device. If you get out of bed to get your device or go sit at your computer, you've moved physically, changed your body position, and changed your location, all of which can reduce your recall of dream details.

Second, electronic devices tend to stimulate the brain, pulling you out of a sleepy state into a greater wakefulness quickly—and when you wake up too quickly, you may lose memory of many dream details. Dream recall is usually most accurate and complete immediately after you wake up from a dream, while you are still in that twilight state. Electronic devices also offer many tempting distractions, such as messages, notifications, and news items. Even a glimpse of such a distraction is likely to pull you out of your sleepy state, causing your dream memories to fade away.

Third, you need the option to include drawings, diagrams, timelines, and notes in the margins—both as you are writing your dream description and during your interpretation process. A drawing of a scene or dream character can help you remember it, as well as help you analyze its meaning later.

You might be tempted to dictate your dream descriptions into a tape recorder or digital recorder, which would be faster than writing them out. However, this may compromise the quality of your dream interpretation process because you may lose some visual details this way, and because dream interpretation is often not a linear process that follows the linear nature of a recording. Also, during interpretation you need the option of easily reviewing, annotating, and illustrating different parts of your dream as you analyze it. If you choose to use an audio format instead of a written format to record your dream descriptions, you'll probably want to translate them into written form before you analyze them.

Use Your Dream Journal Only for Dreams

I recommend a dedicated journal or notebook for dream journaling, rather than a mixed-purpose journal for both dreams and general journal writing. Here's why:

- A journal that is dedicated solely to dream interpretation, and is labelled that way, signals to your subconscious mind every time you see it that dreams are important. The journal becomes a visual reminder to focus on your dreams, as discussed in "Put Energy Toward Dreams and Dreaming" (p. 54).
- The process of choosing, buying or making, and setting aside a book just for dream journaling reinforces your intention to remember dreams. This is important because the stronger your intention to remember your dreams, the more likely you'll be aware of and remember your dreams.
- Some dream journals include helpful questions, instructions, or exercises to assist in dream journaling and interpretation. If you use a blank journal, you can paste in helpful tips and techniques to include in your interpretation process, such as copies of the dream interpretation, the "Quick Reference" (p. 299), and steps from your favorite techniques in "Part III: Dream Analysis Toolkit" (p. 101) and "Part IV: Dream Action Toolkit" (p. 215) later in this book.

The Shelf Life of Dreams

Dreams often have a limited shelf life, or length of time during which their topics are still current or applicable in your life. In general, it's best to interpret the dream as soon as possible after you awake. This section provides some guidelines to consider regarding the time frame for dream interpretation and how long to hold on to dream interpretations once you complete them.

Dreams Have a Short Shelf Life

A dream can be outdated shortly after you've had the dream, such as within a day or a few days. As your life changes, so do your dreams. Your hot-button issues today may not be nearly as important to you by next week—or they may even be resolved by then, such as in the case of a dream about a presentation you're giving tomorrow.

Sometimes a dream is already outdated by the time it ends. For example, you might have a dream in which the dream action is complete within the dream itself, such as a dream in which:

- Transformation or healing took place within you (see more in "Transformative Dream," p. 25).
- You gained clarity about a particular situation in your life.
- You had a dream experience that is complete within itself, such as expressing yourself creatively or flying like a bird.

Don't Wait Until It's Too Late

Most dreams portray something that's going on in your life or mind currently, at the time you have the dream. Like today's "breaking news," dreams deliver up-to-date messages about your innermost thoughts and feelings—sometimes even things that need your urgent attention. Because dreams are often so timely, I recommend interpreting them right away, rather than waiting. Otherwise, you may find yourself learning from last week's dream what action you needed to take last week, and wishing you knew then what you know now.

Dreams Are in the Now

Don't worry about preserving your dreams for posterity. Dreams are always in "the now." They are never more current than when you're actually dreaming them. Except for a few kinds of dreams, such as dreams that provide guidance about life direction, many dreams are providing a real-time snapshot of what's going on in your subconscious mind. Even a dream about your past is likely portraying how you feel now about what happened in the past.

Interpret, Then Move On

A dream interpretation is sort of like a text message: once you get the message, you've gotten it, and there's usually no need to go back and review it again. Once you've interpreted a dream and gotten everything from it that you can, there's often no value in going back to it again later. So, in general I recommend gleaning all you can from each dream, noting any important insights in your journal, and making any appropriate changes in your life and mind. Then let go of the dream and move on.

How Long to Keep Your Interpretations

The length of time you keep your dream descriptions and interpretations is up to you. I don't recommend revisiting old dreams just for the sake of revisiting them; however, there may be other specific reasons you want to keep old dream descriptions on hand. For example, if you're working through a long-term issue in your life, such as a past betrayal and a rebuilding of trust, you might decide to review an older dream as a benchmark for how much progress you've made since then. If you had a dream about a rose last night, you might want to review an old dream about a rose to see what the rose represented in that case.

Dreams also can lead to great realizations, clarifications, and decisions for your life. Sometimes a dream might prompt you to choose one life path instead of another or open a door to an opportunity that you wouldn't have otherwise. Other times, a series of individual dreams each provides the bit of information you need at the time of that dream, and reviewing that series of dreams later can help you see a more complete picture of dream meaning. So, the notes you make during your dream interpretation process can be worthwhile to keep in case you want to revisit them at some point.

Prepare to Sleep

High quality sleep is beneficial to the dream interpretation process, as well as for your overall well-being. Poor sleep can affect dream content, actually changing the course of a dream. For example, you may have experienced situations where noises from the surrounding environment became incorporated into a dream and altered the dream's story. Also, if you're not sleeping well, you may spend less of the night in a dream state, your dreams may be interrupted, and you may not be in much of a mood to interpret your dreams when you wake up. So, if you're interested in interpreting your dreams, it's worthwhile to pay attention to the factors that contribute to a quality sleep experience. Much has been written about this topic elsewhere, so in this section I'll highlight only the factors that I've found to be especially helpful.

Outer Environment

Create a physical sleeping environment that is comfortable, including a supportive bed and pillow. Fresh air can also contribute to a more pleasant sleeping environment, and some people find they sleep better in a cool environment with enough covers to be comfortably cozy. Some people sleep better with a fan running to keep the air moving—and the fan's noise itself can also facilitate sleep, as can a device that generates white noise or nature sounds.

Maintaining a clean bedroom and linens can help avoid respiratory irritation from dust and other particles. You may also want to avoid environmental toxins such as from new products like furniture, carpeting, paint, linens or other fabrics in the bedroom—as well as fumes from a nearby garage or other source of petrochemicals. Lingering chemical fragrances from laundry detergent and fabric softeners can also cause problems for some people.

Do what you can to reduce potential interruptions to your sleep. Use the bathroom just before going to bed, work out agreements with other household members to make sure you all get enough sleep, set a routine of letting your dog out just before bedtime, and take proactive measures to avoid other interruptions wherever possible.

Make the room where you sleep as dark as possible. Turn off all lights and cover any windows that let light in. However, beware of room-darkening curtains or shades that are coated with a layer containing toxic chemicals. You might also want to consider a motion-sensor nightlight that only turns on when it senses movement in the room.

Wear loose, comfortable clothing to sleep in. Choose garments that don't restrict your movements and that won't cause you to overheat. If you get cold you can add more covers, and you won't have to get up and change your clothing in the middle of the night.

Inner Environment

Your inner environment also contributes to your sleep quality. Your physical, mental, and emotional state can have a significant effect on sleep, as well as on dreams. For example, going to bed stressed can result in fewer hours of sleep, and the sleep you do get can be of lower quality. Consider the following suggestions to enhance sleep by helping you fall asleep and enjoy a restful sleep experience.

The physical factors in your body can also affect your mental and emotional state, thereby affecting your sleep and dreams. Therefore, you may want to make a point of eating a healthy diet and avoiding problem substances that could interfere with good quality sleep, such as toxic chemicals, sugar, caffeine, alcohol, tobacco, and other psychoactive substances. Also, avoid using computers or other electronic devices during the hour or so before bedtime to enhance your transition into a healthy sleep mode.

Elevating your inner state before you fall asleep can enhance your sleep quality, may enhance your dreams, and may also help you fall asleep more quickly. Try the following techniques to elevate your inner state after you close your eyes to go to sleep:

- Meditation can help you shift into an inner state that's more conducive to sleep, especially the kind of meditation that focuses on spirituality, love, or peace.
- Visualization can also help release internal distractions and move into a more peaceful state. One example is the Rainbow Visualization(see the full process in "Chapter 3-26: TOOL: Rainbow Visualization," p. 213), during which you visualize sequential colors to shift your mental and emotional state. Another example is visualizing yourself in a relaxing setting such as a sun-drenched tropical beach, embellishing the scene with as much lavish, experiential detail as you can imagine.
- Prayer may also contribute to better sleep. In particular, experiencing spiritual peace and releasing stressful concerns may enhance the sleep process.

• Practicing gratitude and forgiveness before you fall asleep can also elevate your inner state. Gratitude involves listing what you are grateful or thankful for, and forgiveness involves releasing judgments you've made against yourself or others.

Noises can wake you up or affect the content of your dreams while you're sleeping, so do what you can to reduce noise from the environment around you. Establish an agreement among household members to keep things quiet, and make sure everyone has water handy to drink during the night. If you can't avoid noises that wake you up, you can mask them using a device that makes a white noise, nature sounds, or other ambient sounds (but make sure they don't compromise your safety).

Before you go to sleep, take steps to reduce stress and mental chatter. Some helpful techniques include writing down all your mental to-do list items, free-form writing to vent your emotions and mental chatter, deep breathing, meditation, visualization, and soothing music or sounds.

If something is bothering you, address it before going to sleep if possible, or at least decide to set it aside until you wake up tomorrow.

Avoid triggers for Toxic Dreams to reduce the chance of experiencing unpleasant dreams (for details, see "Toxic Dream," p. 31).

PART II

HOW TO INTERPRET DREAMS

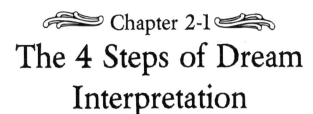

Chapter 2-1

The 4 Steps of Dream Interpretation

In This Chapter:

You're ready to interpret your dream. You've read the whole book up to this point, so you're equipped with the knowledge you need in order to get the most out of your dream interpretation process. (If you haven't read the previous chapters, I strongly recommend reading them before beginning this section, for best results.)

About This Process

This chapter introduces the step-by-step dream interpretation process. At first glance, its four basic steps may appear deceivingly simple. However, what distinguishes this framework is its richness and flexibility. It provides what you need for a robust, customizable interpretation experience in which *you* select the techniques, *you* decide how extensively to analyze, and *you* choose how to use what you learn from your dream—following clear, detailed instructions throughout. For example, during dream analysis, you can select from 25 techniques in "Part III: Dream Analysis Toolkit" (p. 101) to explore the meaning of your dream. Then follow up on what you learned from your dream by choosing from the 15 techniques in "Part IV: Dream Action Toolkit" (p. 215) to improve yourself and your life.

Overview of Dream Interpretation Steps

This dream interpretation process involves the following main steps:

1. **REVIEW**—Review your dream with eyes closed, from beginning to end.
2. **RECORD**—Write a description of the dream, including all elements and emotions.
3. **ANALYZE**—Use analysis techniques to explore until your intuition confirms the true meaning.
4. **ACT**—Apply dream information to improve your life and your mind.

To help you remember these steps, think of the abbreviation **RRAA**.

The next chapter ("Chapter 2-2: Interpret Your Dream," p. 73) provides detailed instructions for each of these four steps. The detailed instructions are also presented in a condensed format in "Quick Reference" (p. 299) near the end of the book.

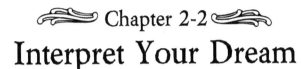

Chapter 2-2
Interpret Your Dream

In This Chapter:

This chapter provides detailed instructions for the four-step dream interpretation process. Each numbered section in this chapter guides you through one of the four steps: "1. Review Your Dream" (p. 74), "2. Record Your Dream Description" (p. 75), "3. Analyze Your Dream" (p. 78), and "4. Act on Your Dream" (p. 87). A condensed version of these instructions is included in "Quick Reference" (p. 299) near the end of the book, which you can use as a handy reference once you're familiar with the process.

1. Review Your Dream

Upon awakening from your dream, before opening your eyes, replay your dream in your mind from beginning to end as if you are mentally replaying a movie you've just seen. This process helps to pull the whole thread of your dream out of your subconscious mind and into your conscious memory so you can remember its details later. If you skip this step, the dream may stay trapped in your subconscious mind once you're fully awake, and you may not remember much.

Review Your Whole Dream

Take your time as you replay the dream in your mind. Start at the beginning and replay every bit of the dream, even if you think you already remember certain parts of it. As the dream plays forward, just let it flow as it did during the original dream. If you can't remember the whole dream, replay the parts you do remember. If you don't remember the sequence of the different parts, just review each part as it comes to mind.

Play the Role of Observer

This dream review is about simply replaying the dream in your mind, and observing it as it plays through. This is not the time for analyzing, commenting on, judging, or reacting to what's happening in the dream. In fact, that kind of mentalizing can actually distract you from remembering important dream details. Instead, just watch the dream as it retells its story.

Assign Keywords

As you move forward through the dream story, choose a keyword to summarize each key event or scene to help you remember the basic dream sequence after you open your eyes. For example, for a dream in which you were driving down a road and then drove off a bridge, after which you swam to safety, you might choose "Driving, Falling, Swimming." For a dream in which you were cooking dinner when a giant squid crashed through your ceiling, and then you ran through the streets to get away, you might choose "Cooking, Squid, Running." Choose short, easy-to-remember keywords or phrases that you can remember until you've finished reviewing the dream. Unless the dream is long or complicated, or you had more than one dream, there's probably no need to write down your keywords until you've replayed the whole dream. Keeping your eyes closed and staying in that post-sleep twilight state until you've reviewed the entire dream can help you stay connected to it and help you remember it later.

If you remember more than one dream when you wake up, assign a series of keywords for each dream.

(For tips to help you remember a dream you just had, see "Tips for Recalling a Dream You Just Had," p. 56.)

2. Record Your Dream Description

A dream description is a written record of your dream. Writing your dream description is important to help you remember as much detail as possible. A written description gives you something to refer to later and add notes to as you interpret the dream. Also, the description process itself may trigger your memory of more dream details. I strongly recommend writing your dream description on paper, rather than on a computer or other device (see the reasons in "The Case for Journaling on Paper," p. 62). For more about the dream journaling process, revisit "Dream Journaling" (p. 60).

Write Immediately After You Wake Up

Your best chance to recall the most dream detail is right after you wake up from the dream, after you've replayed the whole dream in your mind with your eyes still closed. If you wait until later, your memory of the dream may fade during your transition into a fully awake state.

Write Your Keywords

As soon as you complete your dream review, write in your dream journal the keywords you chose to summarize each main event in your dream (as described in "Assign Keywords" on p. 74 of "1. Review Your Dream"). If you didn't choose any keywords, do it now and write them down. Without keywords, by the time you finish writing a detailed description of the early part of your dream, you may have forgotten the later parts. Your keywords help solidify your memories of the dream. They serve as anchor points in your conscious mind as you pull the thread of your dream story out of your subconscious mind into your conscious mind.

Each keyword acts as a touchstone for a particular part of the dream, returning you mentally to that dream scene each time you see the keyword again. In this way, a keyword creates an reentry point back into the dream when you are trying to recall it—which can be particularly helpful if you don't have time to write a full description when you first awaken, and also when you need to reimmerse yourself in a particular dream scene during analysis (in "3. Analyze Your Dream," p. 78).

Write the Date

Write the date you had the dream above your dream description. Not only is this a basic part of the record-keeping process, but the date may end up being especially important for cases in which the timing of the dream is of interest. For example, you might want to look back at dreams you were having during a certain time in your past, such as when you first met your spouse or when you were planning your new business. If you think a particular dream contained a prediction, you would need the date to verify that you had the dream prior to the predicted real-life event.

Write a Description of Your Dream

Next, write a description of your dream from beginning to end in as much detail as possible. Include everything that happened in your dream, just as it unfolded. Include all the details you can remember, including characters, events and actions, settings, objects that stood out, moods, and your feelings during each part of the dream (see more in the next section) and when you woke up. However, don't get bogged down in this list of elements—just write your dream story and include as much detail as you remember.

If you can't remember the whole dream, refer to your keywords to help you remember; otherwise, start writing about the earliest part of the dream you remember. Even a shred of a dream, such as an image and associated feeling, may provide enough for interpretation.

Include Your Emotions

As you write your dream description, include notes about how you felt during the different parts of the dream and when you first woke up, including any associated physical sensations (such as a knot in your stomach). Your emotions during the dream can be a huge clue to dream meaning, since they are likely the same emotions you feel regarding whatever the dream represents in your real life. For example, if your feelings during a dream were "I felt afraid," then "I felt sad about being ignored," then "I felt peace after the person apologized," this sequence could help you identify the sequence of real life emotional events the dream is portraying. For example, perhaps that sequence of feelings represents your real-life fear about your relationship because your partner had become too distracted by her work, followed by a feeling of peace when you two talked and you realized your relationship is strong enough to survive any such challenges.

You may find it helpful to reread your dream description when you finish writing it, and this time add descriptions of your feelings during each part of the dream. Note your feelings and instincts, as well as emotional reactions to characters, actions, and settings as you proceed through the dream. In addition, describe any physical sensations you had during the dream.

Don't Analyze Yet

While you're writing your dream description, it's not yet time to analyze or start guessing what the dream means. If hunches or realizations come forward as you write your dream description, jot them in the margins, but then return to describing the dream. Don't get distracted by trying to figure things out, since this can pull you out of the sleepy state in which your dream memory is still strong. Focus on telling the story of your dream.

Dream Elements to Include

Once you've written the dream description, read through it again and add to it any more memories about the dream that come forward. You can write them in the margins, between lines, or where ever there's room. As you go, notate anything that stood out, seemed significant, surprised you, or seemed odd. Use the following list of dream elements to prompt your memory of dream details:

- **Key Symbols**—Things that stood out, and their contexts and characteristics.
- **Characters**—Identity, appearance, demeanor, intentions.
- **Actions**—Who did what, how, motivations, toward what purpose or result.
- **Words**—Words, letters, or numbers you heard or saw.
- **Time Frame**—Age you were in the dream, other references to a specific time.
- **Setting**—House or building, yard, street, tunnel, graveyard, urban or rural.
- **Setting Characteristics**—Dark, clean, warm, chaotic, rustic, damp.
- **Mood**—Upbeat, depressing, lively, dreary, foreboding, boring.
- **Colors**—Of key symbols or objects, clothing, setting, landscape.
- **Weather**—Sunny, cloudy, rainy, icy, windy, arid, approaching storm.
- **Sensory Information**—Visuals, sounds, smells, tastes, physical sensations, textures.
- **Reactions and Emotions**—Yours, and those you observed or sensed from others.
- **Anything Else**—Things that stood out, seemed important, seemed out of place (such as someone wearing sunglasses at night, or your mother appearing much younger than her age in real life).

Dream Title

Give your dream a descriptive title that indicates clearly what the dream is about. Examples include "Tropical Island Vacation," "Late for Final Exam," "Finding an Abandoned Baby," or "Escaping a Flood." Dream titles help organize your dreams and make it easier for you to find a particular dream if you need to refer to it again later. For example, if you dreamed about a lost cat and you remember that you dreamed about one before, you might want to check what the cat symbolized to you in your earlier dream.

Note a Recurring Dream, Theme, or Elements

If your dream is similar to one you've had before, include that fact in your dream title—such as "Home Invasion Recurring Dream"—or make a note somewhere near the title that this is a recurring dream. You might also want to make a note if your dream contains a theme, symbol, or element that is repeated from a past dream. These notations make it easier to find similar dreams or symbols later so you can analyze them together as a group.

3. Analyze Your Dream

Everything you've written in your dream journal up until this point has focused on describing and labelling your dream. If you don't yet know intuitively what your dream means—or if you think you do, but you're not sure—now is the time to start analyzing your dream.

Dream analysis provides various ways to look at the dream through your mind's eye, until your intuition says "Yes! That's the meaning of this dream." This process involves both your rational mind (your mental level) and your intuition simultaneously. Your rational mind conducts the analysis, looking at the dream in different ways and asking "What about this meaning?", each time giving your intuition a chance to confirm "Yes, that's the true meaning." So, use the analysis process in service to your intuition—to encourage your intuition, clear the way for it, and give it a space in which to operate and recognize true dream meaning.

Sometimes your intuition will confirm the dream's true meaning right away. Other times, you may need to help the intuitive process along by spending more time with the dream, looking at it from various angles using different analysis tools, and finding ways to quiet your mind so you can hear your intuition.

The following sections present the key information you need to know first when analyzing dreams, such as how to begin the process and the most common patterns of dream symbolism to look for in your dream. Once you're familiar with the topics in this section, you can choose from the analysis techniques in "Part III: Dream Analysis Toolkit" (p. 101) to delve further into the meaning of your dream. (After you have determined the meaning of your dream, move on to the final step in the interpretation process, "4. Act on Your Dream," p. 87, to follow up on what you learned from your dream.)

Create a Quiet Space

Make a quiet space for your interpretation process, ideally right after you've woken up, reviewed the dream in your mind, and written your dream description. If you don't have time to interpret the dream at that point, set aside a time later in the day and refer to the notes you wrote when you wrote your dream description in Step 2. For suggestions on how to create a quiet space for dream interpretation, see "Wake Up Quietly" (p. 49).

Write Your First Hunch About Meaning

If you have a hunch or a first instinct about what your dream means, or about what a certain dream symbol represents, write it down and set it aside. You might want to write it on a separate sheet of paper, and then revisit it after you've spent more time with your dream, waiting until you know your dream's true meaning. If you don't have a first hunch about the meaning of your dream, don't worry—maybe you just haven't connected intuitively with its meaning yet.

Open Your Mind

Before analyzing your dream, open your mind. This means letting go of any preconceptions, what you hope or fear the dream means, and any fantasized ideas about what you think it should mean. You've already written down any first hunches about meaning, so those are safe. Now, start from scratch and let your dream speak to you. Create a clear space within your consciousness from which your dream can speak to you. Set an intention to view your dream from a neutral perspective, considering all possible dream meanings that come forward as you explore. (See more about setting intentions in "Chapter 4-7: TOOL: Setting Intentions," p. 234.)

One huge pitfall of dream interpretation is going into the process hoping for a certain outcome, wanting the dream to mean a particular thing. For example, so many clients have sent me descriptions of dreams about getting together with a former love interest, each hoping that it means the person wants to get back together again. These dreams often represent something completely different, such as a wish for emotional intimacy, reminiscing about the past, or the former love interest representing the dreamer's current real-life partner. So, trying to interpret a dream while holding an emotional attachment to a particular meaning is like exploring the countryside while holding a huge picture-book about the city in front of your face. You can't see beyond what's blocking your vision. Interpretation is likely to be more accurate when you let go of any attachments beforehand, or at least suspend them for a while during your interpretation process.

Placing a label on your dream, such as thinking of it as a "bad dream" or a "good dream" can also limit you in the dream interpretation process. Dreams tend to act like a mirror, reflecting your own subconscious thoughts and feelings—and therefore, like reflections from a mirror, dreams are not inherently good or bad. A reflection might be unclear if the mirror is poor quality, but the reflection you see in the mirror is neither good nor bad. The labels of "good" and "bad" exist only in your mind. Although you might label a particular dream as "good" or "bad" or "pleasant" or "unpleasant," the dream itself actually just *is*. Setting aside all labels and viewing your dream from a neutral perspective can help open your mind so you can recognize the dream's true meaning more easily.

Identify the Theme of Your Dream

Identify the main theme of your dream and write it above your dream description in your dream journal. The theme of a dream is the essence of the dream's story, the most basic description of what the dream was about. The theme may not describe everything that happened in the dream, but it describes the main dynamic within the dream. Some common dream themes include:

- Being chased or victimized.
- Being stolen from.
- Boundary invasion.
- Abandonment.
- Betrayal.
- Falling.
- Drowning.
- Being lost.
- Looking for or losing an object.
- Flying or levitating.
- Being naked.
- Illness.
- Pregnancy.
- Death.
- Accident or disaster.
- Failure.

- Being late, or missing a scheduled event.
- Technical problems, such as with a phone.
- Wish fulfillment.

For more clues about your dream's theme, consider the title you chose for the dream, which may point to a certain dream theme. To read more about dream themes and how to identify them, see "Chapter 3-9: TOOL: Dream Theme Analysis" (p. 137).

Connect with Your Intuition

Your intuition is the aspect of yourself that will recognize the meaning of your dream, so I suggest doing one or more of the following to help you tune into your intuition before you begin dream analysis:

- Connect with your intuition by saying out loud or inwardly "I attune to my intuition" or "I call forward my highest inner wisdom."
- Set an intention to attune to your intuition, such as "I intend to connect directly with my intuition"—or shift your focus to your intuition with a statement such as "I call forward my intuition."
- Do a short meditation to center yourself in your intuition. For example, close your eyes for a minute or two and focus on a key word or phrase such as "intuition," "enlighten," or "I attune to the highest wisdom within."
- Say a prayer, such as "I ask for Divine assistance in connecting with my intuition" or "I open to my intuition regarding this dream."

Notice What Stands Out

Think about anything that stands out in your dream—such as events, objects, colors, or physical sensations. Mark each one in your dream description. Then open your mind and explore what each of these elements might represent within your waking life or mind, paying attention to any associated emotion. Remember to explore obvious meanings, as well as less obvious ones. When you come upon the true meaning, you will likely have a distinct experience such as an "Aha!" moment, a flash of recognition, the sudden sense that everything within you is in alignment, and a feeling of peace and completion. If no meaning is obvious, see the following section for more helpful instructions.

The Analysis Sequence

When analyzing your dream, I suggest applying the following approaches to explore the meaning of your dream, in the order shown here:

1. Consider Common Types of Dream Symbolism

Consider whether any of the types of symbolism in the next section, "Consider Common Dream Symbolism First" (p. 82), apply to your dream. If so, this can help inform and streamline your search for dream meaning.

2. Dream Analysis Toolkit: Top Six Tools

Complete the following techniques in the order listed—unless there's one that obviously relates to your particular dream (in which case you'd complete it first):

    3-2: TOOL: Parallels Between Symbols and Real Life (p. 105)
    3-3: TOOL: Generalization Analysis (p. 110)
    3-4: TOOL: Emotion Analysis (p. 114)
    3-5: TOOL: Hierarchical Dream Symbol Analysis (p. 117)
    3-6: TOOL: Character Analysis (p. 121)
    3-7: TOOL: Levels of Existence (p. 126)

3. Dream Analysis Toolkit: Remaining Tools

Explore the remaining techniques in the toolkit in any order you like:

    3-8: TOOL: Caveman Explanation (p. 134)
    3-9: TOOL: Dream Theme Analysis (p. 137)
    3-10: TOOL: Dream Dictionary (p. 141)
    3-11: TOOL: Personal Dream Dictionary (p. 145)
    3-12: TOOL: Timeline Analysis (p. 147)
    3-13: TOOL: Element Relationship Mapping (p. 152)
    3-14: TOOL: Draw Your Dream Symbol (p. 156)
    3-15: TOOL: Dialogue with Your Dream Symbol (p. 160)
    3-16: TOOL: Dream Symbol Monologue (p. 164)
    3-17: TOOL: Dialogue with the Dream Source (p. 167)
    3-18: TOOL: Dialogue with a Higher Source (p. 170)
    3-19: TOOL: Literary Analysis (p. 175)
    3-20: TOOL: Archetype Analysis (p. 181)
    3-21: TOOL: Art Analysis (p. 187)
    3-22: TOOL: Discovering Your Gifts (p. 195)
    3-23: TOOL: Free-Form Writing (p. 198)
    3-24: TOOL: Writing a Shred Letter (p. 203)
    3-25: TOOL: Dealing with Nightmares (p. 206)
    3-26: TOOL: Rainbow Visualization (p. 213)

Consider Common Dream Symbolism First

Dreams tend to incorporate certain patterns of symbolism into their stories. You might think of these patterns as similar to literary devices, which are methods an author uses to convey what she wants to convey in a story—such as through a metaphor. Although some dreams express meaning in a completely unique way, many dreams follow patterns in their storytelling that you'll begin to recognize as you interpret more dreams.

The following items describe some of the most frequently encountered types of dream symbolism patterns. Consider these first when you're analyzing a dream, and this may provide a shortcut to discovering your dream's meaning.

Literal Translation

If the dream people, events, objects, actions, or settings exist in your real life, they may represent those actual elements of your waking life. For example, your mother hugging you in your dream may represent a particular time she hugged you, or her affection toward you in general. Consider whether the dream may be portraying your current life or your past, and whether you recognize thoughts or feelings in the dream that you've experienced in your real life, perhaps recently.

Emotions

The emotions you feel during the dream may very well be the same emotions you feel about the aspect of your real life that the dream represents. For example, jealousy in a dream may point to an area of your life in which you feel jealous of a particular person or situation. If you feel overwhelmed with what's happening in the dream, the dream may be portraying a situation in your real life in which you feel overwhelmed, or did in the past.

Abundance or Lack

The dream may be pointing out something that you feel you have too much of—or something that you do too much of—in your real life. Alternatively, your dream may indicate the opposite—something that you lack or that you do too little of. If your dream contained a pleasant experience, such as doing a good job of finishing a project, perhaps your subconscious mind is pointing out that you'd like more of that kind of experience in your real life. If your dream was unpleasant, such as spending time with people who criticize you, your subconscious mind may be wanting to avoid that kind of experience in real life.

Personal Symbolism

When you think of a specific symbol from your dream, consider what it brings to mind for you personally. You probably already associate each dream symbol with meanings that are specific to you—based on your experience, your perceptions, and other associations you've already made with that symbol in your mind. For example, one person might associate a wolf with fearlessness, while someone else might associate it with loyalty or wildness. The symbol of a baby might bring to mind vulnerability for one dreamer, while someone else might associate it with responsibility or a process of growth. So, when you consider a particular dream symbol, pay attention to the meanings that come to mind when you think of that symbol, since these are the meanings you tend to associate with it.

A particular dream symbol may bring more than one meaning to mind for you. For example, when you think of money, the first thing that comes to mind might be that it's fun to spend, but you might also think of it as power and as a solution to financial problems. So, if the first meaning you think of doesn't relate to anything in your real life, and doesn't resonate for you, see what other meanings come to mind that may parallel what's going on in your life. Some helpful techniques to explore personal dream symbolism are "Chapter 3-8: TOOL: Caveman Explanation" (p. 134) and "Chapter 3-11: TOOL: Personal Dream Dictionary" (p. 145).

Importance

The most important symbols in a dream are often the ones that you tend to notice. These symbols that stood out during the dream are a good place to start when analyzing dream symbolism. Symbols may stand out because they're so huge you can't miss them—like a boulder falling on your house— or they could be small details that happen to stand out in your mind—such as a chip on a teacup that's sitting on a side table. Sometimes an important symbol might be highlighted in the dream with a bright color, illuminated with light, pointed to with an arrow, or emphasized in some other way.

Urgency

If there's a sense of urgency involved in the dream, then the dream could be representing an urgent matter that needs attention in your real life (or in your mind, such as fear). For example, if you dream that there's a fire at work and you're trying to put it out, the dream may be pointing to a real-life situation at work in which a problem has suddenly come up that you feel must be dealt with immediately to avoid a catastrophe.

Subject Context

A dream may be about you, or it could represent your perception of a friend or family member, or a situation you've been aware of lately—even in the media, on TV, or in a movie. For example, if you dream about a girl wearing a cheerful flowered dress that inspires a feeling of fun within you, she might represent yourself feeling happy or wanting to feel happier in real life. Alternatively, she might represent a friend who was in a particularly good mood when you saw her yesterday, a new upbeat song you just heard for the first time, or an optimistic character in a TV show you watched last night.

Time Context

The dream could be referring to past or present events or situations—or to future ones that you expect, imagine, or fear. Elements that might bring to mind a past era include people, activities, clothes, places, music, books, or other things that remind you of a particular time in the past. For example, a dream might indicators pointing to the past such as your elementary school building, a former teacher, a sport you used to play, or fashions from your teen years. A dream that portrays your imagined version of the future might include time-frame indicators such as you looking older than you are, futuristic clothes or hair styles, technologies that don't exist yet, or other forward-looking elements.

Emotional Exaggeration

When a dream portrays a real-life situation that's particularly emotional for the dreamer, sometimes the situation shows up as exaggerated in the dream. In other words, the subconscious mind may amplify the real-life situation as it portrays it in a dream, making a "mountain out of a mole-hill." In these cases, the exaggerations express how strongly you feel about the dream's subject matter. For example, if in real life you saw a baby snake in your yard, and you are very afraid of snakes, the snake might show up in a dream as a huge serpent attacking you. If you stubbed your toe yesterday on a toy fire truck that your son left in the middle of the floor, which really perturbed you because you had asked him three times to put it away, this story might show up in a dream as your son driving a real fire truck over your foot. So, consider whether a situation in your dream could perhaps represent a similar but less extreme situation in your waking life, about which you feel strong emotion.

Apply Techniques in the Dream Analysis Toolkit

After you've considered the kinds of dream symbolism in "Consider Common Dream Symbolism First" (p. 82), proceed to "Part III: Dream Analysis Toolkit" (p. 101) and begin with the first six analysis tools in it. After that, if you still haven't discovered your dream meaning, explore your dream further by choosing among the remaining techniques in "Part III: Dream Analysis Toolkit."

Explore Until Your Intuition Says Yes

Regardless of which dream analysis techniques you choose, the goal is to arrive at your dream's true meaning—when you have a flash of recognition, a sudden sense that everything within you is in alignment, or a sense of peace and completion. (For more about working with your intuition, see "Intuition: The Key to Recognizing Dream Meaning," p. 33, and "Tips for Developing Dream Intuition," p. 39).

The particular dream analysis techniques you choose are less important than the idea of spending time exploring your dream, thereby creating time and space within which your intuition can operate. If you don't experience intuitive clarity about dream meaning right away, try different analysis techniques to turn your dream around different ways and look at it from various angles—which may help trigger that intuitive flash of recognition.

If You Still Can't Determine Dream Meaning

Sometimes you might explore a dream for quite a while—even sit with it a few days—and you still can't figure out what it means. The following suggestions provide ideas for how to proceed when you're having trouble connecting with a dream's meaning.

Set the Dream Aside for a While

If at any point during your interpretation process you are feeling overwhelmed or bogged down with dream details—or if you're just not connecting with dream meaning—you might want to set the dream aside and come back to it later with a fresh perspective.

Share Your Dream

You might find that describing your dream to someone else may help bring forward within you new realizations about meaning. Sometimes the process of telling your dream story to another person can help you connect with your own intuition and recognize hidden dream meaning as you speak. The other person may also offer helpful insights about possible dream meaning, especially if they know you well and are familiar with the details of your life.

Develop Your Intuition

During dream interpretation, intuition is the key to recognizing dream meaning. If none of the meanings you've considered are ringing true for you, you may benefit from reviewing the sections of this book about intuition and how to use it, including "Intuition: The Key to Recognizing Dream Meaning" (p. 33) and "Tips for Developing Dream Intuition" (p. 39).

Consult an Intuitive Dream Professional

An intuitive dream professional may be able provide guidance and suggestions for understanding the meaning of your dream. However, choose wisely who you consult, as discussed in "Working With a Dream Interpretation Professional" (p. 42).

Let It Go

When an issue from a dream doesn't get resolved or a message from a dream isn't received by the dreamer, it often reappears later in another dream or in real life. If you've tried everything and still can't figure out what your dream means, you can try just letting it go. Pressing issues often have ways of making themselves known, sooner or later.

4. Act on Your Dream

Once you understand your dream's meaning, consider what—if any—action to take based on the content of the dream. You now have an opportunity to act on what you learned—to apply the information from your dream in a positive way. Consider what your dream conveyed about what's working and what's not in your life, and any other opportunities to improve yourself and your life. This could mean taking action within your own consciousness—such as releasing judgments, replacing self-defeating beliefs, renegotiating outdated agreements with yourself, finding closure on situations from the past, or clarifying life direction. You might also see opportunities for external follow-up actions—such as solving a problem, inspiring a creative process, trying something new, identifying and acting on your strengths, or completing an unfinished project.

In the following sections I provide suggestions for acting on what you learned from your dream through both inner and external areas of your existence. The step-by-step process in "How to Work Through an Issue" (p. 97) is the cornerstone technique for dream follow-up, which you can use to work through an issue that was brought to light during your dream.

Once you're familiar with the topics in this section, you can choose from the detailed techniques in "Part IV: Dream Action Toolkit" (p. 215), each of which is designed to walk you through a different aspect of dream follow-up.

The Keys to Positive Change

Your dreams may be handing you the keys to a fantastic new life—or at least to a huge improvement—if you listen to and act on what they're telling you. Through your dreams you can discover things about yourself and your life that you've never known, and that you might otherwise never know. Dreams can highlight opportunities for emotional healing, releasing, and closure. They may point to areas for improvement in your inner environment, such as self-defeating patterns, limiting beliefs, or judgments. Dreams can tell you about your unmet needs, so you can then take action to fulfill those needs. You may also find that dreams provide forward-looking information, such as clarity on life direction and decisions, creative ideas, hidden strengths, and unique gifts. The following sections will explore all of these "invitations to action" more closely.

You Are in Charge

Dreams may provide you with information, but the way you act on that information is completely up to you. Some dreams may seem to propel you into action, but ultimately you must decide what, if any, action to take. Do not blindly follow apparent suggestions for action that show up in dreams. If you do, this would mean you're handing over your decision-making power to your subconscious mind, which would be extremely unwise, since the subconscious mind tends to be a poor decision maker. Instead, make your decisions using conscious, careful consideration, taking into account relevant information from all appropriate sources. You—the conscious you—are responsible for every decision and everything you do, along with the resulting consequences.

You may choose to act right away on something you learn from a dream, or you may decide to wait. However, remember that dream information is current at the time you have the dream, and it may become outdated if you wait, as described in "The Shelf Life of Dreams" (p. 63). Use your best judgment in choosing both your actions and their timing.

Examples of Acting on Your Dream

This section shows examples of the many follow-up actions you might take to improve yourself and your life based on information from your dreams. These examples mention various techniques for working through and acting on issues from dreams, such as "Chapter 4-2: TOOL: Acceptance" (p. 219) and "Chapter 4-4: TOOL: Forgiveness" (p. 224). Each of these techniques is presented with detailed instructions in "Part IV: Dream Action Toolkit" (p. 215) later in the book.

Depending on the content of a particular dream, you might decide to follow up in one or more of the ways described in the following sections (or in some other way).

Become more accepting of yourself, someone else, or a situation in your life.

A dream may provide insight about you, someone else, or a situation in your life. For example, the dream might highlight your need for more fun in your life or suggest why a family member acts a certain way. A dream might also clarify a situation in your life, changing the way you think about it. Sometimes, simply the awareness of this new information is enough to trigger a change in how you think about the person or situation. Other times, you may not gain the new insights until you delve more deeply into the issue and your emotions about it (see more about how to do this in the next few sections: "Issues Brought to Your Attention by Dreams" on p. 96, "Resolving Issues by Changing Your Mind" on p. 96, and "How to Work Through an Issue" on p. 97). In order to act on information from a dream that clarifies something for you, you might first choose to accept yourself, the person, or the situation "as is"—and then choose which inner and outer changes you can make to improve your related experience.

Here's an example. After a dream that highlighted your impatience with how long it's taking you to lose weight, you might decide to accept the fact that the process has been slower than you expected (see "Chapter 4-2: TOOL: Acceptance," p. 219). You might also make the following inner changes: decide to be more patient with yourself and the process, and adjust your expectations about how long weight loss will take. You might choose to make an external change of finding ways to ensure that you exercise regularly, such as joining an exercise class or finding new kinds of physical activity you really enjoy.

Forgive a past action.

A dream may trigger a realization that you are still judging someone who you feel wronged you in the past, or perhaps you are judging yourself for wronging someone. Holding onto those judgments means carrying around all that hurt, anger, pain, and resentment within yourself—in perpetuity. Those judgments are creating negative areas within your consciousness that darken and weigh you down. They also keep you tied to the past by effectively "locking in" those past actions within you, which in turn keeps you from letting go of the past and moving on. You can forgive by consciously releasing your judgments of yourself or others as having been "bad" or "wrong" in the past (see "Chapter 4-4: TOOL: Forgiveness," p. 224).

For example, if you dreamed that a horse gave you a golden box and then took it back from you again, you might determine that this dream represents someone in your past who became your friend and then "took the friendship back" by breaking off the friendship. So, you might first process through your hurt feelings about that (see "Chapter 4-3: TOOL: Processing Emotions," p. 222), and then release your judgment against that person as bad for breaking off the friendship (see "Chapter 4-4: TOOL: Forgiveness," p. 224)—realizing that you don't have the ability to fully understand why the person acted that way, what was really going on in her mind, and what problems and inner challenges she was dealing with at the time. You might also remind yourself that, as always in life, you do not have control over other people's actions.

Release limiting beliefs.

A dream might highlight beliefs within your consciousness that are out-dated, irrational, or self-defeating in some way. You can release such a belief and replace it with an updated belief that rings true for you now (see "Chapter 4-6: TOOL: Transforming Beliefs," p. 231).

An example would be a dream in which the wind blew a $100 bill out of your hand, and it repeatedly escaped your grasp as you scrambled to pick it up. You wake up feeling frustrated about money, and you recognize that the dream portrayed your frustrations with your real-life situation of being low on money. When you think of that situation, you hear yourself say in your head: "It's impossible for me to make money" and "I've tried to make money and it doesn't work." You recognize these as limiting beliefs hold-ing you back from earning money. So, you might choose to replace these beliefs with new ones such as these: "I can offer value to others for which they are willing to pay," "I can find a way to earn money that works well for me," and "I can persevere in creative and resourceful ways."

Address or heal emotional wounds.

You may awaken from a dream experiencing strong emotion, such as hurt, anger, or jealousy. If you follow the flow of the emotion, it will likely point to a place in your consciousness that is in need of healing. The issue involved may include several factors, such as judgments (see "Chapter 4-4: TOOL: Forgiveness," p. 224), an opportunity for acceptance (see "Chapter 4-2: TOOL: Acceptance," p. 219), or self-defeating beliefs (see "Chapter 4-6: TOOL: Transforming Beliefs," p. 231).

One example is a dream in which a classmate accuses you of being too nerdy because you enjoy learning and you excel in many subjects. You wake up feeling hurt, and when you follow those feelings (see "Chapter 4-3: TOOL: Processing Emotions," p. 222) they lead to a realization that you are judging yourself as too nerdy, and you believe that your intelli-gence makes you unlikeable. You take the action steps of forgiving your judgments of your "nerdy" and "intelligent" characteristics as being bad things (see "Chapter 4-4: TOOL: Forgiveness," p. 224), and you release your belief that "My intelligence makes me unlikeable" and replace it with "I choose to embrace and celebrate my intelligence" (see "Chapter 4-6: TOOL: Transforming Beliefs," p. 231).

Find closure and peace by working through your feelings about the past.
A dream may bring to light a situation from your past where you still feel
you need closure—where you don't understand why someone did what he
did, or why something happened the way it did, or where you left something unsaid or undone that you wish you had said or done. In this case,
you can use the information from the dream as an opportunity to find
closure within yourself.

For example, you might have dreamed that your mother had a heart
attack and you felt completely helpless. In real life she has not had a heart
attack, but she recently told you that her doctor discovered she has a heart
condition. The dream triggers a memory of you how you cheated on a test
about the heart in high school biology class. You still judge yourself as a
bad person for cheating, and you now realize that you were only cheating
yourself by missing out on that knowledge—which could really come in
handy in understanding your mother's heart condition. You can't go back
and change the past, but you can reach closure by processing through your
current guilty feelings (see "Chapter 4-3: TOOL: Processing Emotions,"
p. 222), then releasing the judgment against yourself as a bad person for
cheating on that test (see "Chapter 4-4: TOOL: Forgiveness," p. 224), and
then studying about the heart to make up for what you missed in high
school (see "Chapter 4-11: TOOL: Completing Unfinished Business,"
p. 249).

Release life situations that are no longer working for you.
In some cases, a dream might portray a situation in your life that is not
working very well for you, such as your friendship with an emotionally
toxic person. You can use this dream information any way you choose.
You might evaluate your real-life friendship and decide to talk with the
friend about your feelings, spend less time with her, or end the friendship
completely.

For example, imagine that you dreamed about a lion that grew bigger
and bigger until his head was touching the ceiling of his cage, and soon he
would be bigger than the cage. You determine that the lion represents you,
and the fact that he is growing represents your skills that are improving in
the workplace. You believe the cage represents your job, which has stayed
exactly the same and has not expanded to make use of your growing skills.
So, you realize that the dream was portraying your feeling that your skill
set has grown enough that you've outgrown your job. You might choose to
act on this dream by first evaluating whether now, in the light of day, you
really feel you have outgrown your job and are ready for a change. If so,
you might ask your supervisor about the possibility of a promotion, or you

might check for other job openings in your company and elsewhere that better fit your current skill set.

Get more of what you want, and less of what you don't want.

Often the subconscious mind explores in dreams either what you enjoy and would like to experience more of, or what you dislike and would like to avoid experiencing. Pay attention to your feelings during the dream. Positive feelings about something in a dream often represent similar positive feelings about what the dream represents in your real life, and negative feelings may indicate something you'd like to avoid.

In an example of a dream that portrays something you'd like to experience more of in your life, you might dream about being hugged by your grandmother and feeling especially loved. Afterward, you realize this dream reminds you how loved you feel when you spend time with your grandmother, and that you miss seeing her. You decide to make plans to visit her more often.

In an example of a dream portraying something you would like less of in your life, you might dream that a bird keeps pecking at your stomach. After a while it starts to hurt a lot. When you awake you realize that the bird pecking your stomach represents the stomach pain you've been experiencing due to stress. This reminds you that you've been intending to reduce stress in your life, and you might decide to begin practicing meditation that same day. You might also decide to schedule a visit with your doctor regarding the physical health of your stomach.

(To learn how to create more of what you want in your life, see "Chapter 4-15: TOOL: Creating More of What You Want," p. 266.)

Solve a problem or work through a challenge.

Sometimes a dream provides an idea or clarification that helps you solve a problem in your waking life. The dream might provide an actual solution, or it might shed light on the underlying cause of the problem so you can then solve it. There are many ways you can apply information from dreams to work through challenges in your life.

One example might be if you dreamed about a whale sucking a whole school of fish into its mouth, carrying them to a coral reef, and releasing them there unharmed. You realize that this dream relates to your upcoming wedding—specifically how to deal with the lack of parking at your reception site. The dream gives you the idea that all the guests could travel together in a large vehicle (represented by all the fish traveling in the whale's mouth). So, you come up with the idea to charter buses to transport your guests from the wedding to the reception.

Catalyze a creative process.

Some dreams provide ideas or inspiration that can stimulate or catalyze a creative process in your waking life. A new idea can pop into your head while you're asleep, just as it can while you're awake. In fact, your subconscious mind is rich with resources that you may not even be aware of when you're awake—such as memories, bits and pieces of things you've seen or heard, and the ability to assemble pieces of a creative puzzle to create something new or unique. Dreams can suggest new ways to think about things, hints about new directions in which to take a creative process, or workarounds for obstacles in your creative process—such as writer's block. Dreams may also help with creative processes beyond typically creative pursuits like art and writing. We all use creativity in our daily lives. For example, you might want to figure out a better way to do something, such as getting all the toothpaste out of the tube or cutting a watermelon for a party. You might need to create a totally new process, like figuring out how to organize your notes for your first event with the debate club or your supplies for your new quilting hobby.

In an example, imagine that in real life you are a scientist who is working on new drugs to reduce dangerous deposits in blood vessels. Imagine that you had a dream about a street cleaner driving through a tunnel, cleaning as it went, and on the ends of its brushes were molecules of a new type that you realize would bind to and remove deposits from blood vessels. You might follow up on this dream by deciding to explore the possibility that these molecules could play a role in developing a helpful new drug.

Clarify your life direction.

Occasionally a dream may offer information about the path you're taking through your life and the direction you're heading. More specifically, dreams might prompt new insights in ways such as the following:

- Clarify or confirm the direction you're going, or a possible readjustment to your direction.
- Prompt you to adopt or continue a particular life purpose, or certain areas of meaningful focus in your life.
- Provide perspective on how far you've come since a particular time in the past, specific accomplishments you've made, or how close you are to realizing a life dream or goal.

Although this kind of information may come forward in dreams, it's wise to make life-direction decisions based on your best judgment and intuition while awake rather than blindly following something that showed up in a dream. Before you set or change a course in your life, make sure that it's clear to you and that it resonates with your inner wisdom. It should feel right to you, with a high degree of certainty.

An example of a dream relating to life direction is one in which you were watching one blackbird flying around and around another blackbird that was sitting in a tree. Suddenly the first bird broke away and rose up, flying toward the sun. As it flew, its color transformed to white. After awaking, you conclude that the bird that was flying around the other bird represents you, its black color represents your negative attitude recently, and flying around the other blackbird represents you centering your life around your current boyfriend, who has also had a negative attitude lately. You realize that the bird breaking away and rising up toward the sun represents you breaking out of that negative mental pattern. You also realize that the bird's color changing from black to white, along with the sun as a source of light, represent a more positive way of existing within yourself. This dream might prompt a greater awareness of your negative mental pattern and a realization that you have a choice of whether to stay stuck in that pattern or break out of it by making some changes. Whether and how you choose to act on this insight is completely up to you. You might decide to process through the emotions that have been darkening your inner world (see "Chapter 4-3: TOOL: Processing Emotions," p. 222), then release any judgments and transform any irrational beliefs that were behind those emotions (see "Chapter 4-4: TOOL: Forgiveness," p. 224, and "Chapter 4-6: TOOL: Transforming Beliefs," p. 231). You might also begin shifting the way you relate to yourself into a more positive and kind relationship with yourself (see "Chapter 4-8: TOOL: Transforming Negative Self-Talk," p. 238).

Identify your strengths and gifts.

Dreams may point to particular strengths or gifts you have—perhaps ones that you aren't using much right now, or even ones of which you aren't yet aware. Maybe you already know that you're an excellent accountant, but perhaps you don't realize that you also have teaching skills that inspire others to learn. Perhaps you spend your days managing a daycare center, and you've forgotten how much you loved to write in high school and how much praise your writing received from your teachers. An awareness of the areas in which you excel, your best skills, and your areas of greater potential can make a huge difference in all aspects of your life—including decisions about life direction, career, business, projects, hobbies, and other pursuits. Dreams can bring to light the strengths and gifts that make you unique and that enable you to enjoy life and provide value to others.

For example, you might dream that you're sitting at your desk at work, when suddenly in the doorway of your office appears a beautiful, large, white bird with a body shaped like an open book. You climb onto the open pages on its back and the bird takes off, carrying you high into the sky. Its strong wings maneuver gracefully as it flies over towns where people look up admiringly at you and the bird, its pages fluttering in the breeze. Upon awakening from the dream you realize that your journey with the "book bird" represents the idea of you embarking on a journey of writing a book—a beautiful piece of work that many people will enjoy. You might decide to lean into this idea (see "Chapter 4-14: TOOL: Leaning into Your Strengths," p. 261) by joining a writers' group, attending a seminar on book publishing, and working on your new book for at least 30 minutes a day for the next month.

Deepen your spirituality.

(Note: In this section, I use the words "the Divine" to refer to the highest power—which you might choose to think of as the holiest of holies, creator, source of pure love, or some other name. As you read, you can substitute whatever name with which you feel comfortable, according to your personal preference.)

Dreams often touch on spirituality and can be a rich resource for creating deeper meaning and experience in your daily life. For example, a dream may open the door to a deep connection with the Divine in that moment, or it might provide clues for how you can deepen your life experience through service to others, raise your consciousness, or change the way in which you view the world around you.

In some cases, you might have a dream in which you receive what seems to be a spiritual message or some form of guidance, but you're not sure what source it came from. As with every dream, you would be wise to focus on whether the message provides any value to you—whether it uplifts you and helps you move in a direction that is positive for you and others. Use your intuition to consider whether the message may have come from a Divine source—whether you sensed the profound love and peace that emanates from the Divine, and whether the dream and its message were consistent with the Divine's love, benevolence, and goodwill for all. As always, it's up to you to evaluate all dream information while you are awake and decide what it means to you, what value it has to you, and what—if any—resulting action you want to take.

An example of a dream that might help you deepen your spirituality is a dream in which a bright white light approached you, bringing with it a profound and overwhelming sense of peace and love. In this light's presence, it felt as if you were swimming in a Divine ocean, with a sense that all was well and an intuitive knowing that you were connected with the Divine. When you awaken, you conclude that this was either a Divine presence or an indication of how it might feel if you experienced the Divine directly. Either way, you decide that you can use this dream as a spiritual touchstone. The feeling during the dream was so profound that you remember it for years, and anytime you recall it you instantly feel spiritually uplifted. (For more about deepening your spirituality, see "Chapter 4-16: TOOL: Deepening Your Spirituality," p. 272.)

Issues Brought to Your Attention by Dreams

Simply put, an issue is something within your consciousness or life that needs your attention. Another way to think of an issue is as an area within your consciousness that is not at peace—for example, an area within which you're experiencing pain, distress, frustration, or darkness. An issue usually requires you to take action within your own consciousness in order to resolve it, or in order for healing to take place.

The issues that come to light during dreams are usually the same kinds of issues that come to light while you're awake, and you can take actions to resolve them both in the same ways. In fact, all of the techniques in this book for working through issues can be applied to any issue, whether it arises during a dream or while you're awake.

Examples of issues that might arise during a dream include feeling overwhelmed with your daily to-do list, a fear of abandonment, feeling guilty about letting a friend down, being upset after losing your job, or a desire for more meaning, fun, or personal connection in your life. As you can see, these issues could all just as easily come up while you're awake as during a dream.

The remaining sections in this part of the book present the fundamentals of working through an issue. Once you are familiar with these fundamentals, explore the techniques in "Part IV: Dream Action Toolkit" (p. 215), which provides many different methods of working with the various dynamics that can underlie an issue. (If at any point you feel overwhelmed or otherwise unable to deal with an issue, consult a mental health professional.)

Resolving Issues by Changing Your Mind

Many issues can be resolved by simply making a change within your mind. Positive changes in the way you think and the way you talk to yourself in your own mind can have a ripple effect in all areas of your life. In other words, improvements within yourself affect your experience of everything—yourself, people, events, the whole world. Sometimes you'll also need to make a change out in the world to resolve a particular issue—such as changing the way you interact with a co-worker or simplifying your to-do list. However, changes within your consciousness—such as processing emotions, releasing judgments, and replacing self-defeating beliefs—can often significantly improve your experience of both your inner environment and the world around you.

How to Work Through an Issue

This section introduces a basic process for working through an issue. If your dream brings to light an unresolved issue, begin with the following three steps, and then add techniques from "Part IV: Dream Action Toolkit" (p. 215), as appropriate. The basic process in this section can be very effective for many issues that arise; however, resolving a larger issue, or one with more extensive underlying dynamics, may require further processing—such as through the more specific techniques in "Part IV: Dream Action Toolkit."

Before you begin, I recommend always setting an intention for your process of working through the issue, such as "I intend to love myself unconditionally throughout this process" and "I intend to take complete responsibility for any reactions and judgments I may have during this process" (for more on setting intentions, see "Chapter 4-7: TOOL: Setting Intentions," p. 234).

1. Express Your Current Emotions

Release emotions associated with the issue by experiencing them (safely)—allowing yourself to feel them—thereby getting them out of your system.

Processing through any emotions involved with the issue first will allow you to then get to the heart of the issue underlying those emotions, so you can resolve it. Emotions include anger, fear, sadness, guilt, jealousy, and resentment, among many others. You can process through emotions and release them from your system by allowing yourself to feel them completely. One way to think of emotions is as bits of energy that flow out of you as you feel or express them. Because emotions often "piggyback on top of" an issue, they can obscure the issue until you have gotten them out of your system. Emotions can also "lock in" an issue, making it impossible to resolve before the emotions have been fully expressed. For example, you might still be judging yourself (a mental dynamic) for missing the winning shot years ago that would have clinched your high school basketball championship. On top of that self-judgment you've piled years of guilt and anger (emotional dynamics), which have further entrenched and reinforced the self-judgment. So, processing through that guilt and anger first will clear the way to then release the self-judgment, thereby forgiving yourself.

(This concept of processing emotions before resolving the issue may not make sense yet, but it will when you're in a situation of trying to release a mental dynamic that's been "locked in" by your emotions, such as trying to release a judgment against someone without first processing through your feelings of anger toward that person, and the judgment won't release. You'll get the hang of this, and it will begin to come naturally.)

One sign of emotional maturity is being able to process through your emotions without dumping them on others. **Be sure you express your emotions in a safe way that will not hurt yourself or others,** such as through free-form writing or letter (see instructions in "Chapter 3-23: TOOL: Free-Form Writing," p. 198, and "Chapter 3-24: TOOL: Writing a Shred Letter," p. 203). Start by expressing how you feel in the moment, and keep those feelings flowing in a safe way until they fade away and the process feels complete. If you can't express your emotions in a way that's safe for you and for others around you, then stop immediately and ask for support from a mental health professional to support you in the safe expression of your emotion.

In some cases, simply expressing your emotions can resolve the issue, which means you don't need to continue to the next step if you already feel complete and the issue has been resolved.

2. Make Inner Adjustments

Transform the inner dynamics that are contributing to the issue, and make decisions about any changes you want to make.

If expressing your emotions did not completely resolve your issue, then it's time to explore and make adjustments to the dynamics underlying the issue. In other words, you will make changes in the dynamics of your consciousness that are contributing to the issue. Often these dynamics are holding onto negativity or self-limitation, such as judgments, irrational or outdated beliefs, or negative self-talk. You can transform these dynamics by first becoming aware of them and then taking steps to shift or release them.

To resolve an issue—in order for real healing to happen—you must deal with all of the emotional and mental dynamics involved in the issue. If emotions come up during this step, repeat Step 1 above until you've processed through them, and then return to this step.

(See examples and techniques for making inner adjustments in "Examples of Acting on Your Dream," p. 88, as well as in the detailed techniques in "Part IV: Dream Action Toolkit," p. 215)

3. Take External Action

Take steps in your life around you, such as in your relationships, career, finances, or environment.

Depending on the particular issue, you may decide that in order to resolve it you need to take external action in addition to any internal adjustments you made in Step 2. You may choose to take steps or make a change in your waking life, such as apologizing to a friend, thanking your mother, or modifying your daily routine. You might also decide you want to take external actions to reinforce any internal adjustments you made in Step 2, such as starting in a new life direction or creating a physical touch-stone to remind you of a new self-supporting belief. Any actions you take are completely up to you. Remember that you alone are responsible for your actions and their consequences, so use your best judgment and act from a place of goodwill toward yourself and others.

To see examples and techniques for taking action, revisit "Examples of Acting on Your Dream" (p. 88), and also see "Part IV: Dream Action Toolkit" (p. 215).

Dreams with No Obvious Actions

Some dreams primarily clarify your thoughts, feelings, situations, or other aspects of you or your life, and in these cases no further action may be needed to resolve issues from the dream. However, you might choose to further explore your feelings about the dream and its specific elements. This exploration may help you identify feelings that indicate deeper, unresolved issues or other areas within yourself that need your attention. For that process, I suggest using open-ended techniques that create space for discovery, such as "Chapter 4-3: TOOL: Processing Emotions" (p. 222), "Chapter 3-23: TOOL: Free-Form Writing" (p. 198), and "Chapter 3-15: TOOL: Dialogue with Your Dream Symbol" (p. 160).

PART III

DREAM ANALYSIS TOOLKIT

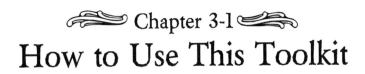

Chapter 3-1
How to Use This Toolkit

In This Chapter:

The techniques in this Dream Analysis Toolkit expand on the third step of the dream interpretation process, "3. Analyze Your Dream" (p. 78). Each technique in this toolkit offers a different way to look at and think about your dream, each providing a new opportunity to process your dream, learn more about it, and trigger intuitive insights about its meaning.

Prerequisites

Before using the techniques in this toolkit, you'll need to:

- Complete the first two steps of the dream interpretation process for your dream: "1. Review Your Dream" (p. 74) and 2. "Record Your Dream Description" (p. 75).
- Read "3. Analyze Your Dream" (p. 78).

How to Work with These Techniques

Begin analyzing your dream using the first six techniques in this toolkit, and then continue (as needed) by using any of the additional techniques in the toolkit.

Of all the techniques I've developed during my years of professional dream interpretation work, I've found these first six techniques to be particularly powerful for getting to the heart of dream meaning. They are listed here in the sequence that I suggest you use them:

However, if one of these techniques seems particularly appropriate for your dream, then start with that technique. For example, if you experienced strong emotion during your dream, you might want to begin with "Chapter 3-4: TOOL: Emotion Analysis" (p. 114), or if you want to explore a dream symbol that really stood out, you might want to start with "Chapter 3-2: TOOL: Parallels Between Symbols and Real Life" (p. 105) or "Chapter 3-5: TOOL: Hierarchical Dream Symbol Analysis" (p. 117).

You may recognize your dream meaning before you've completed all of the first six techniques, and that's fine. You can stop there, or you might choose to continue with additional techniques to understand more detailed symbolism and further meaning.

The remaining techniques in the Dream Analysis Toolkit offer a wide range of ways to explore dream meaning. Use them in any order, and try as many as you like.

Let Intuition Be Your Guide

As you work with any dream analysis technique, keep in mind that your goal is intuitive recognition of the true meaning, as described in "Intuition: The Key to Recognizing Dream Meaning" (p. 33). You may experience more than one of these moments of recognition as you identify the meaning of each different element in your dream, such as symbols, characters, actions, and settings. Sometimes discovering the meaning of one element will trigger an understanding of the whole dream and all of its elements, as all of the pieces of the puzzle fall into place. Let your exploration process unfold organically, and follow your intuition in choosing which dream element to explore next and which analysis technique to use.

Explore Beyond Basic Meaning

After you've discovered your overall dream meaning, you may still benefit from further exploration of your dream. Even the smallest of dream details can carry significant meaning, filling in another color in the dream-portrait that was created by your subconscious mind.

Chapter 3-2

TOOL: Parallels Between Symbols and Real Life

E ach key symbol in your dream likely represents something in your waking life, such as a real-life situation or a matter that has been on your mind. Dream symbol analysis is kind of like detective work. A detective examines a scene for clues such as fingerprints and DNA in order to identify the criminal. In dream symbol analysis you examine the dream's symbols for clues to identify what the dream is saying about you and your life. Examining your dream involves exploring each significant symbol in your dream and looking for parallels with your real life, while watching for flashes of recognition when something about the symbol reminds you of something in your waking life. Then, as you identify a parallel between each dream symbol and an aspect of your waking life, you can "connect the dots" to figure out what the entire dream represents.

Dream symbol analysis is not strictly scientific or logical, nor is it exactly an art. It's more like translating a language with which you're not completely familiar. The good news is that your subconscious mind presumably already knows exactly what the dream means, since that's where the dream occurred in the first place. So, discovering the meaning of a dream symbol sometimes involves a process of "dancing around" with the symbol for a while until its meaning becomes evident. This process for discovering Parallels Between Symbols and Real Life shows you ways to do that "dance of exploration."

The point of this process is to give your subconscious mind a chance to reveal to you what each dream symbol represents in your life. The idea here is to explore each symbol in a way that focuses your mind on it for a while to provide the time and space for flashes of recognition about its meaning. Think of this process as creating a space in your mind within which you can "dance" with each symbol for a while—observe it, listen to it, feel it—as it tells you more about itself and what it represents.

The Process

Here are the steps in the process to explore Parallels Between Symbols and Real Life:

1. Identify the key symbols in your dream—usually the characters or objects that stood out the most during the dream. Write a list of them in your dream journal or on a separate sheet of paper. Keeping notes will help when you get to the end of this process and it's time to pull together all of the clues.

2. For each key symbol, consider what stood out about it. Describe your first impression of it in a few words. Often, whatever you tend to notice about a symbol initially during the dream can tip you off as to what it represents, so make sure you note your first impression before you explore the dream symbol further.

3. For each key symbol, explore the following aspects associated with it, looking for parallels between these aspects and aspects of your waking life.

Feelings—Consider your feelings about the symbol during the dream, and why—what was behind those feelings. Perhaps you recognize a certain time when you've felt that way in your real life. If so, consider what triggered those feelings in real life, and how the symbol might represent that situation.

Physical Symbol—Take note of the symbol's physical characteristics, how it was placed or positioned, its context and attributes, and anything else physical that stood out about it or seemed unusual or unexpected about it.

Setting—Consider the physical setting of the symbol. Think about where the symbol was located—in a kitchen, on a desk, on the lawn, in the air—and what else was around it. Pay attention to anything unusual or unexpected about its setting.

Environment—Notice the kind of environment around the symbol—season, weather, time of day, lighting, and so on. Consider how its environment reminds you of a situation or mood you've felt in your waking life.

Actions—Consider the action(s) involved. If the symbol was an inanimate object, consider what happened to it, and how the dream character(s) related to it. If the symbol is alive, consider its actions and motivations, and whether there was anything unusual or unexpected about them.

Wordplay—Think about what wordplay could tell you about what the symbol represents in your life. Wordplay includes puns, synonyms, sound-alike words or phrases, slang words, figures of speech, and so on (see more in "Chapter 3-19: TOOL: Literary Analysis," p. 175).

4. Review all of your observations, and see if you notice a pattern that reminds you of an event or situation in your life, or an issue that's been on your mind. If the meanings you defined in Steps 1 through 3 don't match anything obvious in your real life, focus on the symbol and your feeling about it and see if another meaning comes forward that resonates with you. If you don't recognize a meaning that relates to your real life, the symbol may represent something in your mind— such as a hope, fear, desire, something you're imagining, or some idea or experience your subconscious mind created during the dream state itself.

Examples

The following examples demonstrate how the Parallels Between Symbols and Real Life process can be used to explore dream symbol meaning:

Example A:

Imagine you dreamed that you were driving at night in an old car, when suddenly the steering failed, causing you to drive off the road. In Step 1 you determine that the car was the main symbol in this dream, and in Step 2 you summarize what stood out about the car as "An old car I was driving that went out of control." In Step 3 you look for parallels between aspects of the dream and aspects of your waking life. First, you describe your feelings during the dream as "I felt panic when I couldn't control the car and I was afraid of crashing." You realize that you recognize this feeling from your waking life—similar to the panic and out-of-control feeling regarding your finances lately, your fear of financial disaster. You describe the physical car symbol as "The car was old, rusty and in need of maintenance"— which you suspect may refer to your spending patterns that could use an overhaul. You describe the car's setting as "The car was traveling on a winding road"—which could represent an unpredictable process or journey somewhere in your life. You characterize the car's environment as "The car was driving at night"—which you suspect could imply something happening without your awareness—something about which you're "in the dark." You summarize the actions involving the car as "The car's steering stopped working and the car veered off the road and crashed"—which you think represents the time in real life when you stopped making wise decisions about spending, after which you experienced financial crisis. You don't see any obvious wordplay, so you move on to Step 4, in which you review your observations and explore the patterns that show parallels between your dream and your real life. When you review each dream element, your intuition flashes to the aspect of your waking life to which it refers. You recognize the out-of-control feeling in the car as similar to your out-of-control feelings about your finances. Veering off the winding road in the dark when the steering stopped working seems to represent your real life situation of poor decision making in the face of unpredictable financial demands, represented by the winding road. This is a pattern of which you've been unaware ("in the dark" about) until now, represented in the dream by the dark setting. The car needing maintenance seems to represent your financial patterns and decision making which need some attention and updating. You conclude that this dream portrays what you've been experiencing in the financial area of your life and the financial trouble that may occur if you don't take corrective action in that area.

Example B:

Imagine you dreamed that a bee that was pestering you. In Step 1, you identify the key symbol as the bee, and in Step 2 you summarize what immediately stood out about it as "The bee kept buzzing around my face." Looking for parallels with your real life in Step 3, you note that during the dream you experienced feelings of fear that the bee would sting you and frustration because it wouldn't leave you alone. You recognize these feelings as similar to a real life situation in which you're afraid of someone who has been pestering you at school. You note the bee's physical characteristic of being bigger than usual, which could imply a pest that "looms large" in your life or has a big effect on you. You note the bee's setting as the inside of your house—which could mean that whatever the bee represents has intruded into your personal space. You note the environment in which the bee appeared was during the daytime while you were trying to get things done—which could represent the idea of something that interferes with your day-to-day activities. You note the actions of the bee, which seemed to be taunting you, repeatedly flying near your face—which could represent someone repeatedly taunting or pestering you at school. You note the possible wordplay—a bee is a type of "bug"—so perhaps it represents something that is "bugging" you. In Step 4 you review your observations and conclude that the bee in the dream represents a girl at school who has been pestering you, intruding into your space when you are trying to focus on your schoolwork. She is relentless, and you are afraid that taking any action against her will result in you getting in trouble—getting "stung." You realize that this dream illustrates the situation from your waking life, but it does not provide any answer about what to do about it. So, you decide to talk it over with someone you trust to give you good advice, and then make a decision about what action to take.

If you complete this process and still need more clues to dream symbol meaning, consider other approaches for finding the meaning of dream symbols, such as dialoging with a key dream symbol ("Chapter 3-15: TOOL: Dialogue with Your Dream Symbol," p. 160) or free-form writing ("Chapter 3-23: TOOL: Free-Form Writing," p. 198) about what the dream symbol could mean.

Chapter 3-3
TOOL: Generalization Analysis

The symbolism in a dream often represents something different in your real life, but the two are linked by some common characteristic. If you can find that common characteristic shared by the dream symbolism and the real-life version, that's often the key to understanding the meaning of your dream. Translating the dream's specific symbolism into a more general symbolism can help you recognize what the dream symbolism refers to in your real life. For example, in a dream in which you received flowers at work for doing a good job, receiving the flowers might represent the congratulations you received in real life from your boss last week for doing a fantastic job on a client presentation. The dream flowers and the real-life verbal congratulations are different, but what they have in common is that they are both specific forms of acknowledgment at work. Figure E shows how this dream story can be translated to a general version, which can make it easier to recognize the related real-life situation.

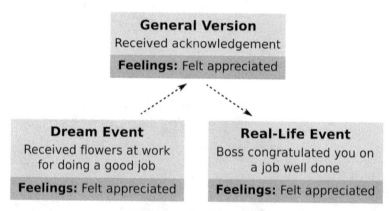

Fig. E. Generalization Analysis

It's important to note—and this is absolutely key—that although the dream symbol and what it represents in real life may seem completely different, you'll usually experience similar kinds of emotions in both the dream and real life. For example, in the dream when you received the flowers with a card saying, "Nice job on the project," you felt appreciated, validated, and acknowledged—the same feelings you experienced in real life last week when your boss congratulated you on doing a great job. Emotions are often so similar between a dream and real life that you can analyze a dream based primarily on your emotions during the dream (see more in "Chapter 3-4: TOOL: Emotion Analysis," p. 114). However, for the purposes of the current technique, we'll focus primarily on the symbolism in the dream.

The Process

Follow these steps to explore your dream using the Generalization Analysis technique:

1. Identify the main idea or event of the dream. If there was more than one, start with the one that stood out the most.
2. Generalize the main idea. In other words, translate it from specific to general. Ask yourself what was the gist of what was happening in the dream? For example, a dream tsunami might translate to "I was suddenly overwhelmed," and a dream grasshopper's huge jumps might translate to "making huge leaps forward."
3. Examine your feelings during the dream for more clues. For example, the dream tsunami may have triggered panic within you, and the dream grasshopper may have triggered awe at his sudden, huge progress forward.
4. Identify what the main idea from Step 2 and your feelings from Step 3 might represent in your real life or mind. For example, in the tsunami dream, the water overwhelming you and your resulting panic may represent the deluge of homework the teacher assigned yesterday and the panic you felt about getting it done. In the grasshopper dream, the grasshopper's huge jumps may represent the huge progress you suddenly made last week when you landed a job in your dream career, and you still have a feeling of awe that it actually happened.

After completing a Generalization Analysis, if you can't find any parallels between your dream and your real life, consider whether your dream may represent something other than an actual life event, such as:

• An imagined situation your subconscious mind mocked up during the dream state, perhaps to play out a fear or a desire.
• A rehearsal for something you expect, imagine, or fear in real life, such as playing in a championship game scheduled for next week.

111

- Something that has been on your mind—either lately or in the past.
- A story portraying a message or "moral of the story" that you can benefit from right now.

Examples

The following are some examples illustrating how to use the Generalization Analysis technique:

Example A:

Let's revisit the dream about the receiving the flowers at work, and walk through a Generalization Analysis of that dream. Imagine that you had this dream, but you have no idea what the flowers represent. No one has given you flowers lately—or any other gift, for that matter. In Generalization Analysis, you translate the main part of the dream into a more general version, so you ask yourself, "What is the most general idea of what happened in the dream?" You determine that, at the most basic level, what happened in the dream is that you received acknowledgment, and you determine that your associated emotion was that you felt appreciated. Next, you consider how this general version and associated emotion relates to your waking life by asking yourself how acknowledgment and appreciation have shown up in your life or on your mind. Then it occurs to you that you received congratulations from your boss last week, which led to you feeling appreciated—and you suddenly experience a flash of intuitive recognition that the work situation is what your dream represents (as described in "Intuition: The Key to Recognizing Dream Meaning," p. 33). You realize that during the dream your subconscious mind was retelling the story of your boss's congratulations using its own symbolic language (receiving flowers), but the general idea of being acknowledged and feeling appreciated was the same in the dream and in real life.

Note: You can apply this technique to explore more than one event or idea in a dream. For example, in the dream in which you received flowers, if the flowers wilted immediately and you felt disappointed, you might generalize this idea to "Receiving acknowledgment that then lets me down somehow." This general meaning would provide another clue about what this dream represents in real life. Perhaps in real life you received acknowledgment from your boss, but then discovered it was not sincere, and you felt disappointed.

Example B:

Imagine you dreamed that you were driving a car that accidentally veered off a bridge into a river. Consider what was really happening in the dream, at the most basic level: one process (driving) abruptly stopped, things went off-course (the car veered off the bridge), and then another process began (escaping from the car, navigating down the river). So, consider how this encapsulated version might represent something in your waking life—going about your day-to-day business when suddenly something unexpected happens that ends that process, and then you suddenly find yourself in a new process—possibly dealing with a crisis. Perhaps you recognize this as a fear you've had that you would get pregnant unexpectedly (represented by veering off the bridge), which would disrupt your life with a new phase (represented by traveling the river instead of the road) involving new kinds of challenges (represented by navigating the river).

Chapter 3-4
TOOL: Emotion Analysis

Emotions are key components of dreams that provide valuable clues to dream meaning. Often a dream is a like an "emotion portrait" depicting the emotional aspects of something from your real life or your mind, as portrayed by your subconscious mind using its own language of symbolism. Although the real-life story may look different when told through the language of symbolism, the emotions are often the same. For example, imagine that yesterday in real life your friend was an hour late to meet you for coffee, and you got annoyed. However, last night your subconscious mind retold that story in a dream in which you went to the post office to mail a letter to a friend, and you were annoyed to find that the post office was closed. The subconscious mind's version is visually different, but still contains the same basic action dynamic and emotion: you went to a place where you expected to communicate with a friend, and then you felt annoyed when you were not able to do so.

Emotions Are Important Clues to Dream Meaning

When you don't understand the symbolism your subconscious mind is using to tell its dream story, your emotion during the dream can be especially helpful in discovering dream meaning. Emotion Analysis of a dream involves recalling the emotion you felt during a dream and then following it as it points to the original situation in your real life that your dream is portraying. Revisiting the dream emotion may shift your mindset back into the real-life situation in which you felt that emotion before. In other words, recalling that emotion-memory can open the door for flashes of recognition, memories, or realizations about what the dream represents.

The Process

Here are the steps to conduct an Emotion Analysis of a dream:

1. Identify how you felt during the main part of your dream or the part of your dream that stands out the most. To help you recall your emotions during the dream, you can replay the dream in your mind from

beginning to end, noticing how you felt at different times during the dream.

2. Close your eyes and feel the emotion from the part of your dream you chose in Step 1. Stay with it, and pay attention to any memories or glimpses of real-life situations that the emotion triggers, since these could be clues to what the dream represents in your real life. The emotion may shift into a different emotion—for example, from annoyance into sadness—and that's okay. Just keep following it. If you lose touch with the emotion, replay that part of the dream story again to recall the emotion.

3. Trace the feeling to its origin. Ask yourself when you most recently felt this feeling, when you typically feel this way, or when you first felt this way. Stay with the feeling until you get an inkling of a real-life situation in which you felt this way. If your dream represents a situation from your real life or mind, the emotion should be familiar to you. Ideally, you'll recognize the emotion from sometime in the past—or currently—and that recognition is a huge clue about what the dream represents in your real life. If during the dream you experienced a series of different emotions—for example, angry and then hurt and then grateful—consider when in your life you've experienced that same series of emotions in that same order.

After completing your Emotion Analysis, if you haven't identified any similar emotions from your real life, consider whether your dream may represent something other than an actual life situation. The dream and your associated emotions may instead relate to one or more of the following:

- A fear or desire.
- Something you anticipate, fear, or hope for in the future.
- Something that has been on your mind—either lately or long term.
- Something new that you've never thought of before, such as a possible new personal strength, project idea, or life direction.
- Subconscious feelings triggered directly by a dream event, unrelated to your events in your waking life.

Examples

Here are some examples of the Emotion Analysis technique in action:

Example A:

Imagine you had a dream in which a tornado swept through and destroyed your house that you've spent a lot of time making into a beautiful home, leaving you feeling devastated. You might recognize that feeling of devastation from your real life, yesterday when your boss swept into your office and criticized your work on a huge project, leaving you with that same devastated feeling. The emotion and main dynamic are similar in both the dream and real-life, providing a link for you to follow from the dream into its real-life meaning. In both the dream and real life, an external force "swept through" your area and wreaked havoc, leaving you feeling devastated.

Example B:

Consider a dream in which you were trying to fill a bucket with water, only to discover with great frustration that the reason it wouldn't fill was that the bucket was leaking in several places. You might focus on and follow that frustrated feeling of "I fill and fill, and it's never enough!" and eventually recognize it from the financial area of your real life—in which you feel frustrated because you work and work, but never have enough money to fill your bank account. The dream conveys the idea that your money supply is "leaking out" in ways of which you're not aware, suggesting that perhaps you'd benefit from paying more attention to your spending. Although the bucket story in the dream looks physically nothing like your money or a bank, the central dynamic of the dream (unseen leaking) and emotion (frustration) are similar.

❧ Chapter 3-5 ❧
TOOL: Hierarchical Dream Symbol Analysis

I n the Hierarchical Dream Symbol Analysis technique, you consider various possible meanings of a dream symbol by translating it into more general symbolism and into more specific symbolism. In other words, you consider the symbol's hierarchy of meaning—from very general ways to define it (a carrot as a type of food) to more specific ways to define it (a particular carrot you saw yesterday that had a rotten spot). Each way you define the dream symbol can suggest a different possible meaning. For example a carrot as a type of food might represent nourishment for the body, mind, or soul. A carrot itself might represent something "underground" or hidden. A particular carrot that had a rotten spot might represent a situation gone bad at work yesterday when an argument sidetracked your meeting.

The point of this technique is to provide a structure within which you can generate many different possible meanings of your particular dream symbol, until you find the one that rings true for you. (Read more about intuition and recognizing dream meaning in "Intuition: The Key to Recognizing Dream Meaning," p. 33.) This process parades a series of possible meanings past your "inner intuitive eye" until it spots the correct meaning in your dream, and it says "Yes, that's it!".

The Process

Hierarchical Dream Symbol Analysis involves finding ways to define your dream symbol in more general ways and in more specific says, and then considering possible meanings for each of those definitions. You can define a symbol in any way that comes to mind and in as many ways as you like. Be creative with your definitions and possible meanings—and remember that your creativity is "great friends" with your subconscious mind, which already knows what the dream symbol represents. The idea here is to watch for a flash of recognition when you come across the true meaning of the symbol.

1. Start with pen and paper. Consider using loose sheets of paper for this process—since it's sort of like brainstorming—and then writing only your final conclusions in your dream journal.
2. In the center of the page write the name of a symbol that stood out in your dream—one that you want to explore.

Use the following steps to draw a hierarchy of symbol definitions—first more general ones and then more specific ones:

3. Think of a general category into which your symbol fits—consider what kind of a thing or character it is. Write the category above the symbol name. (A carrot fits into the more general category of "vegetables.")
4. Think of an even more general category into which the category from the previous step fits, and write it above what you wrote in Step 3. (Vegetables fit into the more general category of "food.")
5. Keep defining categories that are more and more general until you run out. (Food fits into the more general category of "nourishment." Nourishment fits into the more general category of "basic human needs.")
6. Starting with the original symbol again, now think of something more specific about the one in your dream. Write it below the symbol name you wrote in the center of the page. (A carrot with a rotten spot.)
7. Think of something more specific about the thing you defined in the previous step. (The rotten spot on the carrot.)
8. Continue defining more and more specific things about the dream symbol until you run out. (The brown color of the rotten spot on the carrot, or the pattern of light and dark browns in the rotten spot on the carrot.)
9. Translate each definition (both the general and specific ones) into possible meanings, and consider which one resonates with you intuitively as the true meaning. (Vegetables could represent something that grows or is tended to. Food could represent nourishment for the body, mind, or soul. A rotten spot could represent a good situation that's gone bad.)

Also, keep in mind that there are no wrong answers in this process, no incorrect categories or definitions. If you complete this process and you don't recognize your symbol meaning, try it again and create different definitions. (A carrot is in the category of orange things, which could represent the color of a friend's favorite cap. The dream carrot would be just fine to eat if the rotten spot were cut out, which could represent the idea of letting go of something that isn't working for you in your life.)

Examples

The following examples of Hierarchical Dream Symbol Analysis show how you might define a symbol on various levels of specificity, from very general to very specific. For each level of specificity, come up with a definition and then consider what that definition might represent in your life or on your mind. In the following examples, the original dream symbol (the one-to-one representation) is shown in bold, the more general levels are shown above it, and the more specific levels are shown below it.)

Example A:

Carrot dream symbol:

- (Something even more general) Food in general—could symbolize nourishment for body, mind, or soul.
- (Something more general) Vegetables—could symbolize something that grows or is tended to.
- **(Original dream symbol) A carrot**—could symbolize something that is hidden or secret, since carrots grow underground.
- (Something more specific) A particular time I ate a carrot in real life—could symbolize the time frame, feelings, or setting at the time you ate the carrot.
- (Something even more specific) The rotten spot on the carrot you ate in real life—could symbolize a situation that "went bad" or an unpleasant intrusion.

Example B:

Postal mail carrier dream symbol:

- (Something even more general) People who deliver things—could symbolize giving, receiving, or carrying a burden for someone else.
- (Something more general) People you see walking in your neighborhood—could symbolize a certain person who often comes to your house, or your public or social life.
- **(Original dream symbol) Your mail carrier**—could symbolize your actual mail carrier, other delivery person, or someone else who often brings you things or information.
- (Something more specific) The mail carrier delivering a large box to your house unexpectedly—could symbolize the time last week when

you received unexpected good news, or the idea of receiving goodwill from others.

- (Something even more specific) The mail carrier requiring a signature when he delivered a large box—could symbolize feeling the need to prove yourself or your credibility.

Example C:

Wooden door dream symbol:

- (Something more general) Things made of wood—could symbolize something from nature transformed into a practical form, or something that can be shaped as desired.
- **(Original dream symbol) A wooden door**—could symbolize a beginning or ending, an opportunity, or accessibility.
- (Something more specific) The front door of your house—could symbolize the boundary between your personal life and public life.
- (Something even more specific) The broken lock on your front door—could symbolize a fear of someone intruding into your personal life.
- (Something even more specific) The time you tried but couldn't fix the broken lock on your front door—could symbolize a feeling that you've failed to maintain your personal boundaries

Chapter 3-6
TOOL: Character Analysis

A character in a dream—such as a person, animal, other being, or animated object—is one of the most important elements in the story of a dream. A character is anyone or anything in your dream who had the capability of consciousness or who took action. Some wild things go on in dreams, and anything can happen—so, even a table that came to life and danced the can-can could be considered a dream character.

A character can represent itself (your mother in a dream representing your actual mother) or can represent someone different in your real life (your mother in a dream representing someone who has been a mother figure in your life). A character can represent almost anything, although characters often provide clues about what they represent when you examine your feelings about them, their actions, and their characteristics. Often something that stands out about a particular character will point to whom or what that character represents in your real life.

In Character Analysis, you examine the significant characters who showed up in your dream and your feelings about them, searching for clues about whom or what each character represents in your real life.

Character Symbolism Types

Let's look at some ways that character symbolism can show up in dreams. The following list is not meant to be an exhaustive list, but it provides examples to help you understand what the characters in your dreams might represent in real life. Characters in your dream can actually represent anything your subconscious mind knows about or imagines. Sometimes the symbolism is obvious, and sometimes it's cryptic.

Any character in a dream can carry any of the following kinds of symbolism:

A Character Is a Literal Representation

The character represents the real version of itself from your real life (you in the dream represent you, your father in the dream represents your actual father, your dog in the dream represents your actual dog).

A Character Represents a Person

- You (the pilot of a plane represents you being in charge of your life direction, a caterpillar transforming into a butterfly represents your brother moving into a new phase of his life).
- An aspect of you (an artist represents your creative self, a guru represents your inner wisdom, a rock star represents your ego).
- Someone else in real life who looks the same or similar in some way (your sister in your dream represents your real-life friend who's like a sister to you, a clown represents a co-worker who's a jokester).
- A different person in your real life, where the person in the dream does not look like the real-life person he represents (Fred Astaire represents your grandpa who loved to dance, a bull represents the obnoxious stranger in the coffee shop yesterday, an emergency dispatcher represents God—whom you've called for help).

A Character Represents a Group

- A real group or community in your life (three classmates represent your classmates in general, Martin Luther King represents a civil rights or other rights group, Albert Einstein represents scientists, a well-dressed man represents society, an average woman represents all women or "everyone").
- A group defined by you—a symbolic group, not a formal group (a friend represents your social circle, a bully represents "haters," a police officer represents authority figures in general).

A Character Represents a Characteristic or Concept

- A physical characteristic of the actual person in real life (Abraham Lincoln represents your very tall uncle, a delicate baby doll represents your baby sister, a lion represents your muscular classmate).
- A nonphysical characteristic you consider the actual person to have in real life (a chattering bird represents a talkative cousin, George Washington represents your supervisor who is a respected leader, a dog represents your loyal friend).
- A characteristic in general (a famous comedian represents a sense of humor, a corrupt stockbroker represents greed, a long-distance runner represents tenacity).
- A concept (a grandmother represents unconditional love, Indiana Jones represents adventure, an undertaker represents death, a mysterious stranger represents the unknown).

A Character Represents an Activity

An activity from your real life, or a desired or imagined activity (a co-worker represents your job, a clergy member represents your church activities, a train conductor represents the traveling you'd like to do).

A Character Represents a Time Frame

A time frame—a specific time during in your life, a past phase or era, the current time, or an imagined future. A time frame symbol often provides a clue as to the particular time in your life being portrayed in the dream.

- The past (your Senior Prom date represents senior year in high school, your Mom looking 25 years younger represents your life back when she looked like that, bell-bottom jeans represent middle school because that's when you wore them).
- Current times (you sleeping in your bed represents you sleeping in your bed right now, the tooth fairy represents your dentist appointment earlier today, Sherlock Holmes represents earlier this evening when you watched a detective TV show).
- An imagined future (giving a speech represents the time next week when you're actually scheduled to give a speech, a retirement home represents your later years in life, futuristic clothing represents the distant future).

The Process

The following steps show how to use Character Analysis to explore whom or what the characters in your dream represent in your real life:

1. Choose a character from your dream whose meaning you'd like to explore.
2. Consider what stood out about the character—such as what was different than expected; any feeling you got from her; what you liked or disliked about her; actions she took; appearance; nonphysical characteristics; motivations; or her thoughts, fears, or values.
3. Consider how what you wrote in the previous step reminds you of someone or something in your real life (see previous descriptions of the possibilities—Literal Representation, Person, Group, Characteristic, Activity, or Time Frame). If you're still not sure whom or what the character represents, then repeat Step 2, but this time identify something different that stood out about the character.
4. Repeat Steps 1 through 3 for each additional character in your dream whose meaning you'd like to explore.
5. In your dream journal, write any new insights about whom or what the characters in your dream represent.

Examples

The following examples illustrate how to apply Character Analysis to explore characters in a dream:

Example A:

Consider a dream in which you were a guest on a late-night talk show, and the host was interviewing you. You started out very nervous, but the host was so friendly and fun that you were soon enjoying yourself and having a great time.

You complete the steps of Character Analysis in the following way:

1. The character who stood out in this dream was the talk show host.
2. What stood out about this character was that—even though you were so nervous at first—his friendliness, warmth, and sense of humor put you at ease, and he genuinely seemed glad to be talking with you.
3. Considering how your experience of the host reminds you of something in your waking life, you remember a job interview you had last week. You arrived very nervous, but the interviewer put you at ease and genuinely seemed interested in learning more about you. Your intuition confirms that the talk show host in the dream represents the interviewer at the real life job interview, and the characteristics that stood out about him in the dream are the same ones you experienced with the interviewer. You realize that this dream was exploring your memories of the interview, and how someone else's friendliness and warmth transformed a nervous situation into an enjoyable one.
4. The only other character in the dream was you, and you're sure that in the dream you represented yourself experiencing the real-life interview last week.
5. You write in your journal that this dream tells the story of your positive experience at the interview, and the pleasant surprise of a positive encounter on a job interview.

Example B:

Imagine a dream in which you had a miniature donkey as a pet, and you were trying to lead her from her quarters out to a pen in the yard. You pulled her, pushed her, and coaxed her—but she would not go. She was stubborn and had a mind of her own. She planted her feet firmly on the ground and refused to do anything other than what she wanted to do at the moment.

You complete your Character Analysis this way:

1. The character you want to explore is the miniature donkey.

2. What stood out about this character was that she was very stubborn and headstrong.

3. Considering how these characteristics remind you of something in your waking life, you immediately recognize that this seems a lot like your experience with your 13-year-old daughter lately. For the last few days, she has dug her heels in and absolutely refused to help out around the house. You've tried asking nicely, bribing her, and threatening to ground her, but she still would not do her chores. She has seemed as stubborn and headstrong as the miniature donkey in the dream. You conclude that the donkey represents your daughter's recent stubbornness.

4. In the dream, the only other character was yourself, as you interacted with the miniature donkey. Your intuition confirms that your role of donkey-wrangler in the dream represents the way you perceive your real-life experience as a parent recently.

5. In your dream journal, you write your conclusions about the miniature donkey representing your daughter's stubbornness. You also jot a few ideas about how you and your daughter can work together to explore your recent interactions with each other, and what might be behind her particularly stubborn disposition lately.

Chapter 3-7

TOOL: Levels of Existence

An element of a dream can represent its literal equal in real life, such as a wedding in a dream representing an actual wedding you attended last month. However, very often a dream element symbolizes something different in your waking life, such as a wedding representing a desire to be in love, a new beginning in your life, or a commitment made with someone—based on the ideas that a wedding typically involves love, a new beginning, and a commitment being made.

Humans experience life on multiple levels—including physical, emotional, mental, and spiritual levels—and dreams include elements of all these same levels. Dreams can contain physical symbols and settings, mental elements such as thoughts and beliefs, emotions, and spiritual elements such as experiences, figures, or symbols.

Now, here's one reason dreams can seem so cryptic: an element of a dream doesn't always represent something on its corresponding level in real life. For example, a yellow flower (a physical element in the dream) might represent something physical in real life (an actual physical flower you saw yesterday, or a yellow dress), or it might represent something on a different level in real life. The yellow flower could represent something on the real-life emotional level (such as happiness), or something on the real-life mental level (such as intelligence). Determining which level a dream element portrays in real life can help you understand the deeper meaning of the dream element, and what it says about you or your life.

Nonphysical Dream Elements

A nonphysical element in a dream—such as an emotional, mental, or spiritual element—often represents itself or something on the same level in your waking existence. Emotions in dreams—such as feeling angry, afraid, or guilty—tend to represent similar emotions from your real life. For example, if you're afraid of a tiger in a dream, you're probably also afraid of whatever the tiger represents in your real life. Likewise, mental aspects in dreams—such as judgments, belief, and attitudes—tend to represent similar

126

mental aspects from your real life. For example, if you judge a particular person in a dream, there's a good chance that you judge that person in real life. Similarly, spiritual elements of dreams often have to do with a spiritual aspect of your life. For example, an angel in your dream could represent the idea of spiritual assistance in your real life.

Because nonphysical elements of dreams so often correspond to their correlating nonphysical level of real life, the remainder of this section will focus primarily on the more complex symbolism portrayed by physical elements in dreams.

Physical Dream Elements

A physical element—something that you see or otherwise physically experience in a dream—might represent something on any level of yourself or your personal existence. For example, the physical element of clouds that are clearing in a dream could represent you releasing judgments in real life as you forgive a friend who disappointed you, which is a mental-level action. A physical dream element of a flood might represent the emotional overwhelm you've been feeling the last few days, an aspect of the real-life emotional level. The physical dream element of flying might represent spiritual upliftment, an element of the spiritual level.

Now let's consider the two different ways a physical dream element can represent something physical in your waking life. First, a physical dream element can represent itself in real life—as when a shiny, black piano in a dream represents the actual black piano in your living room. Second, a physical dream element can represent something *different* on the physical level of your real life—as when the shiny, black piano represents the new black car your friend just bought.

Next, let's look at how a physical element of a dream can represent something on a *different level of existence*—something on one of the nonphysical levels. For example, the physical dream symbol of a shiny, black piano could represent something on the mental level in real life, such as your goal to become a professional musician—or it could represent something on the emotional level in real life, such as your fear of performing in front of an audience.

Conscious and Subconscious Levels of Existence

When you consider that a physical element can portray something on any level of yourself or your personal existence, keep in mind that "personal existence" here refers to your entire personal existence—including conscious and subconscious experience. In other words, a physical element in your dream might represent any aspect of your conscious or subconscious existence (as shown in Figure A on p. 11)—your conscious mental or sub-conscious mental level, conscious emotional or subconscious emotional level, and so on. This can make dream interpretation a bit tricky. When you consider your dream about a bear, you may not realize that the bear represents a subconscious fear because you're not yet aware of that fear. However, because dreams portray aspects of both your conscious and sub-conscious realities, they can reveal clues about both. In fact, your dreams are an excellent source of information about what's going on in your sub-conscious mind, and that's one reason dreams are such valuable resources. So, as you consider which level of existence each physical dream element is portraying, also consider whether the element could represent something conscious or subconscious.

Levels of Existence Portrayed by Physical Elements of Dreams

Any physical element in a dream—such as a character, object, action, event, or environment—can represent something **conscious** or **subconscious** on any of the following levels. The following list is not intended as an exhaus-tive list of possibilities, and you may discover additional kinds of symbol-ism in your dreams. You may also find that a particular physical element from your dream can represent more than one of the following levels within yourself or your life simultaneously.

Physical Level

A physical element in a dream can represent something on the physical level of your existence, such as:

- Your physical level—such as physical aspects of your body, health, physiology, position (the arm of a cantilever lamp represents your arm, a leaking water heater represents you feeling drained of energy, a pulsing light represents the beating of your heart, a bottle laying on its side represents you laying down or resting in real life).
- Your physical presence and experience in the world (a peacock strut-ting through a gate represents you walking into a party last night dressed in your best, a dog gobbling his dinner represents you enjoy-ing a food that you crave, a fast roadrunner represents your physical running around at work today).
- Anything you can see or otherwise experience physically in the world around you—such as a:

  Person (a slow car in front of you represents a co-worker who slows down your work progress).

Animal (a sphinx represents your cat, a spinning top represents your busy puppy).

Object (a wrapped gift represents the bike you just received for your birthday, a hurdle represents the chair you keep tripping over).

Place (a maze represents your office building, a lily represents your neighbor's flower bed full of lilies).

Environment (an icicle represents yesterday's freezing weather, a wet blanket represents the dampness in your basement).

Event (a cornfield represents your trip to Iowa last June, a motor-boat represents your recent drive to the store through water-logged streets).

Action (a campfire represents lighting a fire in your fireplace, a hammer represents repairing a floorboard).

Emotional Level

A physical element in a dream can represent something on the emotional level of your existence, such as your or other people's fear, anger, happiness, grief, depression, anxiety, or other emotion (a spider represents your fear of spiders, sunny weather represents your elation about your upcoming vacation, a castle fortress represents your emotional walls that keep others at a distance, a tornado represents your brother's anger when you wore his shirt yesterday without asking).

Mental Level

A physical element in a dream can represent something on the mental level of your existence, such as your or other people's thoughts, beliefs, judgments, doubts, goals, aspirations, hopes, desires, intentions, preferences, attitudes, knowledge, decisions, ideas, or other dynamics of the mental level (fog represents your confusion about which direction to take, a cat represents curiosity, a jack-in-the-box represents your surprise when the pop-quiz was "sprung" on you in class this morning).

Spiritual Level

A physical element in a dream can represent something on the spiritual level of your or other people's existence—such as the ideas of spiritual support, guidance, upliftment, or inspiration (a treasure chest full of jewels represents blessings, traveling upward in a hot air balloon represents spiritual upliftment, a spark represents spiritual inspiration).

Imaginary Level

A physical element in a dream can represent something on the imaginary level of your existence—something you haven't directly experienced before in your waking life. This might include experiences you would like to try or you want to explore, desires, curiosities, concerns, pretend situations, or anything else you can imagine (someone asking you on a date represents your desire to be asked on a date, owning a yacht represents your curiosity about what it would be like, singing in front of a large crowd represents your desire to explore a career as a professional singer).

Self Level

A physical element in a dream can represent something within or about yourself, such as aspects of self like inner child, ego, or higher wisdom; roles you play like parent, friend, or boss; and aspects of your personality like enthusiastic, loyal, or shy (a jubilant toddler represents your inner child, Superman represents your inner hero, a cheerleader represents your enthusiasm.)

Time Frame Level

A physical element in a dream can represent a point along a timeline—something that points to a particular time frame in the past, present, or imagined future (your red dress from college graduation represents your early twenties, your favorite stuffed animal represents your early childhood, the county fair represents last summer). This type of symbolism can provide a huge clue to the meaning of a dream by indicating which time frame of your life the dream is portraying.

The Process

The Levels of Existence technique helps you explore the physical elements of your dream to discover clues to their meanings. Follow these steps to explore each major physical element in your dream:

1. Choose an element your dream that stood out, such as a character, object, action, event, or environment.
2. Consider your internal response to that dream element's presence in the dream—what stood out about it, what was different from expected, what you thought or felt about it, what you liked or disliked. Then consider where in your waking life you've had a similar response, and what triggered that response within you. In other words, consider what your experience of that dream element reminds you of in your real life.
3. Once you have an idea of what the element represents in your real life, identify which level of existence the element refers to in your

real life (see previous descriptions of the levels—physical, emotional, mental, spiritual, imaginary, self, or time frame). If you're still not sure what the element represents, consider other clues that may help you recognize its meaning—such as how you felt about it, other elements associated with it, how its place in the dream timeline fits into a series of past events in your real life.

4. Based on the meaning of this element and the level of your existence it represents, consider what it indicates about that aspect of your life.
5. Define any follow-up steps you want to take to resolve any related real-life issues.
6. Repeat the previous steps for other physical elements that stood out in your dream.
7. In your dream journal, write any new insights you gained during this process, and any follow-up steps you've decided to take.

Examples

Here are some examples of how you might use the Levels of Existence technique to analyze a dream:

Example A:

This example shows how the Levels of Existence technique might shed light on the meaning of a dream about a lion chasing away a huge grizzly bear:

1. The element I want to focus on is the lion.
2. My internal response when the lion chased away the grizzly was surprise that she was brave enough to go up against a grizzly, then fear that the lion would be hurt, then relief when the grizzly was gone. What stood out about the lion was that she was wearing a pearl-encrusted collar that reminded me of a pearl necklace of mine. I suspect that the lion represents my inner strength.
3. The lion was a physical element of the dream, and it seems to represent inner strength on the mental and emotional levels within myself.
4. As for what the lion says about me and my life, the ability of a lion to chase away a huge grizzly really says a lot about defending and standing up for oneself. So, I think this dream may be showing me how much inner strength I have to face challenges—more specifically, the challenge of my doctoral dissertation. I've been telling my friends that the dissertation is "going to be a bear," and I'm feeling overwhelmed because it feels like such a "big, hairy" project. However,

after this dream I feel more prepared to face that challenge because I realize I have what it takes to persevere and do a great job.

5. As for follow-up steps, I have decided to take an active step forward on my dissertation by setting up an appointment with my advisor within the next week to discuss my dissertation topic.

6. I feel complete with this analysis and so I don't need to repeat the previous steps.

7. I will write in my dream journal my conclusions about this dream, and I'll also describe the feeling I had seeing the lion hold her ground against the grizzly—such an inspiring feeling that I will use as a touchstone of my inner strength throughout my dissertation process.

Example B:

The following example shows how you might use the Levels of Existence technique to analyze a dream about finding a large, beautiful mushroom along a path in a forest:

1. The element I want to focus on is the mushroom.

2. My internal response to the mushroom was surprise at first, and then awe. What stood out about the mushroom was that it was huge (a little taller than I am), it was bright yellow, and it exuded a strong, exotic scent. I wanted to touch it but was afraid it might be poisonous. When I consider where in my real life I've had a similar response to something, what comes to mind is when I saw a new girl in a yellow dress the other day when I was coming out of biology class. I was surprised because I hadn't seen her before, and then I was in awe of her strong presence and the friendly personality she exuded. I wanted talk to her, but I was afraid of rejection.

3. In this case, the physical dream element of a mushroom represents a person on the physical level in my real life. Its exotic odor is a physical attribute that seems to represent her personality in real life, a mental attribute in real life. The mushroom's yellow color was a physical characteristic that represents her physical yellow dress in real life. I can also see that the forest path represented my path out of biology class, and the forest may represent the old-growth forests we were studying in class that day—on the mental level.

4. As for what this says about me and my life, I notice that my fear of being poisoned by the mushroom seems to represent my fear of rejection (an emotional element representing the same emotional element of fear in real life). It's interesting that I subconsciously equate rejection with being poisoned. Being poisoned in real life would make me sick and could even kill me, but rejection just hurts a little

for a while. It seems like the emotion was exaggerated in the dream, which could mean that it's a big deal in my subconscious mind.

5. As for any follow-up steps, I am setting the following intentions: I intend to explore how to deal with rejection in a different way so that it isn't such a big deal for me. I intend to research helpful resources online, as well as books at the library. (See more about setting intentions in "Chapter 4-7: TOOL: Setting Intentions," p. 234.)

6. I have finished exploring dream symbols, so I don't need to repeat the previous steps.

7. I am going to write my conclusions from this process in my dream journal, and I'll write my new intentions from Step 5 in my regular journal to remind me to follow up on them.

Chapter 3-8

TOOL: Caveman Explanation

The meaning of a symbol in a dream is particular to you, as the dreamer of that dream. Your subconscious mind may tend to choose which dream symbols to use when creating a dream according to the understanding you already have of those symbols. For example, if your impression of weeping willow trees is that they're great at bending but not breaking under high winds, your subconscious mind might choose a weeping willow to represent the idea of surviving a difficult challenge. However, if one of your childhood chores was sweeping the twigs dropped from a weeping willow off of your patio every week, you might think of it mainly as a messy tree, and your subconscious mind might use it to represent a recurring mess in your life.

When considering possible meanings of a dream symbol, there's a good chance it represents something that you already associate with that symbol. So, consider what comes to mind when you think of that symbol—starting with the most basic and obvious. An easy way to shift into this mode of thinking is to imagine you're explaining the symbol to someone who knows nothing about it, such as:

- A caveman.
- A young child.
- An alien from another planet.

When you imagine explaining a symbol to someone who is unfamiliar with it, the meanings that come to mind are often the personal meanings that your subconscious mind associates with that symbol.

The Process

Follow these steps to explore a dream symbol using the Caveman Explanation technique:

1. Choose a symbol from your dream, and imagine that you are explaining what it is to someone who is not familiar with it—such as a caveman, young child, or alien from another planet. The person has

TOOL: CAVEMAN EXPLANATION

no idea what the thing is, how it works, what it does, what it's known for, or anything else about it. Start from the beginning with the most basic explanation.

2. Write the meanings that you used to explain the symbol.
3. Consider which meaning resonates intuitively with you as the meaning of your dream symbol, or which meaning relates to a matter that you've experienced in your real life or that's been on your mind.
4. (Optional) Add this symbol and these personal meanings to your personal dream dictionary (see more in "Chapter 3-11: TOOL: Personal Dream Dictionary," p. 145).

Examples

Here are some examples of using the Caveman Explanation technique to reveal your own personal meanings of a particular dream symbol:

Example A:

Consider a dream in which you were making a phone call to your father, but you couldn't get through because of a bad connection. You might imagine explaining a phone to a caveman this way:

"Okay, Caveman, here's what a phone is. It's a device I can use to talk with other people. I can call them on the phone when I want to talk, or they can call me when they want to talk. A phone lets us talk as if we are standing right next to each other, even if we are far apart. I can also use a phone to call for help."

So, based on your explanation of a phone, the phone in your dream might represent one or more of the following, which you write down:

• Communication, or a desire to communicate.
• One person's availability to another person, such as to talk or listen.
• Bridging the (physical, mental, or emotional) distance between two people.
• A need to speak or be heard.
• Wanting or needing help.

The idea of a phone as a means of communication really resonates with you. In your dream you kept getting a bad connection when trying to reach your father, so you consider how in real life you might be experiencing a "bad connection" when trying to communicate with your father. You realize that you and he haven't been seeing eye-to-eye about how to handle a certain matter. You conclude that the dream was portraying your subconscious mind's view of your disagreement with your father. You then add an entry for "phone" in your personal dream dictionary, along with the meanings you listed here.

135

Example B:

If you dreamed about an apple growing very quickly, you might explore its possible meanings by imagining that you're describing it to an alien from another planet:

"Mr. Alien, let me explain what an apple is. It's red and round, and it grows on trees. It's good to eat, and it's nourishing and healthy. Apples are fruits that take a long time to develop before they are ready. Each apple contains seeds that can grow a whole new generation of apple trees, which can then produce their own apples."

So, based on the way you described an apple, you write the following possible meanings:

- Roundness or redness.
- Something that is created by something else, since an apple is produced by a tree.
- Nourishment—such as mental, emotional, or spiritual nourishment.
- A process, or something that takes time to develop, as an apple does.
- "Seeds" (such as ideas or actions) that can "grow to fruition" and produce desirable results in the future.

In your dream, the apple grew from tiny and green to large, red, and ripe in just a few seconds, so you suspect that the apple may represent a process being completed more quickly than expected. When you think about where in your real life a process went more quickly than expected, you realize that the apple's quick growth represents your financial investment growing more quickly than expected because several of the stocks you chose did very well in a short time. You note this conclusion in your dream journal. You then create an entry for "apple" in your personal dream dictionary, and you include these possible meanings.

Chapter 3-9
TOOL: Dream Theme Analysis

A dream theme is the main subject matter or topic of a dream. It is the universal idea that pervades throughout the story, the overarching nature of the story, the basic gist of what happens in the dream—its essence. Distilling a dream into its basic theme can help you see the dream in a new way that clarifies what it may represent in your real life or your mind.

For example, you might conclude that a dream in which you scared away a monster who was chasing you contained the theme "Triumph Over Adversity." Once you identify this theme, you might realize that the dream represents a particular real-life situation in which you felt that you triumphed over adversity, or one in which you would like to do so.

In another example, consider that you dreamed about seedlings that were sprouting from an old, dead tree lying on the forest floor. You might identify the theme of this dream as "Rebirth," and so you would then look for a parallel situation in your real life in which a new process was able to begin because a previous process had been completed.

A dream can have more than one theme, but often a dream has one primary theme. In the previous example of the monster dream with the primary theme of "Triumph Over Adversity," you might decide that the dream contains a second theme of "Good vs. Evil" because you consider the monster to be "evil" and you to be "good." When a dream has more than one theme, the dream likely represents both of those themes as they exist somewhere in your waking life or mind. Each theme you identify in a dream provides another clue to what the dream reflects about your waking life.

How to Identify the Theme of Your Dream

When pondering what the theme of a particular dream might be, take a big step back from your dream and ask yourself, "What is happening in this dream, at the most basic level? What is the essence of the dream story?" Sometimes it helps to write a nutshell version of the dynamics or actions in the dream, such as "People escaping from a tidal wave." From there, it would be a small step to arrive at a theme of "Human vs. Nature." You might also try writing a nutshell version of the character's motivations, such as "Someone lashes out at me because she is jealous." That might lead you to conclude that the theme of that dream is "Jealousy."

Since a dream is a story, you may find great value in studying how to define themes in literature and other forms of stories. Much information is available about this topic on the internet, which you can discover by searching for "how to identify the theme of a story" or a similar search term. (For more about using other literary analysis techniques to analyze dreams, see "Chapter 3-19: TOOL: Literary Analysis," p. 175, and "Chapter 3-20: TOOL: Archetype Analysis," p. 181.)

Common Dream Themes

Some of the themes that occur frequently in dreams include being chased or victimized, being stolen from, invasion of personal boundaries, abandonment, betrayal, falling, drowning, being lost, searching for a lost object, flying or levitating, being naked, illness, pregnancy, death, accident or disaster, failure, being late or missing an event, technical problems, and wish fulfillment.

Universal Themes as Dream Themes

Another way to explore possible themes for your dream is to consider universal story themes, which are basic stories that are familiar to all of us. They tend to be common across cultures and generations—or even across civilizations. Some examples of universal story themes are:

- Good vs. Evil.
- Transformation and Rebirth.
- Temptation vs. Conscience.
- Cycles (such as the Cycle of Life).
- Human vs. Nature.
- Restoring Order from Chaos.
- Rewarding "Good" and Punishing "Bad."
- Triumph over Adversity.
- Love Always Wins.

We see these universal themes played out again and again in stories— even those from earlier human times, such as myths, legends, fairy tales, folktales—and just about every story ever told. These themes seem so integral to the human experience that it's not difficult to imagine their having been with us as long as humans have existed. It wouldn't be surprising, then, for them to also show up in our dreams.

The Process

Follow these steps to conduct a Dream Theme Analysis:

1. Identify the main theme of the dream. Step back from the dream and view it objectively, then ask yourself, "What is happening in this dream, at the most basic level? What is the essence of dream story?" Consider the title you gave your dream, since it might suggest a theme.
2. Consider how the theme you've identified reflects a similar theme your real life (current or past). Look for a parallel theme in a situation, event, feeling, or thought during your waking experience.
3. Explore the dream in more depth (symbols, setting, and other elements) to confirm whether the aspect of your real life you identified in Step 2 is the one that your dream is portraying. If the symbolism in the dream doesn't line up with that aspect of your real life, repeat Step 2 and look for another aspect of your life the dream may be portraying.
4. In your dream journal, write the theme of this dream, your conclusions about which aspects of your waking life your dream was portraying, and any other insights about dream meaning.

Examples

The following examples show how Dream Theme Analysis can be useful to help understand dream meaning:

Example A:

Consider a dream in which you overslept and arrived late for a test, but the teacher gave you a chance to take a make-up test so you wouldn't fail the class. You might identify the theme of this dream as "Getting a Second Chance." When you consider how this theme has shown up in your real life, you recall last month when you made a mistake on a project at work, and your team leader gave you another day to correct your work. Looking more closely at the details of the dream, you notice that in both the dream and real life a second chance was given to you by an authority figure who evaluated your work—and in both cases you felt grateful for the second chance, and you were determined to make the most of it. You conclude that the dream was indeed telling the story of the second chance given to you at work last month, and you write this conclusion in your dream journal.

Example B:

Imagine that you dreamed about a green and white caterpillar emerging from a chrysalis as an exquisite butterfly. You identify the dream's theme as the universal theme, "Transformation and Rebirth." You suspect that this dream may represent your process of "transforming" into a nurse in real life, since you are currently studying toward a nursing degree. You explore more of the dream's details—including the fact that caterpillar's green and white colors are your university's school colors, and the fact that the butterfly emerged just outside a hospital building. Based on these details and your intuitive sense, you are convinced that this dream definitely represents your transformation process during your nursing education and your subsequent "rebirth" into the world as a registered nurse. You note these dream details and conclusions in your dream journal.

Chapter 3-10
TOOL: Dream Dictionary

It would be nice if you could use a dream dictionary as an easy shortcut to find the meaning of a particular dream symbol, similar to looking up the definition of a word in a regular dictionary. However, the meaning of dream language is much more subjective, complicated, and personal than our spoken and written languages. A dream symbol can mean something different for different dreamers, and can even differ from one dream to another for the same dreamer. There is no standard meaning of a dream symbol in all dreams and for all dreamers. Therefore, no single meaning of a symbol in a dream dictionary can be "the one meaning" for that symbol in all dreams at all times.

A Source of Possibilities

I think of a dream dictionary as a source of *possible ideas* about meanings—as a source of suggestions that can inspire the dreamer's own exploration process. No dream dictionary is a source of definite answers. There is no such thing. No dream dictionary can provide a meaning of a dream symbol that is *always* true for every dreamer and every dream. Just because a book says that a coyote in a dream means you're feeling lonely doesn't mean that's true in your case. Remember that you are the ultimate authority on your own dream. After all, you are the one who created the dream, and your subconscious mind already knows the meaning of the dream and its symbols. As you review possible meanings in a dream dictionary, the hope is that you will experience an intuitive flash of recognition when you encounter the meaning of a particular dream symbol that is true for you in your particular dream.

In my dream dictionary, *The Curious Dreamer's Dream Dictionary* (TheCuriousDreamer.com), I've written the symbol definitions to provide ideas about what each symbol *could* mean in a dream. For each symbol, I include several meanings to help dreamer get started in her own process of exploring possible meanings. Because the subconscious mind draws from many sources for its dream symbolism—such as personal, social, global, intuitive—I include in my dream dictionary some typical and generally understood meanings that are part of our shared experience as human beings. The meanings I provide are based on typical language of the subconscious mind and logical meanings, as well as archetypes, stereotypes, and other shared meanings. My dream dictionary is intended as a jump-starter for the dreamer's interpretation process, rather than as a shortcut to a definitive meaning.

Finding Your Personal Dream Meaning

When you consult a dream dictionary, keep in mind that dream meaning is subjective and personal for each dreamer. For each symbol from your dream, it's important to consider:

- **Personal meaning**—What the dream symbol means to you, what it brings to mind for you, and feelings it triggers within you.
- **Context**—How the dream symbol appears in the dream. For example, in a dream about a bird—consider what the bird was doing, how and where it was doing it, and how you felt about that.
- **Look beyond the obvious**—A dream is often about something other than its obvious meaning. For example, physical events in the dream can represent mental or emotional matters.

The Process

The following process shows how to use a dream dictionary as part of your dream interpretation process. For the purposes of this process, I'm referring to *The Curious Dreamer's Dream Dictionary* (TheCuriousDreamer.com) because it is written specifically for personal growth and enlightenment.

1. Choose a symbol from your dream that you want to explore, perhaps the one that stood out the most.
2. Find that symbol in the dream dictionary, and consider the possible meanings listed. Notice which (if any) resonate with you intuitively.
3. While keeping the dictionary meanings in mind, consider:

   Personal meaning—What the dream symbol means to you, what it brings to mind for you, and feelings it triggers within you.

   Context—How the dream symbol appears in the dream. For example, in a dream about a bird—consider what the bird was doing, how and where it was doing it, and how you felt about that.

   Look beyond the obvious—A dream is often about something other than its obvious meaning. For example, physical events in the dream can represent mental or emotional matters.

4. Using what you discovered in Step 2 and Step 3, explore what the symbol represents on some level of your real life—physical, mental, emotional, spiritual, and so on. If a particular dictionary meaning resonated with you, explore it further by looking for more clues in the dream that point to something parallel in your real life.

5. Write your conclusions about the symbol's meaning in your dream journal, along with any other realizations about the dream.

Examples

The following examples illustrate how you might use *The Curious Dreamer's Dream Dictionary* (TheCuriousDreamer.com) to assist you in discovering the meaning of a dream:

Example A:

In a dream, you watched a giraffe as she tried to eat some leaves high up in a tree, but she couldn't quite reach them. However, she was determined, and you knew she would eventually reach them.

You check the dream dictionary, and it says a giraffe can represent the ability to see different perspectives, to see things differently than others, to see both sides of an issue—or the ability to easily reach beyond what others can see or do. You keep these in mind as you consider the following:

Your personal meaning—When you think of a giraffe, you think of a very tall animal with a long neck who can reach things in high places.

Context—In this dream, the giraffe was trying to reach leaves high in the tree in order to eat them. She was stretching to get food because she needed nourishment, but was having trouble reaching it.

Look beyond the obvious—You haven't seen a giraffe or any references to a giraffe lately in your waking life, so you conclude that the giraffe probably represents something in your life other than an actual giraffe. You think about how perhaps you have stretched to get some kind of nourishment but couldn't quite reach it. You consider all the kinds of nourishment—physical, mental, emotional, spiritual, and so on—and you recognize that in real life you had planned to stretch yourself financially to take an art history class, but you decided it was too much of a stretch right now. You had been looking forward to the class because you're so interested in learning about art and artists from the past—a form of mental and emotional nourishment that would feed your own creative process. Your intuition confirms the dream dictionary's meaning of "reaching beyond," since you are determined to reach beyond your current financial shortcomings as you save money over the next few months so you can take the class. In your dream journal, you write your conclusions about the giraffe's meaning in your dream.

Example B:

Imagine that you dreamed you were enjoying yourself spending money at the mall when you remembered that you had to go home and take care of your dog, who needed to be fed and let outside. You were disappointed about having to leave, but you felt good about fulfilling your responsibility to the dog. In real life you don't have a dog.

The dream dictionary says that a dog can represent loyalty or protectiveness, and that a pet can represent responsibility, unconditional love or acceptance, innocence or other childlike qualities, or your own inner child.

You can't think of a real-life situation during which you had to interrupt a fun time because of someone who was protective, but the idea of responsibility feels on-target to you. In the dream you were leaving the mall to attend to your responsibility of caring for your dog. You keep this in mind as you consider the following:

Your personal meaning—The idea of a dog reminds you of responsibility because when you were a kid, taking care of your family's dog was your responsibility.

Context—In this dream, you knew you had to go home because you had a responsibility to go take care of your dog.

Look beyond the obvious—Because you don't have a dog, it seems that the dog probably represents something else in your life. You consider where in your life you've had to stop in the middle of a fun time to go take care of a responsibility, where you felt disappointed but knew you were doing the right thing by stopping. You recognize the disappointment you felt last month when you decided to stop going to the coffee shop every morning and buying expensive, calorie-laden drinks—and instead enjoying healthier morning beverages at home. Your intuition confirms that the dream portrays your pattern of overspending on expensive drinks you don't really need (represented by spending at the mall), which you stopped in order to fulfill your responsibility to yourself regarding your finances and your health (represented by your responsibility to the dog). You write your conclusions about this dream's meaning in your dream journal.

Chapter 3-11
TOOL: Personal Dream Dictionary

As your subconscious mind creates a dream, it may use particular dream symbols to represent specific things according to your existing understanding of those symbols—based on your past experience with it, your perceptions about it, and the associations you've made with it. Following that reasoning, your subconscious mind may repeatedly use the same dream symbol to represent the same thing across multiple dreams. So it makes sense to keep track of what particular symbols have meant in past dreams.

Keeping Track of Your Dream Symbol Meanings

To keep track of your own personal dream symbol meanings, you can create a personal dream dictionary—adding to it each significant symbol you dream about, along with your personal definition of what it meant in your dream. Similar to a foreign-language translation dictionary, a personal dream dictionary contains symbols you've dreamed about, along with their translated meanings from past dreams you've had. Keeping track of your own past meanings for symbols gives you a short-list to consider first when those symbols reappear in future dreams.

Keep in mind that a particular symbol can have different meanings for you in different dreams. For example, you might dream about a yellow daisy sprouting from a garbage heap, which you might determine represents something good coming out of an unpleasant situation in your life. Then maybe a few years later you dream about a yellow daisy sprouting up in the middle of a formal rose garden, which you determine represents your feeling of "not belonging" at the new school to which you just transferred. It's okay to list multiple meanings for the same symbol in your personal dream dictionary. The idea is that next time you dream about a daisy, you can consider whether any of the previous meanings apply in the new dream.

The Process

Here are some steps to follow when creating a Personal Dream Dictionary that contains dream symbols with meanings specific to you:

1. Choose a place to create your dream dictionary. I suggest using a different book or notebook than you use for your dream journal, so it will still be handy later after you've moved on to a new dream journal.

2. Start with symbols that have appeared in your dreams before. If you like, you can then expand to other symbols that resonate with you or that stand out to you when you hear about them.

3. Write each symbol name, and then write what it meant in past dreams. For a symbol you haven't dreamed about, write what first comes to mind when you think of it. Top-of-mind characteristics are best, since they're probably what you (and your subconscious mind) tend to associate with that symbol. If you get stuck, imagine you're explaining what the symbol is to someone who has never heard of it before. For example, you might describe a tree as "a plant that grows to be big and sturdy, provides cool shade, serves as a home to small creatures, and in some cases can provide fruit as food" (for more ideas, see "Chapter 3-8: TOOL: Caveman Explanation," p. 134).

4. Anytime you have a dream, consult your dream dictionary for possible meanings of key symbols from the dream. If the symbols from your current dream aren't listed, add them—and include what they symbolized in the dream you just had (if you know) and (if you like) any other meanings you tend to associate with them.

Examples

Here are some examples of entries you might create in your Personal Dream Dictionary (except you would replace these meanings with your own):

- **Dog**—Loyal, friendship, love, barks as an alarm, teeth can harm or play-bite.
- **House**—Home, safe, secure, comfortable, relaxed, family.
- **Car**—Drive fast, go places, decisions to turn or stop, always goes home.
- **Baby**—Cute, little, fun, vulnerable, requires help and responsibility, grows up.
- **Red**—Stop sign, danger, attention, blood.

Chapter 3-12
TOOL: Timeline Analysis

The sequence of events in a dream can offer valuable clues about dream meaning, since dreams often portray real-life events in the same order that they occurred in your life. Therefore, examining a dream chronologically can help you map the sequence of dream events to what they represent in your real life. The Timeline Analysis technique involves drawing a timeline of your dream that depicts the chronological flow of events in the dream. A visual timeline enables you to closely study elements of the dream—such as each character's actions and reactions, objects involved, settings and changes of scene, and other elements of the dream—and examine them for clues to meaning.

You can use any format you like as you create your timeline. A basic numbered list is fine, or you could use a words-and-arrows diagram or a flowchart. If you like, you can also add drawings of characters, symbols, and any other major elements of the dream. Since emotions during a dream are such significant clues to meaning, it's a good idea to write emotion keywords along the timeline at the points where you were experiencing those emotions.

The Process

The following instructions show how to use a Timeline Analysis to identify parallels between events in a dream and aspects of your waking life:

1. Start with a full sheet of paper, and have several extra sheets handy. If you prefer, use your dream journal.
2. Near an edge or corner of the page, write a brief description of the first event or situation in your dream, such as "Drifting in a small boat at sea." Next to it in parentheses, write keywords to describe your emotions during that part of the dream, such as "(peaceful, calm)."
3. Draw an arrow leading to the next event in the dream, then describe the event and your associated emotions. (Instead of arrows, you can

147

use a numbered list or any other format that shows the order of events.)

4. Repeat Step 2 and Step 3 for the rest of the dream, depicting each event and associated emotion during the dream, such as "Drifted too far from shore (worried, isolated)," "Called for help (panicked)," and "No reply (disappointed, hopeless)."

5. Distill the entire timeline into a very basic form, such as "feeling comfortable, then realized too late I was out of my comfort zone, but it was too late." (This is similar to the generalization process in "Chapter 3-3: TOOL: Generalization Analysis," p. 110, which may be helpful for you to review.)

6. Look for parallels between the basic version of the timeline and your real life. For instance, in the boat dream example, you might realize that in real life when you started your current math course, you were lulled into a false sense of security because it was easy—but then before you realized it, you were completely lost.

If you recognize what one of the later events in the dream represents in your life, but not the earlier ones, then consider what events in your life happened before the identified real-life event *and* match the emotions you felt during the earlier dream events.

If you can't find any parallels between the dream events and real-life events, try distilling the timeline in different ways to help trigger a memory or realization. For example, you might redefine the timeline in the boat dream as "I isolated myself until I was in trouble and couldn't get help" or an emotion-centered version such as "Calmness shifted into a desperate need for help, which left me disappointed." Remember that the emotions you felt in the dream were likely similar to the ones you felt during the real-life events that the dream represents.

7. Write your conclusions in your dream journal, and if you like, transfer your timeline into your dream journal—perhaps redrawing it more neatly or in a clearer format.

If you can't find real-life parallels with the events in the dream, it's possible that one or more of the dream events was based on something other than your real life, such as:

- An imagined situation your subconscious mind mocked up during the dream state, such as to play out a fear or a desire.
- A rehearsal for something you expect to happen in real life.
- Something that has been on your mind—either lately or long term.

- A story portraying a message or "moral of the story" that you can benefit from right now.

Examples

The following examples show how you can use Timeline Analysis to help identify how a series of dream events represents a series of events in your real life:

Example A:

Imagine that you dreamed you were walking home from school on the last day of high school, feeling happy about the upcoming summer break. Suddenly, you spotted a man in a dark jacket and baseball cap following you. He started chasing you, and you knew he wanted to take something from you. You tried to duck into a nearby bank, but it was closed. Just as the man got within 10 feet of you, you escaped into the office of the local newspaper publisher, and the man disappeared from view.

You create the following timeline to summarize the events and emotions in the dream:

a. Last day of high school (happy about upcoming break).
b. Man following me to take something from me (scared).
c. Tried to escape into bank that was closed (hopeful, then disappointed).
d. Escaped into newspaper building (relieved to be safe again).

You then distill the timeline into this very basic form: Feeling happy and free, then someone is demanding something from me.

Looking for parallels between the timeline and your real life, you note the reference to the end of high school—and just when you were feeling happy about the summer break, someone started following you to take something from you. You realize that this sounds like the real-life situation after you graduated from high school (represented in the dream by the end of high school), when you were so happy to move into your own apartment for the summer, but then bill collectors started coming after you to pay your overdue bills (represented by the man coming after you). In real life, you applied for a job as a bank teller to help pay the bills, but you didn't get the job (represented by the bank being unavailable as an escape from the man chasing you). What happened next in real life also lined up with the dream, since in real life you ended up getting a job at the newspaper (represented by escaping into the newspaper building), which gave you enough income to pay your bills (represented by your escaping from the man in dark clothes). You conclude that the dream portrayed a sequence of events in your real life during the summer after you finished high school, when you were anticipating the freedom of a summer on your own, and then tried to escape the demands of people to whom you owed money—by first trying to get a job at a bank, and then by finding one at the newspaper that gave you the income you needed to escape your debt. You notice that your emotions during the dream were very similar to your emotions during that time in your life: happy, then scared about overdue bills, hopeful and then disappointed about the bank job you didn't get, then relieved to get the newspaper job which enabled you to pay your bills.

Example B:

Consider a dream in which you were at a swimming pool standing on the high diving board. Although you were very afraid of heights, you knew you could make this dive successfully. You took a deep breath and completed the dive with a perfect technique. The swimming pool then turned into a river and you were swept downstream through the rapids. You kept your head above water and navigated around several boulders in the river. Finally, you reached a calm shallow spot, and you pulled yourself out of the water. You noticed your friends at a beautiful house nearby, and they welcomed you for an afternoon of lounging by the pool.

You create the following timeline to summarize the events and emotions in the dream:

a. Diving from the high diving board (afraid, then proud).
b. Navigating the river rapids (afraid but focused).
c. Reaching the shallows (calm, relieved).
d. Joining friends around the pool (happy, glad the challenge was over).

You distill the dream timeline into this very basic form: Proud of doing well, navigating challenges, and relieved when they're over and you're with friends.

Looking for parallels between the timeline and your real life, you recognize the series of challenges (represented by the river rapids and boulders) and then friends being there afterward (represented by your friends at the pool). You realize that these dream events represent a time when you dealt with a series of real-life health challenges while living in a city where you didn't know anyone, and then you moved back to your hometown where your friends still lived. Once you identified what these later events in the timeline represented, you considered what diving off the high dive could represent. You then realize it must represent your original decision to "take the plunge" and move away from your hometown, which was one of the scariest things you ever did. You felt so afraid to leave behind the familiar and relocate to a new city where you didn't know anyone, which was where you experienced the health challenges before eventually moving back to your hometown. You con-clude that this dream was your subconscious mind's portrayal of that period in your life, with the course of water representing the path of your life during that time, the rapids representing challenges through which you navigated, and both pools representing your "safe" hometown (one before you left your hometown, and the other one when you came back and reunited with friends).

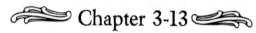

Chapter 3-13
TOOL: Element Relationship Mapping

E lement Relationship Mapping involves creating a portrayal of your dream on paper that shows how you—the dreamer—relate to each major element in your dream. Using this technique, you revisit each major dream element and characterize how you related to it in your own mind during the dream—your relationship to it, feelings about it, attitude toward it, perspective of it. Because the way you relate to a dream element during a dream can be very similar to the way you relate to whatever that element represents in real life, this process may help trigger realizations about the meaning of those dream elements.

Whether you were an active participant or just an observer during the dream, in this technique you always characterize how *you* related to other elements of the dream—*your* connection to other aspects of the dream.

The Process

The following steps show how to use the Element Relationship Mapping technique to explore how you related to various elements in your dream, revealing clues to dream meaning:

1. With pen and paper, write the word "Me" or draw a picture of yourself somewhere on the page.
2. Add a word, picture, or symbol depicting the most significant element in your dream—the one that comes to mind first when you think of your dream. It might be a character, object, place, or anything else in your dream.
3. Draw a line between "Me" and the element you created in the previous step.
4. Along the line, write keywords to describe how you related to the element during the dream. These might include:

Relationship—who or what the element was to you in the dream. A character might have been a teacher, friend, or attacker; an object might have been an obstacle, a distraction, or something valuable to you; a setting might have been a destination or stop along the way.

Feelings, attitudes, or perspectives about the element—you might have felt joyful around your friend, frustrated by an obstacle, or curious about a mysterious object.

Action(s)—any action you or the element took in relation to the other. You might have given your friend a gift, pushed the obstacle out of the way, or studied the object under a bright light.

5. Repeat Steps 2 through 4 to add any other elements that stood out in your dream, connect them to yourself ("Me") in the drawing, and depict how you related to each.
6. Review the diagram you've created, noticing any aspects of the dream elements that remind you of elements of your real life, and write any clues about dream meaning in your dream journal.

Examples

Here are some examples that illustrate how you might use Element Relationship Mapping as part of your dream analysis process:

Example A:

Consider a dream in which you (the dreamer) were actively involved. In this dream you planted a seed that then sprouted and grew into a beautiful flower, and you were in awe of its beauty. You might map the relationships among the elements in this dream as shown in Figure F.

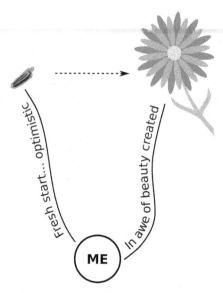

Fig. F. Element Relationship Mapping: Seed Planting Dream

You start by drawing a circle containing the word "Me" and then you draw the seed. You draw a line between "Me" and the seed, and along it you write your perspective and feeling about the seed as "Fresh start...optimistic." You draw the flower, draw a line between "Me" and the flower, and then write your feelings toward the flower as "In awe of beauty created." As you write this last line, you realize that the seed growing into a beautiful flower reminds you of a time when you started painting a small, simple landscape scene which then grew into a wonderful piece of art that inspired the same kind of awe within you.

Example B:

Imagine a dream in which you (the dreamer) were a passive observer. In this dream you watched an ant trying to carry a huge piece of leaf back to its nest, but the ant kept dropping the leaf. You were surprised and impressed that every time the ant dropped the leaf, he just matter-of-factly picked it up again and continued on his way. You noted that instead of getting angry, he seemed calm, persistent, and determined to accomplish his goal. You might map your relationship to the elements in this dream as shown in Figure G.

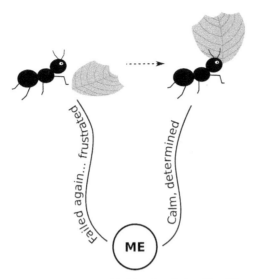

Fig. G. Element Relationship Mapping: Ant and Leaf Dream

You start by drawing a circle containing the word "Me" and then draw the ant as he dropped the leaf. You write your perception of the ant dropping the leaf as "Failed again" and your feeling as "frustrated." You then draw the ant as he picked up the leaf and kept going, and you write your perception of this as "Calm, determined." While reviewing your diagram, what comes to mind is the math problem you've been trying to figure out. Each time you've failed to solve it, you've gotten angry, thrown your pencil, and given up. You then realize that the dream portrays an alternative way that you can handle a challenge that requires repeated attempts—by focusing on the goal and remaining calm and persistent.

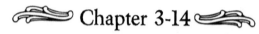 Chapter 3-14

TOOL: Draw Your Dream Symbol

D rawing a picture of a dream symbol from your dream may help you recall it in greater detail and gain a deeper understanding of its meaning. The creative process of drawing can open a channel to the deeper areas of your consciousness—including your subconscious mind, where your dream took place. As your creative process flows, you may notice aspects of your dream coming forward that otherwise might have stayed hidden deep in your consciousness.

When drawing your dream symbol, the method doesn't matter as much as the process. The idea is to just draw, and include all of the details that come forward in your mind. You may find that the longer you draw, the more detail you remember. Also, you might notice better results when you draw soon after your dream, while the symbol is still fresh in your mind.

The Process

Here are the steps in the Draw Your Dream Symbol technique:

1. Have your dream journal or a separate piece of paper ready, along with a pencil or pen. If color was a significant part of your symbol's appearance, you might want to use colored pencils or markers.
2. Close your eyes and visualize the dream symbol. You may find it helpful to re-play the scene of the dream in which the dream symbol appeared.
3. Open your eyes and draw the dream symbol. Refresh your inner image occasionally by closing your eyes and re-visualizing the symbol and its setting. In your drawing, convey what stands out about the dream symbol, including any of the following:

   Emotions
   Color (draw using colors, or write color names)

Mood
Actions
Thoughts and intentions
Size relative to other elements of the dream
Relationship to other elements of the dream

4. Write any intuitive insights about the symbol's meaning that come forward as you are drawing.
5. After you finish, check within yourself for any further insights about the symbol's meaning. Pay attention to how your feelings about the symbol remind you of an event or situation in your life, or something that's been on your mind. If nothing is ringing a bell in relation to your real life, consider whether the symbol may represent something in your mind—a feeling, a fear, an imagined scenario, or perhaps an experience your subconscious mind decided to try out during the dream state. Write any conclusions about meaning in your dream journal.
6. If you're still not clear about the symbol's meaning, set aside your drawing and come back to it later with fresh eyes to see if you get any new insights about meaning.

Once your dream symbol drawing is complete, you can use it to help you connect with your dream symbol when you're using other dream symbol techniques, such as "Chapter 3-2: TOOL: Parallels Between Symbols and Real Life" (p. 105), "Chapter 3-15: TOOL: Dialogue with Your Dream Symbol" (p. 160), "Chapter 3-16: TOOL: Dream Symbol Monologue" (p. 164), and "Chapter 3-21: TOOL: Art Analysis" (p. 187).

Variation: Draw Your Entire Dream

You can also create a drawing of your entire dream rather than just one dream symbol. When drawing your whole dream, you can follow the process just described for drawing a dream symbol, or create your own process and be as creative as you like. The idea is to create a time and space for your subconscious mind to reveal to you clues about the dream's meaning as you draw. You might draw the whole dream or just part of it—maybe just the key characters and symbols, or maybe just the setting to help you connect with the emotions it conveys and to explore how they relate to your waking life. You might diagram the whole dream and how the characters and symbols relate to each other. Another approach is to draw a timeline of the dream from beginning to end, showing the characters and actions they took. You could draw key parts of the dream as if they're scenes on a stage, including the setting, characters, and objects that stood out. I suggest letting your intuition guide you as you begin drawing your dream.

Examples

The following examples show how you might use the Draw Your Dream Symbol technique as part of your dream analysis process:

Example A:

Consider a dream about a sailboat that the wind was propelling forward, but the boat was held back by an anchor deep below. You might portray this dream in a drawing such as Figure H.

Fig. H. Drawing of a Boat Dream Symbol

As you draw the boat picture, you focus on the fact that the strong wind would propel the boat forward quickly if it weren't held back by the anchor dragging behind it. You ask yourself, "Where in my life is forward movement being impeded because of something that is dragging?" You suddenly think of the report you need to finish by next Tuesday in real life, and you realize the boat's impeded movement represents your progress that has stopped because you're waiting for data from a co-worker who seems to be dragging his feet (represented by the dragging anchor). Then you realize that in the dream what's needed to enable the boat to move forward is to bring the anchor up and on board the boat. This gives you an idea: maybe if you can bring your co-worker "on board" in the project and work with him more directly, you can work more effectively as a team rather than just one person just waiting for another person. You realize that if you're both "on board" with the shared goal, you'll have a greater chance of completing the project successfully. You write your conclusions in your dream journal and add a note to your to-do list reminding you to meet with your co-worker.

Example B:
Another example of drawing your dream symbol might look something like Figure I, which depicts a dream in which a giant bee was trying to get back into his hive.

Fig. I. Drawing of a Bee Dream Symbol

The bee has grown so much he can't fit into the hive anymore. He tries repeatedly but can't get in. As you draw this picture, you remember that the bee had a letter R on his back. Because R is your initial, you suspect the bee represents you. You know that the bee is trying to go back home, but he has grown too much to go home. It occurs to you that having "grown too much to go home" in the dream might represent how you've felt since you've been away at college several years—you've changed so much that you don't quite feel like you fit in at home anymore. You feel your family still relates to you as a kid, but you're not a kid anymore. In the dream the hive stayed the same size as always, but the bee grew much bigger—which may represent your feeling in real life that home is still the same, but that you've changed and grown as a person. You add these conclusions to your dream journal, and you decide to use "Chapter 3-16: TOOL: Dream Symbol Monologue" (p. 164) to explore what else the bee symbol can reveal about your situation and feelings.

Chapter 3-15

TOOL: Dialogue with Your Dream Symbol

The Dialogue With Your Dream Symbol technique is an interaction you create in writing, in which you interview a particular symbol from your dream to reveal more clues about its meaning. The goal of dialoging with a dream symbol is to learn about the symbol's meaning from the source that created it in the first place: your subconscious mind. This technique helps open the door into your subconscious mind by creating a space for you to ask questions and to allow your subconscious mind to answer through the voice of the dream symbol.

The Process

Here are the steps to Dialogue With Your Dream Symbol:

1. With pen and several sheets of paper, write your name followed by a colon (for example, "John:"), then write a question you'd like to ask your dream symbol, such as one of the following:

   "Why did you show up in my dream?"
   "What were you trying to tell me in this dream?"
   "Why did you show up specifically as a _____?" (gorilla, tree, or whatever the symbol was)
   "Why did you do what you did in the dream?" (or name a specific action or reaction)
   "Why did you choose this particular time to show up in my dream?"
   "What can I learn from you?"
   "How can you help me improve myself or my life?"

2. Shift into the role of your dream symbol. Write the name of the dream symbol to indicate that you are speaking from the point of view of the symbol, and then answer the question from the symbol's perspective. To help you take on the role of the symbol, you can

160

assume its characteristics such as position, facial expression, or mood. If playing the role of the symbol feels awkward, just think of this as role-playing or a game of pretend. Set aside any skepticism, and you may be surprised what insights come forward.

3. Continue the dialogue, switching between the roles of yourself and the symbol until you feel complete and you have nothing more to say as either yourself or as the symbol.

4. Write in your dream journal any conclusions about the meaning of this dream symbol and the dream, and any realizations about you or your life that this dialogue brought forward.

5. To dialogue with a different symbol or aspect of your dream you'd like to explore, repeat Steps 1 through 4. You can create a dialogue with anyone or anything you like—any symbol, character, place, feeling, or anything else you experienced in a dream.

Variation: Spoken Dialogue with Your Dream Symbol

Sometimes creating a spoken rather than a written dialogue with your dream symbol—in which you physically place yourself in the role of the dream symbol—can prompt your subconscious mind to participate more fully in the dialogue. To do this, modify the Dialogue With Your Dream Symbol technique just described in the following way:

Arrange two chairs so they are facing each other. Begin by sitting in one chair, and imagine the dream symbol sitting in the other chair. Ask your first question of the dream symbol, and then sit in the dream symbol's chair, answering the question while taking on the role of the dream symbol. Continue moving between the two chairs as you ask each new question and then answer it from the perspective of the dream symbol.

Examples

Here are some examples of how you might use the Dialogue With Your Dream Symbol technique to help reveal clues to dream meaning:

Example A:

The following is an example of a written dialogue that a person named Julie might write to explore the meaning of a snake in her dream:

Julie: Hey, snake from my dream—why were you in my dream?

Dream Snake: I was there to tell you something important about something you're afraid of.

Julie: In the dream, you were hiding in the grass, and then you came out suddenly. What does that mean?

Dream Snake: I represent something that lurks unseen most of the time, but could come out at you at any time.

Julie: Let's see. I wonder what in my real life is like that, something that I'm afraid of, that could jump out and surprise me at any time. Oh, it's the pop quizzes in school, like the one Mrs. Kensington gave us yesterday.

Dream Snake: Yes, and notice that in the dream I was moving away from you.

Julie: Yes. That must mean that the scary thing is over, because you were going away.

Dream Snake: Yes, I was a scary thing jumping out at you and then leaving, just like the pop quiz.

Julie: So, what were you trying to tell me?

Dream Snake: I was there to remind you about pop quizzes and how afraid you are that the teacher will give one every time you're in that class. You may not even realize that you sit in that class and worry the whole time.

Julie: Hmm, what could I do so that I don't have to worry so much? Well, if I study and always do my homework, I will always be prepared if Mrs. Kensington gives a pop quiz. I intend to be prepared for her class by doing all the assigned homework from now on.

Example B:

Here is another example of a dialogue with a dream symbol that a person named Simon might write to explore the meaning of a tree symbol in his dream:

Simon: Tree in my dream, you stood out more than anything else in the dream. It's obvious you're important. Tell me more about yourself.

Dream Tree: I was growing inside your office at work. Even though there was no natural sunlight, and conditions weren't ideal for a tree to grow, I started growing and kept surviving.

Simon: So, you grew in a place where it's not easy for a tree to grow. I also noticed that you were producing some kind of fruit.

Dream Tree: Yes, even in those unlikely conditions I was able to produce fruit.

Simon: So, you were productive even when it wasn't easy, even when the odds were against you. Is that what you represent in my real life?

Dream Tree: Yes, that's it exactly.

Simon: Like the way I've been feeling uninspired by my work situation, and I'm having trouble focusing and getting things done because I'm feeling unmotivated?

Dream Tree: Yes. Maybe you can imagine how—without the sun to "motivate" me to grow—I had to find that motivation some other way.

Simon: Oh! So, even if work doesn't motivate me, I can find other ways to motivate myself to do a good job. Even if the environment isn't inspiring, I can do my job. And I can find ways to "open a window and let in some light" by creating more fun and by finding more rewarding ways to think about work. I hadn't even thought about the fact that I can change the way I think about work to make it more enjoyable and feel more motivated. This is great. I'll come up with some more ways to do that.

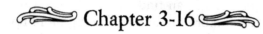 Chapter 3-16

TOOL: Dream Symbol Monologue

If a dream symbol could speak, it could probably tell you a lot about its meaning in your dream. In this technique, you give your dream symbol a voice as you step into the role of the dream symbol and enable it to speak. Through your imagination, you bring the dream symbol to life in a free-form, stream-of-consciousness flow of expression. The goal of this written monologue is to create a space for your subconscious mind to express itself from the point of the view of the dream symbol—in the hope of revealing the symbol's meaning.

The Process

To create a Dream Symbol Monologue, follow these steps:

1. With a pen and paper ready, imagine that you are the particular symbol from the dream. Picture yourself in the symbol's place within the dream, appearing as it did, doing what it was doing, having the purpose it had in the dream. Using your imagination, become the dream symbol.

2. Begin writing, speaking as the dream symbol. Write anything that comes to mind. You might describe who you are, what you represent, your purpose for being in the dream, what message you carry, or anything else that comes to mind.

3. Continue writing until nothing else comes forward in your mind.

4. Write in your dream journal any conclusions about this dream symbol's meaning and any realizations that it triggered about you or your life.

5. If you like, repeat the process from the point of view of a different dream symbol or another element of your dream. You can give a voice to any symbol, character, place, feeling, or anything else you experienced in a dream.

Examples

The following examples demonstrate how the Dream Symbol Monologue analysis tool can shed light on the meaning of a dream:

Example A:

A Dream Symbol Monologue might look something like the following one, from the point of view of an ant as a dream symbol. Imagine that you are the ant from the dream, and then begin to write as if you are the ant speaking:

"I am the ant from your dream, the one whom you dreamed had invaded your bed and crawled onto you. I was bugging you in your dream, and then after you woke up, the idea of me kept you from going back to sleep. I was literally 'bugging' you while you were sleeping. If you think about what has been bugging you while you're sleeping lately, you'll realize that it's your worries about the project that's due next week. Your worries about the project creep in and bug you at nighttime, nagging at your brain, waking you up, and then keeping you awake stewing about your worries. Ants are busy workers, so my showing up in this dream as an ant represents how very hard your worries are working—they are really busy bugging you. However, it's not my job to tell you what to do about the worries. That part is up to you."

Although your dream doesn't tell you what to do about your worries, it does provide some clues about them that can help you come up with a plan to deal with them. Now that you realize how much your worries about your project are disrupting your sleep, you might focus on the fact that your mind spends a lot of time creating a list of these worries, over and over. Then it might occur to you that you could actually write these worries down so your mind doesn't have to keep recreating the mental list. Once you've written a list of all your worries about the project, you might decide to go through them and figure out how to address each one directly, so you won't need to worry about them any more. For example, if you're worried that you won't finish the project on time, you might create a schedule to follow, or set aside a large block of time tomorrow in order to jumpstart your progress. If another worry is about presenting your project in front of a group, you might decide to take steps such as researching your topic thoroughly so you'll feel comfortable talking about it, preparing presentation notes, and practicing your presentation in front of a mirror or a supportive friend.

Example B:

After a dream in which you and your parents went on a bus trip to Chicago (where you currently attend college in real life), you might explore the dream symbol of the bus in a Dream Symbol Monologue. First, you imagine that you are that bus and you picture yourself in the bus' place in the dream, going down the road. Then you begin writing as if you are the bus speaking:

"I am the bus that was driving you and your parents down the winding, bumpy road in your dream, carrying you from your home in Cleveland to Chicago. You were traveling with your parents on your way to begin your first year of college. In the dream, as we drove down the winding road we hit several large bumps along the way. You were worried that the bus would break down and you would never get to college. However, I had no trouble making the trip, and you all arrived safely. Did you notice that I was green, the color of money? Think about the obstacles and bumps on your road to college in real life—the challenges that led up to the time you left for college. There were financial challenges like applying for financial aid and trying to save money from your summer jobs. It makes sense that I—the bus who took you on your journey to college—would be the same color of green as money. Your trip in me represents the bumpy process you went through to arrange the finances so that you could go to college."

After writing this, you realize that this dream was portraying the real-life process you went through to make sure you would have enough money for college when you began as a freshman last year. You and your parents went through a process of putting together a financial plan (represented in the dream by all of you traveling down a road together). There were "bumps in the road" when you were worried that the finances would not come through (represented by your worry that the bus would break down), but ultimately all the finances fell into place, enabling you to go to college (represented by the bus arriving safely in Chicago). You realize that this dream tells the story of a time in the past—of a stressful problem that has since been resolved—and you decide that no further action is needed.

Chapter 3-17

TOOL: Dialogue with the Dream Source

W hen you don't know the answer to a question, you might decide to ask someone who knows or to consult another information source. When you don't know what your dream means, therefore, it might make sense to ask someone who knows about the dream—so, why not ask the one who created it in the first place? In the Dialogue With the Dream Source technique, you create a written conversation in which you interview the source of your dream in the hope of revealing clues to dream meaning.

Instead of getting bogged down trying to identify the exact source of your dream (subconscious mind, imagination, outside source, or something else), for the purposes of this process I suggest you set aside that question and simply direct your questions to "Dream Source."

The Process

The following steps show how to create a Dialogue With The Dream Source:

1. With pen and several sheets of paper, write your name followed by a colon (for example, "Beth:"), then write a question you'd like to ask the source of your dream, such as:

"Why did you create this dream?"
"What is this dream really about?"
"What message does this dream have for me?"
"Why did you choose this particular time to create this dream?"
"What can I learn from this dream?"
"How can this dream help me improve myself or my life?"

2. Shift into the role of your dream source. Write "Dream Source:" (or any other name you'd like to call it) and then answer the question

from the viewpoint of the dream source. To help get into the role of the dream source, try thinking of this as role-playing or a game of pretend. If you can suspend your disbelief, this process can provide great insight into the meaning of your dream.

3. Continue the dialogue, switching between the roles of yourself and the dream source until you feel complete and neither has anything more to say.

4. Write in your dream journal any conclusions about dream meaning or clarifications about you or your life.

Variation: Spoken Dialogue with the Dream Source

Sometimes active, physical participation in a role can elicit different results. To create a physical dialogue, modify the written dialogue technique just described in the following way:

Place two chairs facing each other. Begin by sitting in one chair, and imagine your dream source sitting in the other chair. Ask the dream source a question, and then move to the other chair and answer the question while playing the role of the dream source. Continue moving from chair to chair as you continue the dialogue, alternating between roles.

Examples

Here are some examples of how to use the Dialogue With The Dream Source technique to help understand the meaning of a dream:

Example A:

The following example shows a dialogue that 11-year-old named Claude and might create with the source of a dream in which he discovered he was standing in front of his classmates at school wearing no clothes:

Claude: Why would I dream that I wasn't wearing any clothes at school?

Dream Source: What happened in the dream when you realized you weren't wearing any clothes?

Claude: Everyone was looking at me, and they could see everything.

Dream Source: They could see everything about you, even things you didn't want them to see.

Claude: Yes, and I wanted to run away and hide. I just wanted to get away. Just like I felt last Monday when I had to stand up in front of the class and give my book report, but I hadn't finished the book and so I didn't know what to say. Everybody was looking at me and I wanted to run away. Oh, I think this dream is about how I felt when I had to give my report.

Dream Source: Yes, and what does the dream tell you about that?

Claude: Well, I guess that it would have been a lot better if I had finished reading the book so I would know what to say.

Dream Source: If you had read the book, you would know what it was about. You could give a good book report, and you could feel confident while you're standing in front of the class.

Claude: Yes, I guess I will make sure I'm prepared before my next book report, and I'll start reading the book early so I can finish writing my report on time. Things sure would be a lot easier that way.

Example B:
This example is a Dialogue With The Dream Source that a 31-year-old woman named Beth might write regarding a dream about a flood:

Beth: Is this dream related to something in my real life?

Dream Source: Yes, and you realize that something about the dream feels familiar.

Beth: What about the dream seems familiar?

Dream Source: The feeling of not being in control as the floodwaters rose is something you've felt recently real life.

Beth: But I haven't been around a flood in real life recently.

Dream Source: No, but you have felt "under water" and "in over your head" lately at work.

Beth: Yes, that's true. Not an actual flood, but things had been getting so out of control that I felt overwhelmed. Yes, I did feel that I was "in over my head." So, what is this dream saying about that situation at work?

Dream Source: In the dream, you dealt with the floodwaters rising by calling for help, and a boat came to rescue you. The dream points out that the idea of calling for help is on your mind, maybe because you feel the need for help or because you feel like things are beyond what you can handle on your own.

Beth: Does that mean that I should ask for help?

Dream Source: That's up to you to decide. The dream was merely exploring your subconscious thoughts and feelings about the situation.

Chapter 3-18
TOOL: Dialogue with a Higher Source

If you could talk to someone who knew everything there is to know about your dream, about you, about your life—what would you ask him or her? We all have a wise, inner higher source. Call it anything you like—higher self, inner wisdom, higher power, truth-see-er, Divine intuition, or whatever words you choose. Regardless of the name you give it, there is a source within you who knows—or has access to—more truths than you can imagine. For the purposes of this technique, it's not necessary to be concerned with what it is called or how it works. You merely need to trust that it exists. If you find yourself unable to trust, just suspend your doubt for as long as it takes to finish this technique. You never know what wisdom may come forward that you would miss otherwise, and at the very least you'll be setting aside any skepticism and stepping into a place of clearer inner vision for a while.

This technique involves creating a dialogue to ask this wise inner source some questions about your dream, what the dream tells you about yourself and your life, and how you can use your dream to improve both. For the purposes of these instructions, I'll refer to this wise inner source as "higher source." However, I encourage you to use whatever label helps you connect with the actual source within you.

Recognizing Your Higher Source

You will recognize when you are in touch with your higher source by the sense of calm, peace, well-being, goodwill, or pure love it exudes. The higher source is not excitable or sensational. It exists above any fear, desire, judgment, demand, or any other mental or emotional dynamic. So, if you are expressing any of those lower-level dynamics while speaking in the role of your higher source, you're more likely speaking from some other aspect of your consciousness (such as ego or subconscious mind). If that happens, step aside of those dynamics and refocus on your higher source.

170

The Process

The following steps outline a process for the Dialogue with a Higher Source technique:

1. With pen and several sheets of paper, write your name and a colon (for example, "Joanne:"), then write a question you'd like to ask your higher source, such as:

   "What is the meaning of this dream?"
   "What can this dream teach me?"
   "What can I take away from this dream and apply in my everyday life?"
   "How can I use this dream to uplift or encourage myself and others?"
   "What does this dream tell me about what I need more of or less of in my life?"
   "Why did this dream show up at this particular time in my life?"

2. Shift into the role of your higher source. Write "Higher Source:" (or whatever you choose to call it), and then answer the question from the viewpoint of your higher source. If stepping into this role feels awkward—first, realize that this technique is simply a tool to access higher wisdom. Second, remember that your higher source is actually accessible within you. To direct your focus to it, you may want to try saying, "I call forward my higher source" or "I invite my higher source to speak through me." It's also okay to begin by just pretending to speak for your higher source, and see what useful information comes forward as the process unfolds.

3. Continue the dialogue, switching between the roles of yourself and your higher source, until you feel complete and you have nothing more to say in either role.

4. Write in your dream journal any conclusions about dream meaning or other realizations this dialogue brought forward.

Variation: Spoken Dialogue with a Higher Source

You may find that speaking your dialogue aloud in a physical setting is more effective than writing your dialogue. Sitting in a chair that symbolizes the higher source can help you step outside of any limiting beliefs and allow your inner wisdom to flow more easily. To create a spoken dialogue, modify the previously described written technique this way:

Place two chairs a short distance apart so they are facing each other. Begin by sitting in one chair, and imagine that the higher source is sitting across from you in the other chair. Ask your first question of the higher source, and then move to the "higher source" chair, answering the question while taking on the role of the higher source. Continue alternating chairs as you ask each new question as yourself and then answer it in the role of the higher source.

Examples

The following examples show instances of using the Dialogue With a Higher Source technique to help discover dream meaning:

Example A:

The following is an example of a dialogue that a 70-year-old man named Pete might write regarding a dream in which he found a sailboat and decided to go sailing:

Pete: I was walking along, and I was so surprised to find a beautiful sailboat along the shore. Somehow I knew it was for me—that it was mine—but I had never seen it before. What did that mean?

Higher Source: Think about what happened with the sailboat in the dream.

Pete: I climbed into the boat and hoisted the sail, then I sailed the boat out onto the lake. There were other people out there in their little sailboats, too.

Higher Source: And how does this remind you of something you've experienced lately?

Pete: Well, in the dream I discovered something (the boat) and then used it to try something new (sailing onto the lake), and there were other people around. I can think of one way that I've started something new with other people around, and that was when I started to play string bass in my community orchestra. When I found out about the orchestra, I knew I had to play in it. That's like in the dream when I found the sailboat, I knew it was for me—I knew it was mine. There were other people sailing around me in the dream, too, like there are other people playing around me in the orchestra.

Higher Source: Yes, and is there anything else you can learn from this dream?

Pete: Well, I was glad I found the boat in the dream. It was fun to climb into it and sail around and enjoy the scenery. And that's just like in real life, where I'm really glad I found the orchestra. I really enjoy playing, getting to do what I love, surrounded by others doing what they love. The dream seems to be telling the story of how happy I was to discover the orchestra, and to try something new. I think that next time I have the chance to try something new, I'll be more likely to try it because I enjoyed it so much this time.

Example B:

Here is an example of a Dialogue With a Higher Source by a 24-year-old named Sophia, about a dream in which she was on a ship when a sea serpent came up underneath and tipped the ship so that everyone slid down toward the water. This example shows how a spoken dialogue might sound, in a natural, conversational form.

Sophia: What is the meaning of this dream?

Higher Source: This dream came to tell you something, to give you a message that you can use right now. Think about how you felt during the dream.

Sophia: I felt afraid when the ship tipped because I didn't know what would happen.

Higher Source: Yes. So, think about your fear of the unknown in real life. Your fear is using up a lot of your energy these days. You're devoting a lot of energy to worrying about things going wrong—things that haven't happened and things that will probably never happen. You need to check in with the part of you who worries, and get to the bottom of those worries. Once you understand what those fears are really about and where they're coming from, you can make changes so you're not afraid all the time.

Sophia: Wow, that's a lot of information. What am I supposed to do with this? Where do I start?

Higher Source: Start with the dream. How did you feel when the sea serpent tilted the ship?

Sophia: I was standing on the ship as it tilted, and I started sliding down toward the water. I was petrified. I was so afraid I couldn't move. All I could do was slide toward the water. I had no choice. Now that I think about it, there was nothing scary about the water. What I was afraid of was that the situation was out of my control.

Higher Source: Yes—so the lack of control is what felt scary—before you ever got near the water. And did you ever actually fall into the water during the dream?

Sophia: Well, my foot went into the water, and I almost fell in, but I found a way to crawl back up the ship.

Higher Source: So, you found a way to rescue yourself.

Sophia: Yes.

Higher Source: And what does this say about you and your life, when you encounter a situation that feels out of control?

Sophia: I can find a way to handle the situation. I rescued myself in the dream. I pulled myself up. I looked and saw things to grab onto so I could pull myself up.

Higher Source: So, what do you think this dream is saying?

Sophia: Well, in the dream I looked for a way to help myself. In real life, maybe that means I can look for ways to help myself when things seem out of control—ways to take control—even if its just about having control over myself and my own reactions.

Higher Source: So, what can you learn from this dream about how you can handle fears when they come up?

Sophia: That maybe I'm able to deal with a lot more than I thought I could, and that I can do something about a scary situation even if I'm afraid. And that there's no need to be so afraid of what might happen because I can do something about it if it does. It doesn't just *happen* to me—it *happens* and then I get to *react.* I have the power to do something about it, not just let it happen to me.

Higher Source: Yes. Do you understand the dream now?

Sophia: I get it now. I'm in charge. I'm in control. I may not be able to control everything that happens, but I can control how I react. I control how I handle anything that comes my way. Wow, this feels really different.

Higher Source: And how does this change how you feel about the unknown—about not knowing what will happen?

Sophia: I am not as afraid anymore. I feel more in charge. I get to have a say in things. I may not always have a say in what happens, but I have a say in what happens *next.* This feels really good! I'm going to start thinking about things this way in my life. I feel different already—more in charge of things, like I matter more and I have more of a say. I'm glad I had this dream!

Chapter 3-19
TOOL: Literary Analysis

D reams are stories, so it makes sense that they may contain some of the same kinds of symbolism as stories you read or hear in your waking life. Consider how many stories you've heard during your lifetime—in fairy tales, novels, movies, TV shows, plays, personal stories, and song lyrics. Dreams that originate in your own subconscious mind can draw from anything you already know or you've been exposed to in the past. So, it wouldn't be surprising if your subconscious mind incorporated some familiar story-telling mechanisms into your dreams.

Traditional literary analysis techniques can be a useful set of tools to delve into a dream and expose deeper meaning. To analyze your dream from a literary point of view, approach your dream as if it is a story you've just read or seen in a movie, and consider what literary devices might be at play. For example, once you recognize that an open door in a dream could be a metaphor symbolizing something else, it's a short leap to realizing that since a door leads to somewhere new, an open door could represent an opportunity for a new experience. Likewise, when you think in terms of homophones in a dream (where one word represents its sound-alike word), you might consider whether the sea in a dream might actually represent the word "see"—as in the ability to see something more clearly or examine a situation more closely.

The Process
The following sections describe some literary devices that can be used as tools for dream analysis. Consider how each literary device may come into play in your dream, and how it can shed light on particular symbols and themes in your dream.

Metaphor
You might think of a metaphor in a dream as a type of symbolism in which one element of a dream—such as a character, place, or object—represents something in your real life, based on the similarities between the two things. The subconscious mind very often uses a dream symbol to

represent something different in your real life. Look for metaphor symbolism in your dream by studying the characteristics of the various dream elements, and then considering what elements of your real life have similar characteristics.

Example A:

A dream in which a ray of light revealed a crack in the floor might represent the idea of "shedding light" on an underlying problem somewhere in your life. The ray of light made the crack (representing a problem) visible—and the floor "underlies" everything. So, the light bringing your attention to the crack in the floor may represent a hidden, underlying problem somewhere in your life being brought to your attention.

Example B:

Traveling on a bridge over a river might represent your transition from one phase of your life to the next, such as the transition from a child-rearing phase to an empty-nest phase. A river is a separation between two areas of land, and a bridge is a transition from one land area to another. Therefore, traveling over the bridge in the dream could represent you moving forward from one area (or phase) of your life to another.

Allegory

An allegory is an entire story told through symbolism, in which every character and symbol in the dream represents something else entirely. An allegory typically uses physical characters, events, and objects to represent abstract ideas—like a lion representing courage, or an ant representing productivity. Likewise, dreams are often entire stories told in symbolism. Many elements in a dream actually represent something beyond their face value. An interesting way to analyze a dream is to view it as if it were an allegory: instead of taking the story literally, analyze the dream story by considering what each character, action, and key element represents.

Example A:

In the case of a dream about a frog leaping over a large dog, analyzing this dream story as an allegory might lead you to conclude that those who are seemingly less advantaged (represented by the small frog, who was much smaller than the dog) can accomplish big things (represented by jumping over the dog) by using their unique gifts (represented by jumping, which frogs do very well).

Example B:

If you dreamed about a fish who longed to leave the ocean and go explore the land—only to find that when he got there he couldn't breathe—an allegory analysis might remind you that you create problems for yourself (represented by not being able to breathe) when you refuse to accept a circumstance that you can't change (represented by the fish's respiratory system being built to thrive in water rather than air).

Sensory Imagery

Sensory imagery in dreams refers to experiences of the senses—visual, auditory, touch, smell, and taste—within the dream state. A sensory experience during a dream is often a part of the subconscious mind's way of telling a story. Sometimes a real-life sensory trigger in your physical environment can become woven into the fabric of a dream story, such as the sound of your spouse noisily cooking breakfast that shows up in your dream as a drummer with a bad sense of rhythm.

Example A:

A dream in which you were enjoying strawberry ice cream may point to a craving for that particular flavor or for something sweet, or a desire to experience a particular emotion you associate with strawberry ice cream—such as the happiness you felt on your fifth birthday when you tasted strawberry ice cream for the first time, or the love you felt when your mother used to reward your good grades on your report card with a trip to the ice cream parlor.

Example B:

If in a dream you heard a song you associate with a past relationship, the song might be a part of your subconscious mind's sentimental reminiscence about old times, or a desire to experience the joy that a close relationship with another human being can bring.

Morals

"The moral of the story" is usually a lesson woven into the plot of a story that teaches or warns by showing what happens to the characters when they make certain choices. A fable is one kind of story that includes a moral that teaches a life lesson or warns about potential pitfalls if you make poor choices in life. The story of *The Tortoise and the Hare* teaches the lesson that "slow and steady wins the race," as the tortoise wins the race against the hare through sheer persistence. *The Boy Who Cried Wolf* warns against the consequences of habitual lying, when the villagers didn't believe the boy's cries for help after his repeated attempts to trick them. Like a story with a moral, sometimes a dream explores the consequences of a certain action—either a real action you've taken, or an action your subconscious mind imagines. In some dreams, the consequences that are portrayed are a result of dishonest or malicious actions, such as lying or stealing. Sometimes the consequences are a result of an excess of a certain activity, such as eating too much—or they may result from a lack of a particular activity, such as neglecting to complete your work assignment. It's possible that the subconscious mind creates such dreams to figure out how to avoid negative consequences in real life. Whatever the reason, we can use the negative consequences we experience in dreams to help us avoid trouble in real life.

Example A:
Consider a dream in which you were riding a bike, and when you turned to listen to what your friend was telling you, you ran off the bike path. This dream may remind you to focus primarily on your own business and not get sidetracked by other people's issues or drama.

Example B:
A dream that you punched someone and ended up hurting your own hand might remind you that hurting someone else's feelings also hurts you by creating negativity within your own consciousness—that hurting others also hurts yourself.

Point of View

The point of view of a story is determined by which person it is who tells the story. For example, the story of a child getting in trouble with his mother might sound very different when told from the point of view of the mother than when told from the point of view of the child. In a dream, the point of view is often determined by whether the dreamer is an active participant in the dream or is watching the dream unfold as an observer. Sometimes the dreamer might be viewing the dream action through the eyes of someone else, such as if during your dream you were your cousin, seeing things as you imagine your cousin would see them. The point of view that a dream takes can provide clues about the dream's meaning, and even why it came about.

The subconscious mind may choose an observer point of view—a dream in which the dreamer is an observer and not an active participant—when the dream topic is very sensitive, or perhaps in order to get some distance from the dream events in order to gain a new perspective. Also, consider the reasons that you might choose to observe in real life rather than participate in events with other people, and this may point to some other motivations of your subconscious mind to play an observer role in a dream. If you dream that you are someone else—not that you are you with the appearance of another person, but that you are experiencing events as someone else—your subconscious mind may be trying to "put yourself in that person's shoes" to gain some insight about that person's experience or motivations.

Example A:
If you dreamed you were observing a fox chase a rabbit, and you had no active role in the dream, it's possible that your subconscious mind chose an observer perspective because viewing the action from the point of view of the fox or the rabbit might have distracted you from the dream story. Perhaps your subconscious mind was highlighting the paths they took or the strategies they used, rather than their personal experience or feelings.

Example B:
If you dreamed that you were an eagle flying above your house and looking down at yourself inside the house through the skylight, this could represent the idea of needing a different perspective on yourself in order to see something more clearly.

Homophones

Homophones are two or more words that sound the same but mean something different, such as "flower" and "flour," or "bear" and "bare." In dreams, sometimes a dream symbol represents its homophone, so when exploring the meaning of a dream symbol, consider what word (or words) its name sounds like.

Example A:
If you dreamed that your boyfriend gave you a carrot, the carrot may actually represent a "karat," as in jewelry made of gold or containing precious stones—perhaps representing something valuable you received from your boyfriend in real life (such as jewelry, love, or encouragement).

Example B:
In a dream in which you tripped over the frayed hem of your jeans, "frayed" may refer to "afraid," and the dream might represent the idea of "tripping over" your own fears—the idea of your real-life fears impeding your progress somehow.

Mood

Pay attention to what the mood your dream conveys—such as through color, lighting, and setting. Mood and emotion in a dream often represent your actual mood and emotion about the real-life situation the dream is portraying. So, pay attention to the mood in each part of your dream, and think about when you've felt those same moods or emotions—either recently or in the past.

Example A:

In a dream that took place in a cold, leaky basement on a dreary, rainy day, the physical environment may convey the mood of depression, sadness, and isolation you've been experiencing lately in your waking life because you've been staying home alone and feeling lonely. In this case, your subconscious mind may have portrayed your real-life "dark and dreary" emotions as a dark and dreary physical environment in the dream.

Example B:

A peaceful meadow in a dream with bright sunshine, a gentle breeze, and graceful wildflowers may convey feelings of peace, joy, contentment, or whatever you would tend to feel in that setting. In this dream, your subconscious mind may have been portraying a memory from a time in your real life when you felt those feelings—perhaps a time when you were sitting with your mother who was reading you a beautiful story that took place in a meadow. Another possibility is that your subconscious mind was using this imagery to elicit pleasant feelings that it wanted experience during the dream state.

To explore more literary devices, a quick internet search will show various lists of literary devices, many of which can prompt you to think about your dreams in new ways.

Chapter 3-20
TOOL: Archetype Analysis

An archetype in a story is a typical or stereotypical version of something or someone—often portraying a type of person, a role a person might play, or a pattern of behavior. In a dream, your subconscious mind might use an archetype to tell its story—for example to emphasize how you feel about a particular person or situation, or to highlight something you'd like to experience more of (or less of) in your life. For example, if you dreamed that your best friend was Superman (The Hero archetype), your subconscious mind may have been expressing your perception that your friend is somehow a hero in real life. In another example, perhaps you dreamed that you were a pirate captain (The Rebel archetype) sailing the seas with your loyal crew, which could represent your desire for more freedom and adventure.

By exploring the symbolism of a particular archetype that shows up in your dream, you can shed light on the dream's meaning. For example, if your dream contains a mother figure (The Mother Figure archetype), then the dream likely relates to something in your life involving an actual mother figure or a characteristic you associate with mothering—such as nurturing or love.

The following sections describe some of the archetypes that can show up in dreams, along with examples and possible dream meanings for each.

The Hero

Description: Someone who seeks to do good in the world, acting on honorable intentions.

Examples: Superman, Wonder Woman, Jack in *Jack and the Beanstalk*, Luke Skywalker in *Star Wars*.

Possible Dream Meanings: Feeling heroic yourself, or perhaps feeling you need a hero somehow in your life. Wanting to help other people, help yourself, or receive help from others. Desiring to be a better person or to make the world a better place through goodwill, generosity, or good works.

The Villain

Description: Someone who seeks to harm or destroy, acting on malicious intentions.

Examples: Dracula, the Wicked Witch of the West in *The Wizard of Oz*, Darth Vader in *Star Wars*.

Possible Dream Meanings: Someone in your life whom you feel is trying to harm you or take something from you. Something in your life that you judge as evil or bad. Someone you consider to be a "good person gone bad."

The Mother Figure

Description: A mother or mother-substitute who offers nurturing or who has other qualities you associate with a mother. An idealized version of a mother.

Examples: Mother Nature, Mrs. March in *Little Women,* Maria in *The Sound of Music,* Nanny McPhee in *Nanny McPhee.*

Possible Dream Meanings: Real-life love, help, support, emotional security, or something else you associate with a mother. A desire for more (or less) "mothering" in your life.

The Innocent

Description: Someone young or inexperienced who is threatened by negative or destructive forces in the world.

Examples: Dory in *Finding Nemo,* Tiny Tim in *A Christmas Carol,* Annie in *Annie,* Olaf in *Frozen.*

Possible Dream Meanings: Someone in your life whom you perceive as good, pure of heart, true, child-like, naive—possibly needing protection.

The Explorer

Description: An adventurer, wanderer, seeker, or trailblazer—or an adventurous thinker.

Examples: Alice in *Alice's Adventures in Wonderland,* Captain Kirk in *Star Trek,* Indiana Jones in *Raiders of the Lost Ark.*

Possible Dream Meanings: Discovery, excitement or variety, being true to yourself—which you have experienced, you desire, or from which you would benefit in your life.

The Rebel

Description: Someone who dares to go against the grain, scoff at the rules of established authority, make one's own choices despite others' expectations or opinions.

Examples: Robin Hood, Erin Brockovich in *Erin Brockovich,* Maverick in *Top Gun,* Jack Sparrow in *Pirates of the Caribbean.*

Possible Dream Meanings: Having or desiring more inner strength and backbone. Real-life issues related to feeling constrained by rules or others' expectations, remaining true to yourself despite external pressures, making choices differently than others expect or want you to, standing up for yourself, feeling pressure from within yourself about what you think you *should* do as opposed to what you *want* to do.

The Sage

Description: A wise one, someone who is a source of truth or guidance, a trusted authority.

Examples: Yoda in *Star Wars,* The Oracle in *The Matrix,* Mr. Miyagi in *The Karate Kid,* Morgan Freeman as God in *Bruce Almighty.*

Possible Dream Meanings: Insight or guidance that you've gained in real life, or perhaps that you feel you need right now. Feeling lost or in need of direction on your life path.

The Ruler

Description: An authority figure with real or contrived power—who exercises power that was either given by permission or taken by force.

Examples: King Arthur, Zeus, the Queen of Hearts in *Alice's Adventures in Wonderland,* Don Vito Corleone in *The Godfather.*

Possible Dream Meanings: Power or control issues—perhaps feeling powerful in real life, or feeling powerless and desiring more power. Leadership, visionary capabilities, or the idea of managing your own life—being your own leader or feeling more in control of your own life.

The Magician

Description: Similar to the Sage, but with the power to manipulate the world in order to create that which is desired—often in seemingly powerful and mysterious ways. Sometimes known as a healer.

Examples: The fairy godmother in *Cinderella,* Merlin in the King Arthur legend, Gandalf in *The Lord of the Rings,* Prospero in *The Tempest.*

Possible Dream Meanings: Feeling powerful. A desire for more control or power, for help, or for a certain thing, situation, or experience.

The Underdog

Description: Someone who faces a seemingly insurmountable challenge, where success seems out of reach. The underdog often defeats the odds against him, often through discovering a previously hidden strength.

Examples: The Ugly Duckling in *The Ugly Duckling,* the tortoise in *The Tortoise and the Hare,* Frodo Baggins in *The Lord of the Rings.*

Possible Dream Meanings: Feeling like an underdog yourself due to a challenge in your life or within yourself. Feelings of empathy for someone in your life who's experiencing a challenge. A desire to see the "good" or "deserving" person win.

The Trickster

Description: A mischievous troublemaker who stirs things up, refusing to play by the rules. Someone who creates havoc—for his own entertainment, to manipulate others for his own gain, or for some other reason.

Examples: Bugs Bunny, Tom Sawyer in *The Adventures of Tom Sawyer,* Puck in *A Midsummer Night's Dream.*

Possible Dream Meanings: A feeling or fear of being manipulated or fooled, or of someone trying to take something from you—such as money or other object of value, your time, your energy, your attention, or something on an emotional level.

The Savior

Description: Someone who rescues someone else, or who saves the day—usually altruistic and often self-sacrificing.

Examples: Aslan from *The Chronicles of Narnia* series, Doctor Who in *Doctor Who,* Neo in *The Matrix* trilogy.

Possible Dream Meanings: Feeling the need to be rescued, or wanting to rescue someone else—perhaps due to a situation that feels out of control or a challenge that seems impossible. Issues of co-dependence, or always putting others' needs above your own in a way that creates an unhealthy imbalance. A desire to feel the joy of helping others in need.

If you'd like to explore these and other archetypes further, you can find a wealth of information on the internet and in books.

The Process

Archetype Analysis of a dream involves exploring which major characters and other elements of your dream may represent archetypes, and considering how those archetypes can contribute to your understanding of the dream. This is a free-form exploration process involving the following basic steps:

1. Explore how the major characters and other elements of your dream might reflect particular archetypes through their characteristics, actions, choices, story lines, or in some other way.
2. For each archetype you identify in your dream, consider how it portrays something in your real life or on your mind.
3. Determine what you can learn from the archetype and what it says about the part of your life or mind it represents.
4. Decide how you can use what you've learned from this archetype in a positive way, and what action steps you'll take to follow up.

Examples

The following examples show how Archetype Analysis can be applied as part of the dream analysis process:

Example A:

Consider that you dreamed you were an astronaut who discovered a fascinating planet. In the dream you were thrilled to be the first person to set foot on this planet, and you immediately set off into its lush, forested landscape to see what you could find. In an Archetype Analysis, you consider which archetype might be present in the dream. You decide that your role of astronaut in the dream matches The Explorer archetype because as an astronaut you were on an adventure, and you were a trailblazer who was the first to visit the new planet. You notice how excited and happy you felt to be on this adventure, and you realize that you haven't felt that way for a long time because you've gotten stuck in your daily routine. You determine that this dream reflects your desire for more adventure in your life, to experience a sense of freedom, and to discover new things. Using what you've learned from The Explorer archetype, you make a plan to try at least one new thing every day—such as tasting a new kind of food, talking to a new person, or taking a new route to work. You also decide to plan two trips during the upcoming year to explore places you've never visited before.

Example B:

Imagine you dreamed that your real-life boss, Amanda, was a queen ruling over your workplace, sitting on a throne instead of at a desk, and wearing a bejeweled crown. In the dream, no matter what gifts you presented to the queen, she refused them and sent you away on a quest to find something else. In your archetype analysis, you realize that the queen is similar to The Ruler archetype. In real life, your boss has authority over you and your co-workers, just as a queen has authority over her subjects. As for what this dream scenario might say about your real life, you recognize in the dream a frustration similar to your real-life frustration when your boss repeatedly finds fault in your work and asks you to try again. No matter how hard you try, she isn't happy with the results. Finally, you consider how you can learn from The Ruler archetype in this dream. You realize that in the dream, the queen was not very specific when she described your next quest. She didn't clearly communicate what you needed to know to complete the quest successfully, and it occurs to you that this may also be happening in the situation at work. You decide to ask more questions next time your boss asks you to do something, so that you'll know ahead of time exactly what you need to do to complete the task to her specifications.

Chapter 3-21

TOOL: Art Analysis

The Art Analysis technique can be applied to dreams by analyzing your dream as if it were a painting or other work of art—exploring, examining, and asking the kinds of questions used in traditional art analysis. The technique described here adapts a traditional art analysis process to enrich the dream interpretation process through examination of the "artistic elements" of a dream, which can help you view your dream from different perspectives and reveal new clues about dream meaning.

Think about your dream as if it were an abstract painting created by someone else. You may even want to make a drawing or painting of it (see "Chapter 3-14: TOOL: Draw Your Dream Symbol," p. 156). Step back and imagine what the "artist" was trying to convey in this painting, as if you were viewing it for the first time. Consider the "look and feel" of the painting and what it might be trying to say. Think about what story it's trying to tell or what message it's trying to convey. Consider what is going on in the main character's mind and emotions during the dream, and how that may relate to something in your real life. Think about how you would interpret this painting if you were a student in an art class, and remember that there are no wrong answers.

The following sections explore how the framework of traditional art analysis can be applied in the dream analysis process, and how each element of art analysis can provide value in the search for dream meaning.

Line

Just as a line in a painting leads your eye through a painting—following the curve of a river or the soaring spire of a building—lines can also guide you through a dream. Lines may play an important role in the dream story as representations of boundaries or edges. For example, a fence around your house in the dream may represent the boundary between your personal life (represented by the house) and your life out in the world (represented by the area beyond the fence). A line could also indicate where one thing stops and another begins—conveying the concept of an ending of one phase of your life and the beginning of another. A line can also represent a guideline or limitation, such as the lines painted along the edge of a highway representing the guidance that keeps you on-track as you proceed forward through your life. The idea of crossing a physical line in a dream could symbolize a real-life situation in which someone has "crossed a line" by doing something you consider unacceptable.

Another kind of line in a dream is the timeline, the chronological "line" of the dream's story from beginning to end. Mapping out the timeline of your dream on paper (see "Chapter 3-12: TOOL: Timeline Analysis," p. 147) may help you recognize the story from your real-life that your dream is portraying. Once you've created a visual timeline by mapping out the dream's events, you may begin to see a familiar pattern of events or associated emotions that fits a particular time in your past.

You may also want to follow the "line of emotion" throughout the story of your dream. Consider your changing emotions as the dream progressed from beginning to end. Creating a visual representation of the "emotion story" may help you recognize a similar series of emotions you've experienced in your real life, pointing to what the dream is portraying. You might choose to draw your line of emotion as a path winding through various emotions, like a path winding through one setting after another. Another alternative is to label your emotions as negative or positive, like a line on a graph. In that case a line moving downward would indicate more negative feelings (angry, afraid, disgusted), and a line moving upward would show a transition into more positive feelings (happy, excited, optimistic, peaceful). For example, perhaps your dream started out with you feeling sad on a rainy morning, and then when your mother came to see you the weather shifted to sunny and you felt happy. If you charted a line to represent the emotion in this dream, it would start out low (negative) and then move upward (positive) as the dream events unfold. (For more about exploring the emotion in a dream, see "Chapter 3-4: TOOL: Emotion Analysis," p. 114).

Shape and Form

Shape and form define how objects appear in space within a work of art. In art, shapes are two-dimensional (as in a painting) and forms are three-dimensional (as in a sculpture). Let's explore several ways you might apply the concepts of shape and form to view your dream from a new perspective and examine its symbolism.

For example, you might consider what form the overall story arc of your dream would take if you translated it into physical form. Maybe in the dream you circled back to where you began, and the story arc might form a circle. Maybe you began the dream and then progressed continuously, and the story arc would form an upward slope. The form of the story arc may help you recognize a similar story arc in your real life that the dream is portraying.

You might also examine what stands out about the shape and form of physical elements of your dream, such as the characters, objects, or aspects of the setting or environment. A character might have appeared taller than in real life, which could represent your perception of her great importance, intimidation, or inflated ego. Your house in a dream might seem more convoluted or have more rooms than in real life, which could represent the idea of your life seeming more complicated or involved than usual. The setting may seem off somehow—such as floors being slanted, which could represent your feeling that something foundational that you've always taken for granted (such as a belief or a family member's availability) is now shifting or is not available in the same way.

Also, look for specific geometric shapes that stand out in the dream, which can convey a meaning of their own, depending on context. A circle might represent wholeness, a cycle, or femininity—while a square might represent solidness, logic, or symmetry. For more clues, consider what the shape in its particular context means to you personally.

Space

In art, space refers not only to the two- or three-dimensional aspects of the space within the painting, but also to how the artist uses that space. If we translate that idea to apply in dream analysis, we might examine the patterns and amount of space in a dream. For example, the main character being in an enclosed space such as a closet might represent a mental limitation imposed by self or others. If the main character is in an open space such as on the open ocean, this might represent unlimited opportunity or feeling lost, depending on the context.

The amount of physical space between two elements in a dream can tell you a lot about the story your subconscious mind is telling about them. For example, the amount of physical space between two people in a dream can represent the dreamer's idea of the actual or desired closeness of their mental and emotional relationship with each other. A dream that your friend is far away from you, where you can't get to her, may represent the fact that she seems mentally or emotionally distanced from you in real life, or the idea that she doesn't seem very available to you right now.

Color

Color in a dream can convey meaning and nuance just as it does in art. In a dream, color often represents a mood, or the color of a particular dream element can represent a characteristic the dreamer perceives that element to have. For example, a red sunrise might represent an angry mood, and a white hat might represent a character's benevolent intentions.

As in artwork, there are no concrete definitions of what different colors represent. In a painting, the artist may have intended to express a certain meaning through a particular color, but unless the artist is there to explain herself, a color's interpreted meaning is in the eye of the beholder. However, when you're interpreting your own dream, you *were* the artist who created the dream (at least subconsciously)—and so you *do* have the capability of understanding what the artist (your subconscious mind) intended to express through color.

When you see or think of a particular color, it's likely to bring something to mind or to evoke a certain feeling within you according to your innate responses, your preferences, your experiences with that color, and other personal factors. For example, bright orange might immediately evoke joy within you whenever you see it, or it may feel overwhelming to you. Purple may remind you of playfulness, or it might bring to mind strength because your grandmother often wore purple and she was such a strong woman.

Your interpretation of a color in a dream will often be obvious to you as soon as you see or think about the color, so pay attention to your immediate reaction. Your subconscious mind didn't stop to analyze before choosing that color to use in the dream. It chose the color based on your own subconscious impression of that color. Mental machinations to analyze what the color might mean may cause you to get sidetracked, whereas first impressions are often very telling about the meaning of the color in the dream. However, it's possible that you may have more than one strong associated meaning with a particular color.

In both art and dreams, the context in which the color appears can affect how you interpret that color. Pale yellow as a skin tone might seem to portray weakness or illness, whereas pale yellow as the color for a baby's room might convey cheerfulness.

Your preconceived notions affect the way you interpret the meanings of colors. In society in general, and also in particular cultures, certain colors have typical meanings that may become incorporated into your dreams. For example, the national colors of a country might represent patriotism—or a color's meaning might be based in common phrases, such as using "He was red in the face" to describe someone who was angry. You are the ultimate authority on what a particular color represents to you, since you are both the creator and interpreter of your own dream.

In art, color can be analyzed in terms of the following factors:

Hue—The basic color (green, red, purple).

Value—The lightness or darkness of the color (pale, medium, or deep).

Intensity—The brightness or saturation of the color (pure and bright, or subdued or muted).

In dreams, all three of these factors can help convey meaning of a particular color. The hue can connote a particular meaning, such as green representing freshness or blue representing tranquility. The value of a color—its lightness or darkness—can add more depth to that meaning, or change it completely. Pale blue might represent peacefulness to you, while navy blue might represent your father who wore a uniform of that color. Likewise, the intensity of a color can modify or completely change its meaning to you. Periwinkle blue might represent happiness to you because you used that color in your wedding, whereas dull gray-blue might represent disgust to you because it reminds you of bleu cheese, which you dislike.

Texture and Pattern

Texture in a work of art evokes a particular response that you might have if you were to actually touch that kind of texture. In both art and dreams, when you see a texture it may instantly trigger a particular feeling or mood within you, or it might evoke a certain kinesthetic experience of that texture as if you were touching it. For example, the roughness of burlap might trigger an imaginary sensation of the uncomfortable scratchiness of the burlap against your skin. The smoothness of a well-worn river stone might evoke a feeling of calm as you imagine its soothing coolness in the palm of your hand.

Pattern is the repetition of a shape, texture, or other element in a work of art. In art, pattern usually refers to the repetition of physical elements, but in dreams a pattern could show up in almost any way. A physical pattern in a dream might take the form of three identical pillows on a couch representing triplets, or 200 airplanes representing the 200 graduates in your high school class embarking on their life journeys. A temporal pattern (repetition over time) might take the form of a friend repeatedly ignoring your text messages, which might represent the multiple instances of her being unavailable to you in real life.

As you analyze your dream, note any textures and patterns that stand out or that provoke a response within you, since they may hold clues to meaning that you might otherwise miss. Pay attention to the response they evoke within you, and consider where in your waking life you've felt that response before.

Time and Motion

Time and motion are elements that can portray story, emotion, and mood in dynamic types of artwork—such as dance or performance art. Likewise, the movement of the characters and objects in your dream often carries significant meaning. To delve into this meaning, explore each significant movement itself, as well as the manner of the movement—how the character or object moves, its direction and speed, why it moved, and so on. The movement and its characteristics may provide important clues about the particular real-life action or change the dream is portraying. For example, a person trudging begrudgingly away from his house may represent someone in your life feeling sad to leave home, while a car careening down a winding road might represent someone in a hurry or crisis, or someone in your life acting hastily or carelessly.

The Process

This technique adapts a traditional art analysis process (Observe, Describe, Analyze, Interpret, Evaluate) for use in dream interpretation. Before beginning this process, make sure you've read through the preceding descriptions of the art elements so they are fresh in your mind.

1. **Observe**—Close your eyes and replay the dream in your mind from beginning to end. Don't try to figure out its meaning or put any labels on it. Just observe the dream as it passes through your mind.

2. **Describe**—In your dream journal, write a description of your dream as if you were retelling its story to yourself. Only describe, do not interpret possible meanings at this point. (Optional: create a drawing or other artistic version of your dream, as described in "Chapter 3-14: TOOL: Draw Your Dream Symbol," p. 156.)

3. **Analyze**—Look for any art elements (lines, shapes, colors, or others in the preceding descriptions) that stood out during the dream, and note them next to those parts of your dream description or drawing.

   Consider your emotional reactions to what happened in the dream, and indicate those by writing emotional keywords alongside the corresponding points of your dream description.

   Imagine that you are asking the artist who created this dream questions like "What were you trying to say in this dream?" and "What is the message of this dream?" Write the answers below your dream description.

4. **Interpret**—Consider what the dream means, based on all the evidence you've gathered so far. Interpreting a dream is different than

interpreting art, which involves interpreting what the artist intended. You have an advantage here because *you* were the "artist" who created your dream—even if you're not yet aware of its meaning. You are the one who already knows the artist's intended meaning, and you can access that information using techniques and suggestions in this book (such as the tips in "Chapter 1-3: Intuition: Your Dream Translator," p. 33).

5. **Evaluate**—In traditional art analysis, this step would involve evaluating the quality of the work of art. In the case of dream interpretation, instead of evaluating the quality of the dream itself, it makes more sense to evaluate what you learned from the dream—the value it provides to you. Consider the meaning and message of the dream, and how it contributes to your understanding of yourself and your life, and how it helps you see potential areas for improvement. Decide what action, if any, you want to take based on what you've learned.

Examples

The following examples demonstrate how you might apply the Art Analysis technique to explore the meaning of a dream:

Example A:

Consider a dream in which you were driving a bright red car. While driving it, you felt confident—you felt like you could do anything and go anywhere. During the Art Analysis technique of this dream, you ask yourself (as the artist who created the dream), "What were you trying to say in this dream?" The answer that comes forward is, "The way I felt when I was driving the bold, red car is how I feel when I am doing what I love in real life. In that car I feel like I can go anywhere I want to go." You realize that red color of the car symbolizes both the boldness and the love of life you experience when you are doing something you love. Next, you evaluate this interpretation, and decide that the value in this dream is the message about the importance of engaging in meaningful, fun work. You realize that your work life has been suffering because you don't enjoy that part of your life as much as you could. You decide to explore how you can find more meaning and enjoyment in your work, either in your current job or perhaps on a new career path.

Example B:

Imagine that you dreamed about a prism that was splitting a ray of sunlight into separate colors of the rainbow. In the dream you noticed that the prism was wedge-shaped, and that what it was doing was breaking apart the ray of sunlight to reveal all the different colors the sun's light contains.

You felt intrigued and inspired. In analyzing the dream, you ask yourself (as the artist who created the dream), "What is the message of this dream?" You think about the wedge shape of the prism, which brings to mind the idea of something that "creates a wedge" between two people—like an argument, misunderstanding, grudge, or some other challenge in a relationship. You suddenly realize that experiencing a challenge (or "wedge") in a relationship tends to reveal "what makes up" a person—their character, values, priorities, and so on—just as the prism reveals the individual colors that "make up" sunlight. You decide that the message of this dream is that dealing with relationship challenges is what really shows "what kind of stuff a person is made of." In other words, a "wedge"—or a challenge—in a relationship reveals deep truths about a person that might not be obvious during more pleasant times (without that "wedge"). Finally, you evaluate this interpretation and decide that the dream provides a new perspective on relationships, and a different way to view challenges when they arise in relationships. When you think about it, you remember several situations in the past in which challenges revealed your partner's "true colors." You decide to begin viewing each relationship challenge as an opportunity to better understand the other person and their needs, perspectives, and values.

Chapter 3-22
TOOL: Discovering Your Gifts

If you pay attention, your dreams can reveal a lot about what makes you special and unique. Dreams often point out your special gifts—strengths, abilities, characteristics, tendencies, or other areas where you really shine. Your gifts might include things like leading, teaching, inspiring, problem solving, resourcefulness, creativity, keeping calm in a crisis, painting, or composing music.

A dream can reveal gifts that you could be making better use of in your life, ones you can develop further, or even ones you didn't realize you had. Sometimes you may not even recognize a particular gift within yourself until you follow a hunch to explore it and discover you're great at it. When you're aware of your gifts, making the most of them can lead to more fulfilling and meaningful life experiences. When you integrate your gifts into the way you live, both you and other people can benefit from them—which is a win for you and a win for others.

How Dreams Speak About Gifts

Dreams can provide insights about your gifts and strengths in many ways. You may notice yourself doing something new that you're particularly good at in a dream, such as giving a presentation to an enthusiastic crowd. You might notice in a dream that a certain activity resonates with you, feels meaningful to you, or comes naturally to you. A dream might force you into a situation beyond your comfort zone, in which you try something new you didn't realize you could do—perhaps something at which you excelled in the dream, and also could in real life.

Even a seemingly negative dream can tell you something about yourself. For example, if you dreamed you were being chased by an angry wolf and you came up with a really creative way to escape, you might notice that this dream highlights your gifts as a quick thinker and creative problem solver.

Indicators of Your Gifts in Dreams

Discovering gifts in your dreams can sometimes be fairly straightforward because your feeling about the gift often becomes obvious when you're using it during the dream. Pay attention to the following types of indicators that could be pointing out your gifts in a dream. These don't necessarily point out gifts in every case, but they are definitely worth exploring.

• Something you did really well in your dream.
• Something you really enjoyed in your dream.
• Something for which people sought you out in a dream.
• Something on which other people complimented you in a dream.
• A situation in which you felt proud of yourself, your abilities, or your actions.
• A situation in which you made a great impression on others.
• A situation in which you felt happiness or joy regarding what you were doing.
• A situation in which others were benefitting from your actions.
• A situation in which you were expressing yourself well.
• An activity in which you felt a sense of meaning or purpose.
• An activity that came naturally to you or for which you demonstrated an innate ability.

The Process

The following steps show how to use the Discovering Your Gifts technique to explore how a dream might be highlighting one or more of your gifts:

1. Review your dream from beginning to end by replaying it in your mind. Pay special attention to things you did well, enjoyed, or other indicators in the previous list.

2. For each indicator in your dream, imagine making more use of that gift in real life and pay attention to how that feels. If imagining it brings a sense of fulfillment, meaning, well-being, or upliftment, then consider the idea of actively integrating that gift into your life to a greater extent.

3. Take steps to "lean into" your gift and explore how you want to put it to use. You might begin by setting an intention (see "Chapter 4-7: TOOL: Setting Intentions," p. 234) and then taking action to create more of what you want, depending on how you want to use this gift (for example, using the technique in "Chapter 4-15: TOOL: Creating More of What You Want," p. 266). You may find some additional

196

ideas and inspiration in "Chapter 4-14: TOOL: Leaning into Your Strengths" (p. 261).

Examples

The following examples show how the Discovering Your Gifts technique can help you understand what your dreams reveal about your special gifts:

Example A:

Imagine a dream in which someone asked you to teach a class about one of your real-life interests. At first you hesitated because you had never taught a class before, but you finally decided to accept. Suddenly, you were teaching, standing in front of a group sharing your knowledge and expertise in the subject area—and thoroughly enjoying yourself. The group was fascinated and was asking you questions, which you answered readily. The dream ended with you feeling fulfilled and happy about providing value to others, which created a wonderful experience for both you and the students. In reviewing this dream, you notice how during the dream you felt as if you were enacting a part of your life purpose through teaching. Something just felt right about it. Next, you imagine how it might feel to teach a class in real life, and although it seems a little outside your comfort zone, you feel a similar sense of purpose and fulfillment. So, you decide to "lean into" this possible gift by taking these first steps: teaching a friend who's been wanting to learn about this topic, signing up for a public speaking course, and writing a course outline for a class you could offer through your local community center.

Example B:

Consider a dream in which you were on the beach playing in the sand. It was low tide, and so there was a good supply of wet sand with the perfect texture for creating sand sculptures. Suddenly in the dream, a vision of a fantasy village appeared in your mind, and your hands began shaping the sand to match the image in your mind's eye. Every movement happened naturally, and you knew exactly how to produce the results you desired. When you finished, you stepped back and admired your beautiful sculpture. After awakening, you replay the dream in your head, taking note of how the creative process took over and you were completely engaged in it. You've never felt as alive as you did during this dream. So, although you've never considered yourself an artist, you decide to enroll in a sculpture class to explore the artistic experience further.

Chapter 3-23

TOOL: Free-Form Writing

F ree-form writing is basically what it sounds like: a process of writing freely, continually expressing on paper whatever flows into your stream of consciousness. It's a great tool for reaching into deeper areas of your consciousness that aren't always easily accessible. The following process applies the technique of free-form writing with the specific goal of tapping into the subconscious mind as a source of insight about dream meaning. The idea here is that if the subconscious mind created the dream, then it already knows what the dream means. Free-form writing can create an outward flow through which your subconscious mind can reveal its secrets and provide a more direct look at dream meaning.

Choose Your Focus

You can use free-form writing to explore a whole dream or any aspect of a dream: a character, symbol, location, color, and so on. Simply start writing about whatever you want to explore, and let your mind wander freely as you write. It doesn't matter if what you're writing at the moment makes sense or is helpful. The idea is to write anything and everything, without any self-editing, judgment, or evaluation of content. Then when you're finished, review what you wrote for clues to a dream meaning that resonates with you.

The Process

Use the following steps to apply Free-Form Writing as a tool in dream analysis:

1. Sit down with pen and plenty of paper. Do not use your dream journal. Instead, use separate sheets of paper because you will be discarding them when you are through.
2. Write your topic, question, or a starting sentence. This is optional, but when using this technique as part of dream analysis (as opposed to general free-form writing), it may be helpful to start by focusing

your mind in a certain direction, such as the aspect of the dream that stood out the most.

3. Start writing anything and everything that comes to mind. Don't worry about your handwriting or spelling because you will be the only person who ever sees this. As you write, make a check mark anywhere you have a flash of recognition of dream meaning (see "Intuition: The Key to Recognizing Dream Meaning," p. 33). If your mind goes blank, just write "I am going to keep on writing" and keep going. If you get stuck for a long time with nothing to write, refocus on your original topic, ask yourself a question, or prompt yourself with a statement such as "If I had something to say, it would be..." or "If I knew what to write, it would be...."

4. Keep writing until you feel complete and there is nothing left to be said.

5. When you are finished, review what you wrote—paying special attention to the parts with the check marks denoting flashes of recognition. In your dream journal or on a separate piece of paper, write any conclusions, insights about the dream, clues to dream meaning, or anything else that you want to keep.

6. Tear up or shred the original writing pages to let your subconscious know you are releasing everything that you can't use after you've made notes about what you can use.

Free-Form Writing to Move Beyond Mental Blocks

To explore the meaning of a particular dream, try starting your free-form writing with "If I knew the meaning of this dream, it would be this..." or "If I knew what this dream symbol means, it would be this...", and then write whatever comes forward in your mind. This approach often provides a way to step around any mental blocks and more directly access the subconscious mind. You may feel like the description you're writing is just coming from your imagination, but that's okay because—first, you may not know for sure where it's coming from—and second, even if it is from your imagination, your imagination is "great friends" with your subconscious mind, where the dream came from in the first place. Your imagination may be inspired by content in your subconscious mind, which is how your subconscious fears and desires often show up in stories you create.

Free-Form Writing for Follow-up After a Dream

Free-form writing is also helpful for exploring your thoughts, feelings, desires, and needs that may arise during or after a dream, and to create a space in which they can be expressed. Perhaps your dream triggered some memories or emotions you'd like to explore further, or perhaps you could benefit from expressing those emotions in order to release them and reach closure within yourself. Your dream may have brought up an issue you'd like to resolve, and perhaps Free-Form Writing can help you clarify how to do that. Free-form writing provides a time and space within which your voice can be heard, you can talk things through with yourself, and you can clarify any follow-up that's needed—such as forgiveness, releasing negative patterns, renegotiating agreements with others, or changes in life direction (for more about follow-up actions, see "4. Act on Your Dream," p. 87, and "Part IV: Dream Action Toolkit," p. 215).

Examples

The following examples show how Free-Form Writing might be used to enhance the dream analysis process:

Example A:

In this example of a Free-Form Writing process, a 54-year-old man named Evan explores the possible meaning of the previous night's dream in which he was wearing a suit of armor in bed:

"Topic: The armor that I dreamed that I was wearing.

"Why would I dream that I was wearing a full suit of armor in bed? That doesn't make any sense. I would never be wearing armor in bed in real life. I wear regular pajamas to bed, and they don't look anything like armor. Let's see. If I wore armor to bed I couldn't move very well, and I couldn't turn over very easily. It would be pretty uncomfortable, and the metal might make me cold. Well, maybe the armor relates to my waking life. I think of armor as something that is worn for protection. So, how do I feel like I need protection in my waking life? What really stands out about the armor is that I was wearing it in bed, when I was sleeping, which is when I am most vulnerable because I'm asleep. Also, my bedroom is a personal space, not an area that very many people see. So, maybe the armor represents some kind of protection when I feel vulnerable, in a personal area of my life. This armor might represent my tendency to push people away when I feel like they're getting too personal. I know sometimes they are just being friendly or trying to show they care about me. But sometimes it feels like they are getting too close, like they are trying to meddle in my business—and it's exactly that—MY BUSINESS. I don't like it when people ask too many questions or get nosy about my personal life, like when Melissa asked me the other day if I was feeling all right. Okay, I think I've discovered what the armor represents in my real life. It represents when I put a wall up around myself to protect myself from others.

But, in writing this, I realize that a lot of times what I'm 'protecting' myself from with the armor is actually genuine friendship and caring. I'm going to pay more attention to this pattern in the future and consider being more open to goodwill from others."

Evan then writes the following conclusion about this dream in his dream journal: "Sometimes in the past I've tried to protect myself from others by wearing a virtual suit of armor, especially when it felt like people are getting too close. However, I know that a lot of times, people are just showing they care. I intend to be more open to friendship and goodwill from others." He then shreds the Free-Form Writing pages in the shredder—releasing all that he expressed on those pages, and feeling a much greater sense of clarity.

Example B:

The following is an example of a Free-Form Writing process by a 42-year-old woman named Kristen, after a dream about a tropical setting:

"Topic: My dream about the tropical island.

"In the dream, as I was floating in a peaceful bay of tropical water. The sun shone down and warmed my body. I could hear the calls of tropical birds all around and the rustling of the palm trees in the breeze. A feeling of peace pervaded my whole being, and it still does now as I write this. I would like to experience more of this feeling at other times in my life, too. I'm tired of my daily routine that includes no time for me. Everything I do is for someone else. I need time to stop and just *be*. I'm angry that I'm always doing things for others and never for me. Who am I angry at? I don't know. I don't know what to write now. My mind is a blank. But I will just keep writing. I'm writing this sentence now to keep the flow going. I feel angry. I feel aggravated. I feel frustrated, not just that I don't have any time for myself, but because I don't know what to do about it. I want to have more time for me, and I want to have more relaxation time when I don't have to do anything for anyone else or think about anyone else. Not all the time, but just sometimes. I am ANGRY, ANGRY, ANGRY!! I just want to let all of this anger out, to get it out of my system. I need to say what I need to say, even if it doesn't feel right to say it. I have spent too long taking care of everyone else and not me. NOT ME. Oh, I see. 'Not me' is the problem. The problem is not the time I spend taking care of others, it's the lack of time taking care of me. I don't resent giving my time and energy for others, but I see that I'm shortchanging myself by not spending time on me. Doing things for others doesn't keep me from taking care of myself if I make a decision to make time for myself on a regular basis. I think I've been blaming others for me not getting what I need, but that's not accurate. It's up to me to make sure I find ways to take care of myself, to nurture myself emotionally, mentally, and spiritually. I've been choosing to focus solely on others instead of myself, when what I really want to do is to focus on both myself and on others. I am going to find ways to make sure I give myself the time and space I need more of the time. That has to start with me knowing what I need. I don't know what I need right now in this moment, but I intend to remain open and mindful about what I need as I go forward. I can make this easy for myself by starting small, doing something easy on a regular basis. Okay, starting today, I'm going to check in with myself during my drive to and from work, and also when I first wake up and before I go to sleep. I'm going to ask myself how I'm doing, what I need more of, and what I need less of. I'm going to ask myself what needs are not being met. Then I'm going to ask myself how I can meet those needs. When I start work in the morning, all I want to do is sit quietly for 10 minutes with no interruptions and plan my day. People always have lots of questions first thing in the morning, but I could close my door and put up a fun sign that says what time I'll be available. Or I could arrive early while the building is still quiet. Okay, well, now I have a new approach to build more 'me focus' into each day. This feels like a good plan, and I'm excited to see how it works. Now I realize that this peaceful dream provided the kind of inner experience that I want more of in my life, and I feel like I'm on a path to building more of that peace into each day."

Kristen then writes the following conclusion in her dream journal just below the island dream description: "This dream reminds me of the inner experience that I want more of in my day-to-day life: more 'me' time, and more focus on what I need. My free-form writing led to a plan to do regular check-ins with myself about what I need more of or less of at that time. See my regular journal for more details."

Then before Kristen destroys the free-form writing pages, she writes the details of her plan in her regular journal: "I made a check-in plan after my peaceful island dream. Starting today, I intend to check in with myself during my drive to and from work, and when I first wake up and before I go to sleep. I intend to ask myself how I'm doing, what I need more of, and what I need less of. I also intend to ask myself what needs are not being met and then how I can meet those needs. I intend to do this every day for the next month."

Kristen then shreds the free-form writing pages and carries the shreds out to the recycle bin. In doing so, she feels an emotional weight lift from her.

TOOL: Writing a Shred Letter

This technique involves writing a letter to express what's present in your consciousness—anger, blame, an apology, acknowledgment, thanks, gratitude, or anything else—evaluating what you've written for clues to dream meaning, and then shredding the letter instead of sending it.

When you write a shred letter, you write everything you have to say and then destroy the letter as a symbolic way of sending it—thus providing closure. You can say anything you want in this letter, because the only person who will ever see it is you. The process of writing this letter is actually *for you*. It provides the aspects of you who need to be heard a chance to express themselves, which can sometimes be enough to resolve any underlying issues. The expression and release that happens during this process can enable deep healing of your relationship with yourself as well as your relationship with others.

This process of writing a letter can bring forward from your subconscious mind new clues to dream meaning, such as memories of events or emotions in your real life, issues or emotions of which you were previously unaware, or aspects of past relationships about which you've forgotten.

You can write a shred letter to absolutely anyone, real or imaginary. Examples include:

- A character or symbol from a dream.
- Someone living or someone who has died.
- A real person you know, or someone you don't know, such as a public figure.
- A historical figure, such as Leonardo da Vinci or Socrates.
- An imaginary person, such as a comic book hero or a stereotype.
- A group, institution, company, political party, cause, or social movement.
- Society, the world, or the entire universe.

- Yourself or an aspect of yourself, such as your inner child or higher wisdom.
- A spiritual figure, according to your beliefs.

The Process

The process for Writing a Shred Letter involves the following steps:

1. Sit down with pen and plenty of paper. Write on paper you don't need to keep, because you are going to destroy it immediately when you're done.
2. Write the name of the person (or thing) to whom you have something to say.
3. Write what you want to express. Keep writing until you feel you have written everything you have to say and you feel complete, and then sign your name at the bottom.
4. Read through the letter, and in your dream journal write notes about clues to dream meaning or issues that need further attention.
5. Immediately destroy the letter by shredding or tearing it up as a symbolic way of sending it. This indicates to your subconscious mind that everything you've expressed has been "sent." **Do not** send the letter, and **do not** keep it.

Examples

Here are some examples of how the Writing a Shred Letter technique can be used in the follow-up process after a dream:

Example A:

A young man named Brian sits down to write a letter to the monster from his dream last night. In the dream, the monster intruded into his bedroom and came after him. He has things to say to this monster, and his shred letter might look something like this:

"To the monster in my dream:

"You intruded into my personal space where you do not belong. I want to make it clear that you are not allowed in my personal space. I banish you from this space and send you off into whatever is next for you on your journey, and I hope that you will use your future experiences to become a better individual so that you don't bother other people like you bothered me. I am sending you goodwill in the hope that it will help you feel better about yourself, so you don't have to pick on others to feel good about yourself.

"(*Signed*) Brian"

Brian then rereads the letter and realizes that the issue of intrusions into his personal space has been coming up a lot lately in his life. It seems like he's been getting upset a lot lately about people interfering in his business and trying to tell him what to do. He writes a note in his dream journal to explore boundary issues further, as a follow-up to this dream. He then tears the letter into small pieces, takes them outside, and throws them in a garbage can.

Example B:

A woman named Kate dreamed about her grandfather taking her fishing. It was just like old times, and it brought back so many treasured memories of spending time with him before he died many years ago. Kate has so much to tell him, and she writes the following shred letter:

"Dear Grandpa Joe,

"I was so happy to see you again in my dream last night. It reminded me of all the fun times we had out on the lake near your farm. I didn't realize then how fortunate I was to have you as a grandfather and to get to spend time with you, just the two of us. Back then, I thought that we were just shooting the breeze, but I actually learned some of the most important things in life from you during those chats. You were such a wise man. I still miss you so much, but most of all I feel so honored to have known you and to have had you in my life. I love you so much."

"With love and gratitude,

"(*Signed*) Kate"

Reading through the letter again, Kate realizes that not only does she miss her grandfather, she also misses the sense of safety and security she felt whenever she was with him. Lately she has noticed she's been feeling as if she's lacking a sense of security or an emotional foundation within herself. She wonders if maybe the dream showed up right now because she's been experiencing these feelings. She makes a note in her dream journal to explore these feelings further. She then shreds the letter, as a symbolic way of "sending" it.

Chapter 3-25

TOOL: Dealing with Nightmares

Nightmares and Toxic Dreams can be analyzed just as any other kind of dream—such as by looking for parallels with situations in your real life, while paying special attention to possible links to subconscious fears and recent traumatic experiences (real or virtual, such as watching a movie). However, some nightmares may simply have been triggered by your toxic state at the time of the dream, and therefore may offer no useful meaning to interpret.

Nightmares and Toxic Dreams can wreak havoc by scaring the bejeebers out of you. Not only do they affect you during the dream state, but they also often leave you with a negative emotional and mental residue that can last hours or even days. Often when you wake up from a nightmare, you may suddenly realize that it didn't really happen in real life, but you're still in a mental and emotional state as if it did. You may also notice physical effects like a pounding heart, sweating, or even crying. You might feel residual mental and emotional effects such as fear, anger, hate, a desire to run away from or punish the "meanie" in your dream, or you might just experience a general "yuck" feeling.

From the point of view of your subconscious mind, the events in the dream really happened, so why wouldn't you have a genuine reaction to them? Furthermore, the reaction can linger, just as it would after you experience disturbing events in your waking life. Over the next few days or even months, recalling the dream can be like returning to the scene of a crime. Every time you recall the dream, you revisit that same negative, traumatic state within yourself—and why would anyone want to do that?

The following techniques are ones I've used to deal with "problem dreams" such as nightmares and Toxic Dreams. The idea is to glean any value from these dreams that you can, and then release them so that they no longer affect your subconscious or waking consciousness. I've listed the following techniques in the order in which I suggest they be used, and I suggest using them immediately after waking up from a nightmare or Toxic Dream.

Rainbow Visualization

The Rainbow Visualization is a technique to help you lift out of the negative emotional state left behind by an unpleasant dream. If you're feeling afraid or otherwise upset after waking up, you can use this technique to shift into a more positive emotional state. This technique is also wonderful at bedtime to help release the effects of the day and help you fall asleep. The idea is to visualizing individual colors throughout the rainbow from a lower to a higher wavelength (or frequency), which can help shift your consciousness from a "lower" to a "higher" state.

For full instructions, see "Chapter 3-26: TOOL: Rainbow Visualization" (p. 213).

Detach From the Dream

This technique is intended to help get a nightmare out of your system—to remove its effects from your consciousness, to empty them out of your mind, emotions, subconscious mind, and all other aspects of you. You can complete this technique with eyes open or closed, but some people find the visualization easier with eyes closed.

1. Ask for the presence of the Divine within you (or substitute another name according to your personal preference).
2. Send love to and release all judgments against all who were involved in the dream. This step is just as much for your sake as for theirs, so that your judgments or grudges do not lock the negativity of the dream into your consciousness. If you can't bring yourself to send love and forgiveness, then send thoughts that you hope all involved will be healed, filled with love, and become kinder.
3. Release the dream and all negativity associated with it. One way to do this is to say inwardly, "I release this dream and any negative residues from it."
4. Visualize the whole dream leaving you and floating into the Divine presence that is already in and around you. Alternatively, visualize the dream leaving your body and floating into a Divine white flame, where it disperses on contact.

Example A:

After waking from a nightmare about a very tall woman trying to harm you, you begin by calling forward a Divine presence. You then send love to and release judgments of all involved in the dream, including to the woman and to the "you" who was in the dream. You immediately feel the negativity within you begin to dissipate. Next, you release the entire dream by saying, "I release this dream and any negative residues from it." You visualize the whole dream floating out of you and into the Divine presence, and you observe as the dream disappears completely into Divine light.

Example B:

Consider a nightmare that your house was on fire and you were trying to phone for help, but you couldn't press the right buttons on the phone. After you awaken, you ask for the presence of the Divine, and then you send love to all involved in the dream, including yourself. You release the dream by saying, "I release this entire dream and any negative residues from it," and you visualize the entire dream leaving your body and dissolving in a Divine white flame.

Rewrite the Dream in Your Mind

A dream can leave you feeling a certain way when it's over, just as movie leaves you in a particular mental or emotional state at the end. Using the following technique, you can change your inner state by "rewriting" the ending of your dream in a more positive way, to resolve any outstanding issues and tie up any loose ends. In other words, you can give your dream a happy ending. For example, in a dream that ended with you falling off a bridge into a river, you could visualize the story continuing with a large air cushion deploying below you, on which you land safely. Re-envisioning the outcome this way can help release any emotional distress you are still feeling and shift into a more positive state.

1. Close your eyes and visualize the last thing that happened in your dream.

2. Create the rest of the story, giving it any ending you choose. Imagine that you're watching the rest of the movie, and give it a positive ending with a satisfying resolution. I suggest using positive, win-win strategies rather than lowering yourself into negativity and creating more negativity within your consciousness. Examples of positive strategies include:

    Send Love—Shoot love or peace toward your attacker until his negativity is dissolved. For example, imagine using a Ghostbusters-type gun that drenches the attacker with pure love—or a peace-breathing dragon who breathes out peace instead of fire—which not only stops the attacker in his tracks, but also fills him with love or peace.

    Disarm With Humor—Imagine that a purple polka-dot cow flies in and eats your attacker's weapon or chases him away, or imagine your attacker wearing huge clown shoes and a big red nose and doing a silly dance off into the sunset.

Bring in a Helper—Imagine a source of help neutralizing the negative element in the dream. You can imagine any figure—past, present, or created in your mind—stepping in and neutralizing the negativity in the dream through positive action. For example, you might imagine a superhero surrounding your attacker in a cloud of pure love—or a fairy godmother waving her magic wand—and the negativity then drains from him.

Eject the Negative—Tell the attacker that it must leave. Say something like "You are not allowed here. This was my dream, this is my consciousness, and I am in charge. You must leave now." Then envision white light filling your consciousness and pushing him out of it.

Lift Above—Imagine yourself climbing into a beautiful hot air balloon and being lifted up out of the scene and into a bright, white, light cloud of love and peace, or imagine that by generating love within yourself you can levitate upward and float away to a peaceful place.

Rewind and Redirect—Rewind the dream story by envisioning everything happening quickly in reverse until you get to a point before a problem developed. Then play the story forward, but this time redirect the story your way—in a positive way. For example, you might rewind a dream in which someone steals your wallet, and redirect it to tell a story in which you deploy a protective rubber bubble around yourself, which the would-be thief just bounces off of when he tries to approach you.

Example A:
Imagine a dream in which a mean man was chasing you and was just about to catch you, and then you woke up. Upon awakening, you close your eyes and visualize the last moment of the dream, when he was close enough to touch you. You then visualize another ending to the dream—one in which you dissolve his negativity with love. You visualize yourself pivoting around and "shooting love" at him through your eyes—bright white love, inundating him with caring and goodwill. You feel yourself actually wanting him to become kind, to be healed of whatever emotional wound has brought out the meanness in him. As the love engulfs him, you visualize it replacing the meanness within him, and the angry expression on his face is replaced with one of kindness and relief. Now he is a grateful, happy guy.

You visualize him thanking you for helping him and then going on his way until he fades from view.

Example B:

Consider a nightmare in which you're adrift in a small inflatable boat in the middle of the ocean, when a storm begins tossing you on huge waves. The boat then loses air and begins taking on water. A huge wave is towering over you, ready to crash, when you wake up. You close your eyes and visualize yourself in the sinking boat. Then you visualize an ending to the dream in which the sky suddenly clears, the storm clouds are replaced with happy, fluffy clouds, and the waters become calm. Then a hot air balloon floats down from above. You climb into its basket, and you feel an overwhelming sense of love and well-being. The balloon begins lifting—and the higher it goes, the greater your sense of love and well-being. You close your eyes, feel the warm sun on your face, and enjoy the experience.

Do a Reality Check

One of the reasons that nightmares are so disturbing is that they tend to feel so real. Otherwise, we wouldn't respond to them in such an extreme emotional way. If the subconscious mind experiences the events in a nightmare as a reality, you may be able to erase the nightmare's effects by doing a reality check—by proving to your subconscious mind that the nightmare is not your current reality. You can do this by replacing the dream reality with your current waking reality. You might find that the most effective way to do this is visually and through your other senses, by "showing your subconscious mind" a physical reality that is different from the one in the nightmare.

Example A:

Perhaps you dreamed that your mother died in a car crash. You might do a reality check to erase this nightmare from your consciousness by "showing your subconscious mind" that your mother is alive and well by calling, visiting, or video-chatting with her. This waking version of reality conflicts with and replaces the nightmare version of reality.

Example B:

Imagine that you woke up from a nightmare about enemy planes dropping bombs on your house during the night. You might do a reality check by "showing your subconscious mind" that:

- It is daytime (not nighttime), by noticing the daylight shining into your room.

- There are no planes flying over your house, by looking out the window at the empty sky and listening to the silence.
- Your house is intact, by walking around and viewing the intact structure.
- There are no reports of any bombings in your area, by checking the news on TV or the internet.

Find the Value in a Nightmare

Many nightmares don't have much useful value to help you improve your life. Often you want to escape the nightmare and its effects, and you don't want to spend any more time with it than you have to. I recommend not writing descriptions of nightmares and not revisiting them once you've released them—because doing so can plunge you right back into all that negativity. However, there are some less direct ways you might find value in a nightmare, such as these:

- **Identify troublesome triggers**—If the nightmare was a Toxic Dream, determining what triggered the dream can help you avoid more Toxic Dreams in the future. For example, if you ate too many sweets the day before you had the dream, you might decide to reduce the amount of refined carbohydrates in your diet.
- **Identify your fears**—Nightmares may portray some of your worst fears. After all, if you hadn't had such an emotional reaction to the nightmare, you wouldn't have considered it a nightmare. Knowing what kinds of things you're afraid of might help you avoid those things in real life, or help you deal with your fears directly with the help of your therapist. For example, if you know that you tend to feel claustrophobic in enclosed spaces, you might choose to avoid them—such as opting for an open MRI test instead of the enclosed version.
- **Discover clues about unresolved issues**—If your nightmares tend to have a recurring theme—such as falling, being chased, or your home being invaded—this could point to a related issue in real life that could benefit from further attention. For example, if you repeatedly dream that someone is breaking into your house and coming after you, it's possible that you feel unsafe in your real life somehow—physically, mentally, or emotionally—or that you've felt unsafe in the past. If the real-life issue is that you feel your personal boundaries are being invaded by a certain person harassing, demanding from, or taking advantage of you, then you might decide that you would benefit from practicing assertiveness, minimizing your interactions with that person, creating more personal space, or taking some other action.

Look for a Physical Cause

Because physical factors can trigger nightmares (as discussed in "Toxic Dream," p. 31), when you have a nightmare you would be wise to consider possible underlying physical causes. If you determine that the primary factor contributing to the nightmare was a physical one, then it's probably not worthwhile to spend time interpreting the dream. Also, once you identify a physical trigger of a nightmare, you may be able to make changes on the physical level to avoid more similarly-triggered nightmares in the future. (For details on the physical factors that can trigger nightmares, see "Toxic Dream," p. 31.)

Chapter 3-26

TOOL: Rainbow Visualization

The Rainbow Visualization technique helps you lift into a higher, more peaceful and positive state. The basic idea of this technique is that visualizing individual colors in order from a lower to a higher wavelength (or frequency) can help you shift from a "lower" to a "higher" state of consciousness.

This consciousness-lifting process can provide great benefits during and after dream analysis, and you can apply it in several ways. Completing this visualization before you begin dream analysis (Step 3 of the dream interpretation process) can help clear your mind and elevate your perspective, so you can access higher wisdom more directly. This technique can also help reduce negative mental residues left behind by a dream that could otherwise interfere with your analysis process. You can also use it to help attenuate huge or chaotic emotions, such as after an overwhelming dream, so you can analyze the dream more objectively. After you've finished analyzing your dream, you can use this technique to shift into a clearer state before you begin addressing any issues that arose during the dream.

In general, you can use the Rainbow Visualization technique anytime you want to shift out of stress and negativity and into a more peaceful, positive, elevated state of consciousness. When used at bedtime, this technique can help you release the stresses of the day, help you fall asleep, and create a more positive state of consciousness that may result in more pleasant dreams. After a nightmare or Toxic Dream, this technique can help you clear out any lingering negativity and move into greater peace.

The Process

An easy way to remember the Rainbow Visualization technique is that it progresses through the sequence of colors in the visual spectrum—from the lowest frequency (red light) to the highest frequency (violet light), and then finishing with very light shades of gold, silver, white, and clear light.

1. Close your eyes, and call forward a Divine presence within you (or another name according to your personal preference). Alternatively, bring forward a feeling of love within yourself by thinking of a loved one or a favorite pet. (This step is the foundation for the whole process: make sure you complete it before continuing.)

2. Visualize that you are floating inside a huge rainbow, inside its red band of colored light. Visualize this red light filling and surrounding you for 15 to 20 seconds. Then float over to the orange part of the rainbow, and let the orange light fill and surround you for 15 to 20 seconds. Continue until you have visited all the colors in order as listed below. To visualize each color vividly, think of something beautiful in that color—red rose, orange sunset, yellow lemon, leafy green tree, and so on.

Red
Orange
Yellow
Green
Blue
Purple
Violet

3. Visualize yourself rising above the rainbow into a light shade of bright golden light that fills and surrounds you for 15 to 20 seconds. It then changes to a light shade of bright silver light and you continue floating in it another 15 to 20 seconds. Then repeat similarly for a bright white light, and then clear light.

Gold
Silver
White
Clear

If you'd like to extend this process after you finish the last color (clear light), you can visualize a white light filling and surrounding you for as long as you like. If you have trouble visualizing any of the colors, you might find it helpful to look at a color wheel online for inspiration. Use your favorite search engine to search for "labelled color wheel" and then click an image to view it.

PART IV

DREAM ACTION TOOLKIT

Chapter 4-1
How to Use This Toolkit

The techniques in this Dream Action Toolkit expand on the fourth step of the dream interpretation process, "4. Act on Your Dream" (p. 87). This toolkit contains a collection of powerful, transformative techniques that facilitate personal growth and healing. Although you can apply these techniques in any area of your life, they are presented here as tools for acting on the information that comes forward during your dreams and your interpretation process. Some of these techniques may seem deceptively simple, but even the most basic ones can lead to great transformation and healing.

Prerequisites

Before using the techniques in this toolkit, you'll need to:

- Complete the first three steps of the dream interpretation process for your dream: "1. Review Your Dream" (p. 74), "2. Record Your Dream Description" (p. 75), and "3. Analyze Your Dream" (p. 78).
- Read "4. Act on Your Dream" (p. 87).

How to Work with These Techniques

When a dream brings to your attention a particular issue—an area within your consciousness that is not at peace—begin with "How to Work Through an Issue" (p. 97). Then supplement that process with techniques from this toolkit based on whatever arises during that process. For example, if you discover a certain way you are judging yourself, release that judgment using "Chapter 4-4: TOOL: Forgiveness" (p. 224). If your process reveals a self-defeating belief, transform it using "Chapter 4-6: TOOL: Transforming Beliefs" (p. 231). Continue working with the techniques in this toolkit until your process feels complete—until you feel at peace and you are not aware of any other inner issues needing your attention.

The particular techniques you choose from this toolkit will depend on:

- The content of your dream.
- The particular kinds of issues your dream brought to light.
- The underlying dynamics that are revealed as you process through those issues, such as judgments and outdated decisions.
- The types of follow-up actions you feel are indicated by all of the above.
- Any other steps you need in order to feel complete with your dream interpretation process.

To see examples of ways you can take action to follow up on a dream, revisit "Examples of Acting on Your Dream" (p. 88) and see the examples throughout this toolkit. As always, be responsible when working through issues, always work in a way that is safe for yourself and for anyone else around you, and if you feel unable to handle something, seek help from a mental health professional.

Chapter 4-2
TOOL: Acceptance

Acceptance means admitting to yourself that something *is the way it is* right now, or *was the way it was* in the past. In other words, acceptance means acknowledging that right now in this moment, a certain thing (you, someone else, a situation) is the way it is, or was the way it was—regardless of whether it is the way you want it to be or was the way you wanted it to be, or whether it might be different in the future.

For example, if you're out of money, you can choose to accept that you don't have any money right now, even if you you're not happy about it and even if you plan to change that situation. Accepting that you're low on funds doesn't mean you're agreeing that you like being that way or that you'll always be that way. Acceptance simply means that you're acknowledging to yourself that right now you don't have any money. Your acceptance of that fact enables you to break out of current patterns such as denial ("I really don't have money problems"), escapism ("I don't have money problems if I distract myself from that fact"), excuses ("I only spent all my money because my favorite store was having a big sale"), and wallowing in misery ("Being without money is so awful—I'm so upset that all I can do is watch TV all day"). Acceptance interrupts those patterns and enables you to start fresh in finding a path to a better situation.

Likewise, you can choose to accept something that happened in the past, such as the fact that you dented your car when you backed into a telephone pole. Accepting that you hit the telephone pole doesn't place blame or judgment on you. Acceptance simply means you are acknowledging to yourself, "I did it," which allows you to move immediately into "...and so, what next?" Perhaps next you will decide to release your judgment against yourself as a bad person for having hit the pole, set an intention to focus more on your surroundings when you're driving, and start today setting aside money for your car repair.

Benefits

Acceptance can bring great peace, immediately. Once you accept that something is the way it is (or was the way it was), you may be surprised how much energy you were putting toward fighting against it, denying it, thinking about it, or trying to avoid thinking about it. You may suddenly feel a load lift off of you when you stop fighting what is, or what was.

Once you accept something, often you can see the situation more clearly. You may be less afraid to look at and explore the situation than when you were fighting or avoiding it—and that deeper understanding of the situation is important to help you decide what your next step will be.

Accepting something can immediately shift your awareness into the actual issue and its underlying dynamics, such as judgments, guilt, blame, or self-defeating patterns of denial or excuses. This awareness gives you the power to work through those issues by shifting their underlying dynamics. (Read more about working through issues and their underlying dynamics in "How to Work Through an Issue," on p. 97, as well as in "Chapter 4-4: TOOL: Forgiveness" on p. 224, "Chapter 4-6: TOOL: Transforming Beliefs" on p. 231, and other techniques in "Part IV: Dream Action Toolkit" starting on p. 215.)

Acceptance allows you to move into the mode of "What's next?" rather than remaining hung up in the past, whether it's the distant past or the past of just a few minutes ago. Acceptance moves you into the now. When you accept, you are accepting *right now,* in the moment.

Acceptance creates a clear space from which you can more easily move forward and change things. Although you accept something, you may still not be happy about it and want to change it—which is fine. However, in order to change something, you must start from the way it is *right now* and make changes from this point forward. In any moment, all you have is now, and so that's where you must start when making a change. The very first step is acceptance—and then you can move forward from there.

The Process

The process of acceptance has only one step: Say inwardly or outwardly, "I accept..." and then describe what you're accepting right now, in the moment. Remember that by accepting something, you don't necessarily have to like it, agree with it, or want it to stay the way it is. You are merely accepting that something *is* or *was,* and you still have the ability to change it or change the way you relate to it.

The process just described only includes acceptance, which is often the first step of working through an issue or changing the way you relate to a situation. Therefore, you may choose to follow up with additional steps.

For example, if you are feeling strong emotions, you might process through them using "Chapter 4-3: TOOL: Processing Emotions" (p. 222). To work through an issue, you might follow the steps in "How to Work Through an Issue" (p. 97) and the various techniques in "Part IV: Dream Action Toolkit" (p. 215). If you'd like to change how you relate to a situation, see "Chapter 4-5: TOOL: Reframing" (p. 228).

Examples

Here are some examples of acceptance statements:

- "I accept that the teacher marked a grade of C on my homework."
- "I accept that I arrived late to work again this morning."
- "I accept that it is hot outside today."
- "I accept that the stoplight is red right now."
- "I accept that my parents cancelled their plans to visit me."

TOOL: Processing Emotions

Emotions are like pent-up energy that can be released through allowing yourself to express the emotions fully. Working through emotions involves expressing whatever emotion you are feeling in each moment until the emotions have run their course and subsided.

When expressing your emotions, you must do it in a safe way that does not harm yourself or others. You do not need another person with you to express yourself to—you only need to express how you feel in words. The point is *expressing*, not expressing *to* someone. However, if at any time you feel the emotion is such that you might harm yourself or others, seek assistance from a health professional to facilitate you with your process.

To process through emotion, express in words what you are feeling—such as "I feel sad" or "I feel angry"—using words to give a name to the emotion and characterize what you are feeling. You can express these words inwardly, or you can express them outwardly through spoken or written words. You may find that speaking the words out loud is more effective in facilitating the flow of emotion. Begin each emotion statement with the words "I feel," and do not judge or evaluate any emotions that come up. Emotions are not right or wrong, or good or bad—they just *are*. It may help to think of emotions as energy waiting to flow. By their nature, they only tend to stick around until they are fully expressed.

Benefits

Processing emotions can eliminate emotional stress you're holding in your consciousness, which can decrease your inner quality of life and color your experience of everything in your life. Carrying around anger, resentment, guilt, and depression can weigh heavily on you. Releasing them can provide great inner healing. Working through emotions provides relief as the emotional burden lifts, and it also facilitates self-validation as the aspects of yourself that are harboring those feelings get a chance to be heard.

Allowing emotion to build up within yourself by not expressing it creates not only emotional pressure but also toxicity within yourself. That toxicity can be destructive to yourself and also to your relationships with others. Then when you finally do express those built-up emotions, they provide more to deal with than if you had been regularly expressing your emotions in a healthy way. Think of a tea kettle with steam building up inside—you can vent the steam a little at a time, or it can come out all at once, but it's coming out one way or another.

Sometimes emotions obscure or even "lock in" an underlying issue (such as a judgment or grudge), and processing through the emotions first allows you to then access the underlying issue so you can resolve it.

Processing emotions can also lighten your inner environment, facilitate inner peace, help you find closure by working through your feelings about the past, among many other benefits.

The Process

The basic instructions for processing emotions are simple in concept: express your emotions. You can do this by speaking or writing the words that express your emotions, such as "I feel afraid" or "I feel upset." The emotions don't need to make sense, don't need to seem justified, and don't need to have a reason. You feel the emotions you feel, and that's okay. Accept all emotions as they show up, and just keep expressing. Don't judge them or label what you feel as "bad" or "good." Don't judge yourself for feeling the emotions, and don't tell yourself you shouldn't feel that way. Let the emotions flow as you express them in a safe way, and keep expressing them until they subside completely and there is no more emotion present to express. After you're done, you may need to take further action to fully resolve an issue, since emotion often overlies deeper dynamics that need your attention. Therefore, I strongly suggest completing this Processing Emotions technique as a part of the larger process of working through an issue (see instructions in "How to Work Through an Issue," p. 97, the first step of which is processing emotions).

Examples

Examples of emotion statements include:

- "I feel sad."
- "I feel angry."
- "I feel afraid that I will run out of money."
- "I feel jealous of my co-worker who received a promotion."
- "I feel hurt after Patricia made those comments about me."
- "I feel anxious about giving my presentation tomorrow."

Chapter 4-4
TOOL: Forgiveness

Forgiveness involves releasing judgments that you have created or that you have allowed to exist in your consciousness. A judgment is a value statement that puts down yourself, someone else, or something else—often criticizing them as falling short of some standard or ideal in your mind. One way to think of a judgment is as a label of "bad" or "wrong" that you place on yourself or on something out in the world, such as "I'm a bad daughter" or "His fashion sense is so bad" or "Society is wrong for valuing money." (Note that a judgment of "wrong" here refers to the denouncement of something, rather than an inaccuracy such as a wrong math calculation or wrong phone number.)

A judgment is like a wedge that you drive between yourself and whomever you are judging. When you judge yourself, you are rejecting or separating from the part of yourself that you're judging. When you judge someone else, you are essentially rejecting her and pushing her away, creating within your mind a wall between yourself and her. Judgments are also mentally "heavy." They're like weights you've tied to yourself that drag you down and make life miserable within your own consciousness. A judgment you've created stays in place until you release it, sometimes remaining for years without your awareness.

A judgment includes two aspects: the value statement (the aspect you consider as bad or wrong) and the object to which you're applying that value statement (the person or thing to which you're applying it). For example, if you judge your cousin as too greedy, the value statement is "bad for being greedy," and the object to which you're applying the value statement is your cousin. The object of the judgment can be yourself or someone else, or almost anyone or anything: a group, institution, society, the world, the Divine, the universe, or "everybody." However, regardless of whom or what you're judging, you can release the judgment.

A judgment is often "locked in" by emotions that you've attached to it. For example, if you judge your friend as a bad friend for forgetting your birthday, you might have a lot of anger and hurt riding on top of that judgment. Before you can release a judgment, you must process through the emotions associated with it. If you ever try to release a judgment, but can't, it may be a sign of unexpressed emotions that are holding the judgment in place and that need to be expressed before the judgment will release. See instructions for expressing emotions in Step 1 of "How to Work Through an Issue" (p. 97) and in "Chapter 4-3: TOOL: Processing Emotions" (p. 222).

It's possible for a judgment to contain positive terms but still be making a criticizing value statement, such as "I'll be good and not eat that pizza" or "I'm much more worthy of love than he is." Despite using positive words, in these cases you are still assessing your (or others') value according to some standard in your mind. In the pizza example, you are placing a label on yourself as "good" if you don't eat the pizza, implying that you're "bad" if you do eat the pizza. In reality, you are *you*—you are never actually "good" or "bad." Those words are simply labels you create in your own mind, and they are not in your best interest. Their effect is to threaten yourself with punishment or with bringing yourself down, both of which are self-defeating. In the example in which you claim you are more worthy of love than someone else, you are putting the other person down in an attempt to elevate yourself. You are labelling yourself as superior to the other person—when, in fact, you are both individuals living your lives in your own ways, and any ideas of comparative worthiness of love are just labels you've created in your own mind. Again, it doesn't serve your best interest to view yourself as intrinsically superior to or inferior to another human being. When you accept yourself as you are, you don't need to judge others to feel better about yourself. Instead, celebrate yourself and others as individual souls who are living a human experience, each in his or her own way.

Forgiveness has nothing to do with who is at fault or whom you consider to blame. You can release a judgment regardless of the details of the situation.

Forgiveness does not mean forgetting the past, nor does it mean agreeing to stay in an unhealthy situation or toxic relationship. Forgiving merely means letting go of your judgment—releasing the negative label you created that puts down whomever or whatever you're judging. Once you release the judgment, any other decisions regarding the matter are completely up to you.

Releasing judgments is more about you than it is about the person or thing you're judging. *You* created the judgment, it has been living in *your* mind, and now *you* are choosing to release it. Releasing the judgment benefits you. Sometimes it helps to remember this fact, particularly when you are having trouble finding compassion for the object of your judgment. Forgiveness also becomes easier when you remind yourself that maybe you don't know that person's whole story—you aren't aware of everything that has happened to him in life, how he deals with things, what it's like to be him, what it's like inside his head, the inner stresses he is experiencing in any particular moment. Most of us are doing the best we can, given what we have, what we know, our situations, and our state of consciousness in any given moment. However, people sometimes do things, react, or handle situations differently than what you expect or want.

Forgiveness becomes easier when you can do it from a place of kindness and compassion. Processing through all the emotion attached to your judgment creates a clear space within which you can connect with the part of yourself who can forgive as you would like to be forgiven, who can give others the benefit of the doubt or a second chance as you would like to receive, and who can look at the other person and see their essence— acknowledge the soul that exists beneath their issues and behaviors. Remind yourself that each of us is at a different point in our own learning process. We all need space to learn—to make missteps and then to figure out how to do better next time. Choose to give yourself and others the space for their own learning process. Take every opportunity to celebrate yourself and those around you—regardless of where each person is in their own learning process—and you will likely notice that forgiveness begins to come more naturally to you.

Benefits

A judgment is a piece of negativity that you create and then hold in your consciousness—like a dark spot in your consciousness that constantly emits mental toxins such as resentment, guilt, or envy. When you release a judgment, you're releasing that dark spot—thus eliminating its negative effects and allowing that spot to fill with something more positive.

Releasing a judgment can often start a broader cascade of healing within yourself. Some of the specific results you might experience within yourself when you forgive include a greater feeling of peace, acceptance of yourself and others, a more positive mental environment, and "room" in your consciousness for more enjoyable ways of thinking. You may notice improvements in your relationships with people around you as you release your judgments of them. You may also find yourself enjoying new opportunities that you never would have before when your judgments were acting as walls between you and those opportunities.

Over time, you may notice a shift into a more pleasant life experience resulting from your practice of forgiveness and a non-judgmental attitude.

When developing a habit of forgiveness, you may start to recognize immediately when you've created a judgment (and then release it), then after more practice you may start to catch yourself even before you make a judgment and you can redirect your consciousness in a more loving and accepting direction. Eventually, you may break your habit of judgmental thinking altogether.

The Process

The following process shows how you can forgive by releasing judgments:

1. Say inwardly or outwardly to yourself, "I release my judgment of (say whom or what the judgment is about) as (specify what you labelled as bad or wrong)."
2. After you've released the judgment, visualize the space it occupied within you as being filled by white light or love.

If you can't seem to release a particular judgment, first express your emotion about the situation involving the person or thing you've judged until there's no more emotion to express (see instructions in "Chapter 4-3: TOOL: Processing Emotions," p. 222, and Step 1 in "How to Work Through an Issue," p. 97). Then release the judgment.

Examples

The following are examples of how to release judgments in the process of forgiveness:

- "I release my judgment of myself as unworthy of love."
- "I release my judgment of my boss as wrong for not giving me a raise."
- "I release my judgment of Dad as wrong for not letting me go to the party."
- "I release my judgment of the world as wrong for not being the way I think it should be."

Chapter 4-5
TOOL: Reframing

In your day-to-day activities, the way you perceive yourself, someone else, or a situation can limit you—even without your awareness. When you encounter something—such as an external event or a thought in your head—your experience of it is shaped by the way you choose to see and interpret it, what you tell yourself about it, and the labels you put on it. You might immediately label something as "good" or "bad," "wanted" or "unwanted," "fun" or "boring," instantly creating an inner frame of reference that colors your experience of that thing. Think about how differently you might experience your first day on a new job if your frame of mind was "I intend to enjoy this new adventure" rather than "I'm probably going to dislike this company and everyone who works here." The good news is that you are in control of your frame of reference, and you can change it.

Here's an example of how your internal frame of reference can make all the difference. Consider what it would be like to view a beautiful painting while wearing glasses with green-colored lenses. Everything would look greenish to you, and you couldn't see the full range of beautiful reds, yellows and blues. You might completely miss the beauty of the painting, and you might declare the painting to be boring and ridiculous. However, if you remove your limiting glasses, you can see the range of colors, experience the painting as it actually is, and enjoy its full expression. In your day-to-day life you can change the "inner glasses" through which you view yourself and the world so you can see more clearly, in a way that works better for you. This inner shift is called reframing.

Benefits

Reframing gives you power over how you experience things in your life. Even when you can't control what happens around you, you *can* control your inner reaction to and your experience of what happens. Anything that you might tend to interpret in a self-defeating way can be transformed, creating a more self-supporting, positive, and uplifting inner experience. For example, you can use reframing to transform a failure into a win ("Look what I learned") in your mind, or to transform an obstacle into a stepping stone to whatever is next ("I can use this to move forward"). Used in a positive way, this technique can transform the environment inside your head into a much more pleasant place.

Reframing can entirely shift the way you relate to yourself, others, events, and situations. Since labels and judgments can create a kind of "blind spot" obscuring your view of a situation, reframing can restore your full range of "vision" of a situation—allowing you to see it more clearly for what it is, and perhaps revealing opportunities you couldn't previously see. For example, if you're busy viewing a situation as a failure, you might not spot an opportunity in its midst—which is why we have products like bubble wrap, which originally failed as a textured wallpaper before it was repurposed as an innovative packaging material.

Since this Reframing technique helps you change the way you see things, you can use it to help see your way forward when you're feeling blocked or stuck. When you're trying to solve a problem that you just can't seem to move past, instead of using the label "unsolvable problem," you might reframe the situation as "an opportunity to get really creative" or "a great chance for collaboration with other people"—or some other perspective that helps you work through the problem.

The Process

The Reframing technique involves shifting your internal frame of reference through which you are viewing something—such an external event, situation, or person—or an internal event, situation, thought, feeling, or other dynamic. You can reframe any situation that seems challenging or that's not working for you, or that you think you'd benefit from seeing in a different light. Some telltale signs of an opportunity for reframing include judgments, self-defeating language, and frustration, or when you notice that you're fighting against a particular thought, feeling, or situation in your life. Consider how you might reframe the situation in a way that works better for you, that highlights an opportunity or lesson, that can help move you forward and upward, and that is a win-win situation for you and others involved. In other words, think of how you can remove your distorted lenses of negative or limited perception, and shift into a lighter, more self-supportive way of seeing.

The reframing process involves these two steps:

1. Identify something within or around you that you would like to reframe.
2. Create a new frame through which to view the situation by removing the current frame (your current perspective and labels) so you

229

can see the situation more clearly (neutrally). Create a new frame through which to view the situation that is more accurate, neutral, positive, or beneficial to you (and to any other people involved).

Examples

The following examples illustrate how you might use the Reframing technique to shift the way you relate to a particular aspect of your life:

Example A:

Consider a dream in which you were riding a slow turtle to work. You realize afterward that this dream was portraying how much you dislike the long, boring commute to work on the train. You might decide to reframe your commute time as "dream time," during which you work toward your personal dreams and goals, such as writing the book or screenplay you've always wanted to write, or studying for your next career. Another idea is reframing your commute as "fun time," for surfing the internet, reading the latest bestseller, or other activities you enjoy. Another possibility is reframing it as a chance to plan your day and catch up, updating your to-do lists and reading messages or reports so you can devote your time at home to relaxation. Yet another option is reframing your commute as a quiet time when you meditate, pray, or reconnect with yourself.

Example B:

Imagine a situation at work in which a new co-worker keeps bugging you with questions about how to complete engineering reports according to your group's guidelines. You view the co-worker as a pest who won't leave you alone so you can do your own work. You might choose to reframe this situation to see it in a different way that works better for you. You could begin by shifting your frame of view of your co-worker to view her as a team player who is eager to learn and contribute to the group. This new frame of view may change your attitude about that person and make your interactions more pleasant. You might also shift your frame of view about the situation, seeing it as an opportunity to practice your training skills. Your experience training this co-worker in group procedures would even enable you to add "procedural training" to your performance report and resume. You also could also reframe the situation as an opportunity to improve your team process by documenting your group's report guidelines, thus streamlining the group's work, reducing future interruptions with questions about report guidelines, and also allowing you to add "documentation experience" to your performance report and resume.

Chapter 4-6
TOOL: Transforming Beliefs

Beliefs are ideas that you take as fact, whether or not they are accurate or have been verified in any way. We form some beliefs based on what we observe in our own experience, such as the belief that "It gets dark at night." Beliefs can also come from other people, such as from scientists telling us that "Eating vegetables helps keep us healthy." We also form beliefs by coming to our own conclusions or making assumptions, such as "My sister is trustworthy." Some beliefs show up in our consciousness without us even realizing where they came from, such as "I don't deserve a decent income" or "People don't like me."

Just because you believe something, that doesn't mean it's accurate or rational, or even that it rings true for you or works well for you. In fact, some beliefs can work against you, such as the following types of beliefs:

- **Outdated beliefs**—Beliefs that you formed in the past but that no longer ring true for you, such as beliefs that you formed when you were too young to know any better. Examples include a belief that "I'm not a good learner" that you formed based on your experience in second grade, or a belief that "My opinions never matter," which you based on your parents ignoring your opinions when you were a child.

- **Irrational beliefs**—Beliefs that have no logical basis or no basis in reality, or that conflict with verifiable facts. Examples include the belief that "No one loves me," when in fact you have family members and friends who love you very much, or "If I don't get an A on this test, I'm a complete failure in life," when in fact the result of one test won't likely destroy all of your chances for success in the future—and besides, "success" and "failure" are completely subjective. Irrational beliefs are often weighted down with emotion waiting to be expressed (for more about expressing emotions, see "Chapter 4-3: TOOL: Processing Emotions," p. 222, and Step 1 in "How to Work Through an Issue," p. 97).

- **Implanted beliefs**—Beliefs that were not originally your own, but that you adopted by picking them up from another person, group, the media, or another source outside yourself—perhaps without your awareness, and in some cases through no conscious intention on the part of the source. Just because a belief was implanted doesn't mean it doesn't serve you well, but because implanted beliefs were not yours to begin with, they are worth re-evaluating. One example is an implanted belief that you can never be an artist, which was based on overhearing your first grade music teacher tell your mother that you have no artistic potential. Other examples include creating a belief that you're only be acceptable if you wear a certain brand of sunglasses, based on ads you saw depicting that idea—or creating a belief that it's okay to steal if you are doing it to help someone else, which you picked up while watching a movie depicting such activity as acceptable. A belief can also become implanted into your consciousness as a result of hearing it repeated over and over again. Repeated statements from others can be particularly tricky because they can slip past your critical thought process and lodge into your consciousness without your awareness. One example might be a belief that women must always wear makeup, which became imbedded in your consciousness after repeatedly hearing your grandma say, "You're never fully dressed without your makeup." Another example is a belief that you could never start your own business, which you formed after repeatedly hearing that successful entrepreneurs are all big risk takers (which you feel you are not).

Beliefs we create in our own minds can become self-fulfilling prophecies. For example, if you create the belief that "I can't trust anyone," then you probably can't—not because all people are untrustworthy, but because this belief keeps you from allowing yourself to even try to trust people. You have closed your mind to the idea of trusting people. If you create a belief that "I can't do anything right," it can become like an affirmation as you repeat it to yourself, and it may start affecting you subconsciously in a way that leads to mistakes you wouldn't otherwise make, such as by undermining your confidence.

Benefits

You may choose to transform your beliefs that you decide are inaccurate, irrational, or don't ring true for you because you feel they are holding you back, causing you to miss valuable experiences, or simply polluting your inner environment. For example, think about how your interactions with people might change if you transformed the belief that "People are basically unsocial" into "People are basically friendly," or if you transformed the belief that "I'm not good at talking to people" into "I'm learning to be a better conversationalist." Beliefs can color your perception of everyone and everything you experience in life. You give beliefs great power when you let them take root in your consciousness, so be wise about what you choose to believe. When you consciously decide what you believe, you take back your own power. Your beliefs about yourself can deny your worth and bring you down, or they can support you and lift you up—you get to decide.

The Process

Here are the steps in the process for Transforming Beliefs:

1. Identify the outdated, irrational, or other belief you've decided to change because it's not serving you well.
2. Release the belief by saying inwardly or out loud, "I release the belief that (*say the belief you want to transform*)."
3. Choose a new belief to replace the one you just released. Be sure that it rings true for you, and that it supports you (and others, if applicable) in a positive, uplifting way.
4. Replace the old belief by saying, "I replace the old belief with the belief that (*say the new belief you are creating*)."

Examples

The following examples illustrate how to release and replace beliefs:

- "I release the belief that I'll never find work that I love, and I replace it with the belief that I can find or create a livelihood that brings me joy."
- "I release the belief that I am a loser unless everyone likes me, and I replace it with the beliefs that I have no control over other people's opinions of me, and that by being myself I'll attract the kind of friends I want to be around."
- "I release the belief that I'm a bad person if I'm not constantly doing nice things for others, and I replace it with the belief that my value is based on who I am rather than what I do."

TOOL: Setting Intentions

An intention is a kind of commitment you make within yourself to act or think in a certain way. It is a determination toward a certain action or result. Setting an intention helps you commit to and follow through on something you want to do, change, or create in your life or your consciousness. When you state that you intend to take a particular action, that action automatically gets added to your mental to-do list, and a portion of your mental energy becomes dedicated to making sure you follow through on it.

Within your consciousness, an intention dedicates more mental power for follow-through than a want, hope, or possibility. If you say, "I intend to call my friend tonight," that's a stronger commitment than saying, "I want to call my friend tonight," "I hope I can call my friend tonight," or "Maybe I'll call my friend tonight." You could say, "I will call my friend tonight," but that doesn't take into account unforeseen circumstances, such as your mother needing your help this evening, or you ending up at the hospital all evening with a broken ankle. Because you can't always control future circumstances and events, you can't say with 100% certainty that you *will* do something—so you might be making a promise to yourself that you can't keep. However, "I intend" leaves room for unforeseen circumstances that you may choose to give a higher priority, allowing you to keep the agreement you made with yourself in case something else comes up.

When you set an intention, it creates changes within your consciousness in specific ways. An intention tends to focus you toward action, and it "flips the switches" in your consciousness that will help you follow through on the intended action. When you say "I intend to...":

- You place yourself in an *active role* for taking a certain action, rather than a passive role of waiting or hoping for it to happen.
- You create a *connection* between yourself and that action in your mind, which makes you more likely to complete that action.

- You *commit* to taking that action, which goes beyond simply saying you'd like to do it or you want it to happen.
- You add the intended action to your *mental to-do list,* and it now will be tracked by the part of you who monitors which to-do items have been completed and which have not—again, helping you follow through on your intended action.

You can set intentions to create more of what you want in your life (and less of what you don't want) in any area where you have control or influence. One excellent way to use intentions is to set an intention before beginning to process through an issue, such as "I intend to love myself unconditionally throughout this process" and "I intend to take complete responsibility for my reactions and judgments during this process." You can also set a pre-sleep intention to help you recall your dreams—such as "Tonight I intend to remember my dreams that are beneficial to re-member" (for more details, see "Set a Pre-Sleep Intention," p. 51). You can set an intention for an external action, such as "I intend to go to the coffee shop at 7:30 tomorrow morning," or for an internal action, such as "I intend to reframe my current situation." You can also set an intention for an ongoing process, such as "I intend to stay present in the moment," or for a manner of doing something, such as "I intend to relate to myself as my own best friend," or for a way of thinking, such as "I intend to focus on the value in every situation." Intentions can be powerful tools for com-mitment and change in all areas of your life.

Keep in mind that you can only intend things regarding matters in which you have influence or control. For example, you can't intend some-thing for someone else. "I intend for John to loan me $50" doesn't make sense because it's up to John whether he decides to loan you the money or not, and you are not in control of his decision. You also can't intend some-thing out in the world where you don't have influence, such as "I intend for the hurricane to move away from our area." You may *want* the hurri-cane to go away, but you can't *intend* for it to go away because the hurri-cane is not within your control.

You also can't intend something in a situation in which you're involved but you have no control. For example, when traveling on a plane, you couldn't effectively set the intention "I intend for this plane to land safely." As a passenger, you may *hope* the plane lands safely or *want* it to land safely, but you have no control over landing the plane safely unless you're involved in flying the plane. If you were the pilot of the plane, you could intend to land the plane safely, but as a passenger you can only intend things over which you have control, such as in the intention "I intend to stay calm and breathe deeply during the landing process."

You can release or replace intentions if they become outdated, circumstances change, you change your mind, or for any other reason. However, once you set an intention, your consciousness relates to it as a commitment: the intention remains in effect in your consciousness until you cancel it (similar to the way your consciousness relates to a decision, as described in "Chapter 4-10: TOOL: Revisiting Past Decisions," p. 247).

Benefits

Intention setting is an extremely effective tool of self-empowerment—bolstering your own power to act, change, and create what you want in your life. Intentions place you in charge of your own life—enabling you to direct your inner life and the way you interact with the world around you. When you set an intention, you prompt yourself to act and you motivate yourself to follow through on that action. In the moment that you set an intention, you place yourself in an active role, connect yourself to that action, and begin tracking that action on your mental to-do list. When you set an intention, your mental energy instantly starts moving toward that action, generating a momentum that carries you forward through the completion of the action.

An intention also directs your consciousness to "focus on this action or direction" rather than on some other action or in some other direction. Therefore, you can use intentions to redirect yourself away from self-defeating habits or ways of thinking. For example, you might set an intention such as "I intend to pack a delicious, healthy lunch for work every day" to avoid being tempted by unhealthy food in the cafeteria. You might set an intention of "I intend to notice every time I talk to myself in a self-defeating way," so that you can then replace each instance with positive self-talk.

Once you start working with intentions, you may discover that you are more powerful than you realized, and you're able to create situations and experiences that bring joy beyond what you've ever imagined. Don't be afraid to think big and think happy.

The Process

The following steps show how to set an intention:

1. Decide what intention you would like to set. Remember, you can only set an intention in an area of your life that is within your control.

2. State your intention within yourself or aloud by saying, "I intend (*say what you intend*)." This intention will remain as a form of commitment in your consciousness until you cancel or release it.

Examples

Here are some examples of setting an intention:

- "I intend to finish interpreting my dream before I get out of bed."
- "I intend to celebrate the uniqueness of each person I meet."
- "I intend to notice judgments I make about myself and others, and release them immediately." (See more about releasing judgments in "Chapter 4-4: TOOL: Forgiveness," p. 224.)

Chapter 4-8

TOOL: Transforming Negative Self-Talk

Self-talk is the way you relate to yourself within your own mind, the inner conversation you have with yourself as you go about your daily life. Some people refer to self-talk as the "tapes you play in your head," meaning the things you tend to say to yourself. Negative self-talk—relating to yourself in a negative or self-defeating way—can include self-judgments, self-defeating beliefs, or any other dynamics in your consciousness that put yourself down instead of lift yourself up. Examples include telling yourself "I can never do anything right," "I'm such a loser," "I'm not as likable as that person is," or "I don't deserve to be happy."

You are the only one in control of how you interact with yourself in your head. You get to choose in every moment whether to build yourself up or tear yourself down, whether your consciousness is a pleasant or unpleasant place to be, whether you live in a toxic or healthy inner environment.

The goal of transforming negative self-talk is to consciously shift your inner narrative into one of unconditional love. One way to think about this is speaking to yourself in the same way you would speak to someone whom you love dearly, a precious child, or someone you admire—or in the way that someone who loves you would speak to you. Be kind, gentle, and encouraging with yourself. Instead of punishing yourself, be patient and remember that you're doing the best you can with what you have and what you know, and you are still in a learning process (as we all are, for as long as we're alive). For inspiration, you can think of someone who is a role model of unconditional love—perhaps a family member, friend, celebrity, historical figure, or someone else who always loves, encourages, and uplifts—and imagine what that person would say to you in any moment as you are going about your life.

Sometimes positive self-talk can feel less than genuine when you're not really "feeling it"—and that's okay. Do it anyway. Keep it up, and it will likely start to come more easily and naturally. After practicing it enough, it eventually will become second nature to you—the genuine way you interact with yourself.

Benefits

Using positive self-talk is one of the most effective ways to immediately and directly improve the quality of your day-to-day experience. If negative self-talk creates a toxic environment within your consciousness that can limit you and darken your experience of everything in your life, then shifting to positive self-talk can cleanse, lighten, and open your "inner doors" to new possibilities.

Transforming your inner dialogue from self-defeating to self-encouraging can improve self-esteem and confidence, as well as remove inner blocks to personal growth. It can also transform your interactions with the world in all areas of your life. Consider how different life might be if you replaced an inner tape of "Life is boring and difficult" with "I find the humor and joy in every situation."

Possibly the most profound benefit of positive self-talk is that your love for yourself becomes contagious and you begin to radiate it to others around you. The kindness and gentleness with which you treat yourself begins to extend to others around you as it becomes second nature. When you are filled with love and goodwill, it can't help but spill out to others around you.

The Process

Here are the steps for Transforming Negative Self-Talk:

1. Set an intention to engage in positive self-talk ongoing, and set another intention to transform any negative self-talk you hear within yourself to positive self-talk. You could even set an intention for a "bell to go off" or a "red flag to pop up" in your mind when any negative self-talk occurs. (Read more about setting intentions in "Chapter 4-7: TOOL: Setting Intentions," p. 234.)
2. Pay attention to your inner narrative as you go about your daily life. When you notice negative self-talk, stop your inner dialogue and pause for a moment. Release what you just said to yourself, without judging it.
3. Replace the negative statement with a positive one. Consider what would be a more gentle, supportive, uplifting, and encouraging thing to say to yourself. Be kind, gentle, and patient—the way you would

239

talk to someone you love dearly, a precious child, or someone you admire—or the way someone who loves you unconditionally would speak to you.

4. Repeat Step 2 and Step 3 throughout your daily life, paying attention to your inner dialogue.

Examples

The following examples illustrate how to go about Transforming Negative Self-Talk:

Example A:

You catch yourself saying to yourself, "I can never do anything right." You pause and release that statement, and then replace it immediately with something like "I intend to learn from every situation," "I'm using every opportunity to do better next time," or "I'm doing the best I know how to do, and I intend to learn and improve."

Example B:

You notice a well-dressed person and think, "If only I could be like that person, then people would like me so much more." You catch yourself in this negative self-talk, pause, and release that statement. Then you immediately replace it with "I celebrate my own uniqueness and all that I have to offer the world," "I accept myself for who I am, regardless of what I'm wearing," or "I intend to look beyond appearances to see the value in the person, including the value in myself."

Chapter 4-9

TOOL: Exploring Projections

A projection can be described as a mental dynamic wherein you subconsciously deny something about yourself—such as a particular characteristic or tendency—and instead you attribute it to someone else. Another way to describe a projection is when you recognize an aspect of yourself in someone else, at the same time denying that aspect within yourself. A projection is a way to avoid accepting and taking responsibility for something that you judge or reject about yourself.

The classic version of a projection is a negative projection, in which you project your judgment of yourself onto someone else. You judge someone else as having an undesirable aspect, and at the same time deny that same undesirable aspect of yourself. Examples include:

- Someone who is often dishonest accusing others of being dishonest.
- Someone who judges his own body as less than perfect judging others bodies as less than perfect.
- A person who is very stingy with her money judging others as stingy.

Sometimes a projection takes the form of blaming someone else, such as:

- Someone who dislikes another person claiming that the *actual* problem is that the other person doesn't like *him.*
- Someone who often picks arguments blaming her partner for always starting arguments.

Through the process of a projection, you are maintaining a false self-image by denying in yourself the very characteristic you are projecting onto someone else. In this way, a projection can be a defense mechanism. By projecting your own characteristic onto another person, you avoid experiencing your own self-judgment, and you avoid taking responsibility for your own characteristic and dealing with any of its ramifications (such as self-judgment). So, unfortunately, your judgment of yourself gets perpetuated, rather than you getting an opportunity to recognize it and release it—and your self-judgment continues to poison your consciousness.

Projections often occur completely subconsciously. As dynamics of the subconscious mind, your projections can show up in dreams—which can help bring the projection to your attention and perhaps provide clues about the issues involved. The good news about projections is that once you become aware of them, you can see them for what they are and work through the underlying dynamics. A projection often stems from your *lack of awareness* of your own inner dynamics such as self-judgments and negative patterns—and dreams can deliver the gift of awareness so that your projection can no longer rule over you.

Negative and Positive Projections

Just as you might project your own undesired characteristic onto someone else, it's also possible to project your own desired characteristic onto someone else—which is called a positive projection. In both positive and negative projections, you are denying a particular characteristic in yourself. A positive projection involves externalizing a characteristic you view as positive—denying that you also have that characteristic, or the potential for it. Examples of positive projections include claiming that you could never be a good leader like a certain leader you admire, or telling yourself you could never be as likable as your older sister. Another way to describe a positive projection is when an aspect of yourself "resonates" with that same quality in another person, but you deny that aspect or potential within yourself. For example, the part of you with the potential to inspire others through public speaking "resonates" when you see your favorite inspirational speaker on TV, but you deny your own potential to be an inspirational speaker by telling yourself, "I could never be an inspiration to others."

The Object of a Projection

The mechanism of a projection involves not only personal denial of your own characteristic, but also an external target onto which to project it. That external target can be any external entity—a person, group, society, people, the world, or just about anything within your world view. For example, a projection onto society might take the form of a corrupt government official claiming that we live in a corrupt society. In a projection targeted onto the world, a vengeful person may see the world as a vengeful place. A projection can use almost anyone or anything as a target.

A projection is all about *you*—it's completely *within you*—and really has nothing to do with the external target, except that the target happened to trigger your subconscious recognition of something within yourself.

Dissolving Projections

First, realize that a projection is not a "bad" thing. It's just a dynamic that your subconscious mind has created within your consciousness. More than anything, it's a pointer to an area within yourself where you don't feel at peace, an area that needs your attention.

You can dissolve a projection by accepting and taking responsibility for the aspect of yourself you are denying. Recognizing a projection removes its power over you. Awareness of a projection deflates its power, like a pin bursting a balloon and letting all the air out. Once you realize that you're projecting your own issue onto someone else, take responsibility for that issue by accepting that it is *your* issue, and then you can resolve that issue within yourself. The person you're projecting the issue onto may or may not also have that same issue, but his issue is not yours to resolve. You can only resolve your own issues.

Benefits

A projection indicates a particular area within your consciousness that needs attention. Projections often point to underlying dynamics that perpetuate negativity within yourself, such as self-judgments and limiting beliefs—dynamics of which you might not otherwise become aware. Each projection that you identify offers you the gift of self-awareness, as well as a golden opportunity to work through related issues and release underlying dynamics that have been holding you back or bringing you down.

Each time you project your own judgment of yourself onto someone else, you may also be reinforcing that judgment of yourself. Therefore, working through those projections allows you to release your self-judgments, thereby lightening the load of negativity within yourself and improving your inner environment.

Because projections can create walls between you and others onto whom you're projecting, dissolving those projections can also improve your relationships and interactions in the world.

The Process

Important: Remember that this process is completely for your benefit. We all project onto others sometimes. Instead of judging yourself for projecting, use every projection you identify as an opportunity to transform and heal an area within you, like untying a knot that has been binding you.

The following steps outline a procedure for exploring projections and using them as opportunities for inner transformation:

1. Explore whether your dream involves a projection:

Look for negative projections: For each major character (or group), ask yourself whether there's anything about the character that bothers you—anything you judge to be bad or wrong.

Look for positive projections: For each major character (or group), ask yourself if there's anything about the character that inspires you, that you admire, or that you would like to emulate—but that you think you could never aspire to or hope to emulate. Ask yourself whether the character is reflecting some positive aspect or potential within yourself that you're denying.

2. Identify the projection:

For a negative projection: Consider how the character may reflect back to you an aspect of yourself that you've labelled as wrong or bad. Look for that aspect in yourself—even if it's just a little, or just the potential to be or think that way.

For a positive projection: Look within yourself and acknowledge that whatever inspires you about that person may also exist within you. Consider how you may already have that characteristic or ability, or the potential for it.

3. Acknowledge that the projection exists and accept it:

For a negative projection: Say out loud or within yourself, "I acknowledge that I was projecting a judgment of myself onto someone else, and I accept that what I was judging in that dream character I am actually judging in myself."

For a positive projection: Say out loud or within yourself, "I acknowledge that I was projecting my own positive characteristics or potential onto someone else, and I accept that what I was admiring in that dream character I was denying in myself."

4. Take responsibility for the aspect of yourself (or the potential for it) you were seeing in the dream character by saying out loud or within yourself, "I am the responsible owner of (*describe the characteristic or potential*) within myself."

5. Allow yourself to feel any emotion that comes up, and let it continue to flow (safely) until it runs its course and disperses.

6. Release your judgments of yourself—anything you label as bad or wrong. For each judgment, say inwardly or out loud, "I release my judgment of myself as (*specify what you labelled as bad or wrong*)." Let go of the judgment, and visualize love or white light replacing it.

Repeat this step for each judgment of yourself that comes to mind. Every judgment you release lightens your consciousness even more. (For more on how to release judgments, see "Chapter 4-4: TOOL: Forgiveness," p. 224.)

7. Release any judgments of the person onto whom you were projecting. For each judgment, say inwardly or out loud, "I release the judgment of (*say whom the judgment is about*) as (*specify what you labelled as bad or wrong*)." As you release the judgment, visualize it being replaced by love or white light. Repeat this step for each judgment of the other person that comes to mind.

8. Take action to transform the dynamics within yourself related to this projection that are no longer working for you. For example, you might decide to transform negative beliefs or self-talk, and then set an intention for a new way of thinking. (For more about follow-up techniques, see "Chapter 4-6: TOOL: Transforming Beliefs," p. 231, "Chapter 4-8: TOOL: Transforming Negative Self-Talk," p. 238, "Chapter 4-7: TOOL: Setting Intentions," p. 234, and other techniques in "Part IV: Dream Action Toolkit," starting on p. 215.)

Examples

Here are some examples that illustrate the Exploring Projections technique:

Example A:

The following example shows the process of exploring a negative projection that came to light in a dream:

You dreamed about a bully bothering you, and you don't recognize anyone from your waking life whom the bully might represent. You then realize that he may represent a part of you who has a tendency (or the potential) to bully others or to bully yourself. You open your mind to the possibility that what you see in this bully character also exists within you, to some degree or in some form. You ask yourself how you might be bullying others or yourself, whether there's somewhere in your life you could be less overbearing or controlling, whether you've bullied someone in the past, or whether perhaps you're afraid you have the potential to act that way in the future. You recall bullying your little brother and some of the kids in school when you were a child. Next, you acknowledge your projection of bullying onto the other dream character by saying, "I acknowledge that I was projecting my judgment of myself onto someone else, and I accept that what I was judging in that dream character I am actually judging in myself." You take a few moments to experience the sadness you feel about hurting others when you bullied them in the past. Then you release your judgment of the bullying aspect of yourself by saying, "I release the judgment of myself as a bad person because I bullied others," and as you release the judgment, you visualize it being replaced with white light. You release judgments of the people you bullied by saying, "I release my judgments of the people I bullied as deserving of my bullying," letting each judgment go and visualizing white light filling its place. You follow up by setting an intention to be respectful during future interactions, and to accept each person at whatever point he happens to be in his own personal growth process.

Example B:

The following example shows the process of exploring a positive projection that surfaced in a dream:

Imagine that you dreamed about your grandmother being very loving and caring with everyone around her (as she was in real life), and you think, "I wish I were like that—I could never be that kind to people." You consider that perhaps the loving and caring you observe in the grandmother dream character also exists within you to some degree or in some form—and you then realize that the part of you that resonates so strongly grandmother's kindness is the part of you that's actually capable of great kindness. You decide to step fully into that part of yourself and own it. You accept the idea that you, too, have the potential to show such love and kindness to others. You allow yourself to feel the emotions that come up—including the sadness that you underestimated yourself so much, and joy upon realizing that you *do* have great kindness within you. Next, you acknowledge your projection onto your grandmother by saying, "I acknowledge that I was projecting my own positive characteristic onto my grandmother, and I accept that I was judging myself as inferior to her." You then release your judgment of yourself by saying, "I release my judgment of myself as incapable of great kindness." As you let go of the judgment, you visualize it being replaced with white light. You then follow up by setting an intention to practice more kindness in your interactions with others.

Chapter 4-10

TOOL: Revisiting Past Decisions

S ince childhood you've been making decisions about yourself, your place in the world, and how you interact with others. At age three you might have decided that you were going to be independent and do everything yourself with no help from others. At age eight perhaps you decided that you would do whatever it takes to get the other kids at school to like you. At age 14 you may have decided that being pretty or handsome was more important than anything else, and that you would make that your highest priority. At age 16 you may have decided that you wanted to be nothing like your parents and you set out to do everything as differently from them as possible. You may not realize that these decisions can stay "locked into" your consciousness until you consciously release or replace them. Decisions you've made in the past that are now outdated can limit you, the way you think about yourself, and the way you relate to the world—even if you're unaware that those decisions are still in effect.

Identifying outdated decisions can be challenging, especially if you don't remember making them. You can find clues about them by considering what in your consciousness isn't working for you. For example, if you suddenly realize you're not willing to spend an hour every day on your beauty routine, you might delve into why you started spending that much time in the first place, which may prompt you to remember your old decision to make beauty your top priority—thus providing you an opportunity to revisit that decision and release it.

Benefits

Since outdated decisions can limit you in ways you no longer desire, releasing them offers freedom and a fresh start. Starting with a clean slate, you are no longer held to old rules or constraints of the past. You might choose to replace the old decision with a new one that propels you forward into the kind of life experience you desire, or you might simply enjoy your newfound freedom from your limiting decision.

Outdated decisions may be influencing your priorities, current decisions, and actions even without your awareness. Identifying and releasing the ones that no longer work for you can instantly improve your life, enabling you to live and think in a less affected way and to live more freely and authentically.

The Process

The Revisiting Past Decisions technique includes the following steps:

1. Identify a past decision that is now outdated—that no longer serves you well or enhances your quality of life.
2. Release the decision by saying to yourself or outwardly, "I release the decision to (*say what the decision was*)." Alternatively, you can write the decision on a small piece of paper and then tear it up or shred it.
3. (Optional) Make a new decision to replace the one you just released. Consider its potential effects or limitations in the future, and be sure that it's a decision that's wise to make. Alternatively, you can replace the old decision with an intention or other dynamic.

Examples

The following statements are examples of releasing outdated decisions:

- "I release the decision to be completely independent and never accept help from anyone."
- "I release the decision to make my top priority trying to control what other people think of my appearance."
- "I release the decision to never love anyone else after my most recent relationship ended."

The following statements are examples of releasing and replacing outdated decisions:

- "I release the decision to hide my intelligence so that others don't judge me, and I replace it with a decision to apply my abilities to benefit myself and others."
- "I release the decision to do whatever I have to in order to fit in with others, and I replace it with a decision to instead foster a few great friendships with people who accept me and appreciate me as I am."
- "I release the decision to not be anything like my parents, and I replace it with a decision to accept them just as they are, and I set an intention to learn what I can from my experience with them."

⤙⤚ Chapter 4-11 ⤙⤚
TOOL: Completing Unfinished Business

U nfinished business from the past can leave you with a sense that you've left something incomplete, unsaid, or otherwise unfinished. Perhaps you didn't get to say goodbye to your grandmother before she died or you never thanked your favorite teacher for changing your life. Maybe you left a promise unfulfilled, neglected to say you're sorry for a wrong you committed, or never got around to doing something you promised yourself you would. Unfinished business creates a sort of "pregnant pause" within your consciousness, wherein a part of you keeps expecting something more to happen in order to complete the action that was left incomplete. These incompletions can nag at you constantly from the back of your mind—often subconsciously—sapping valuable mental energy until you take steps to complete or release them.

If you have unfinished business that involved another person, it's possible to reach closure regardless of whether you interact with that person now. Sometimes taking action within yourself is sufficient—such as expressing your feelings, saying what was left unsaid, releasing judgments and outdated promises, and releasing the matter into the past. If you made a promise or had an agreement with someone, and it's not too late, you can fulfill that promise or agreement, and give the other person the opportunity to fulfill her part of it. Alternatively, you can renegotiate the agreement and change the terms, or even cancel it if you both agree to do so (see more in "Chapter 4-12: TOOL: Renegotiating Outdated Agreements," p. 252).

Unfinished business comes in many forms that can exist all around you in your life: items on your to-do list, projects you began and never finished, things around the house that need to be repaired, and anything you've ever told yourself you'd do. Even the dishes in the sink, unpaid bills, and baskets of unfinished laundry are incompletions. As long as they remain undone, they are sapping bits of your mental energy. When you complete them, the mental energy previously devoted to tracking them suddenly becomes available again.

Benefits

Think about the satisfaction and sense of accomplishment you feel each time you complete and cross an item off of your to-do list. Each completion lifts a weight from your consciousness and frees up the mental energy that was previously required to maintain that item on your mental to-do list. To get an idea of how much energy is involved, starting listing in your mind all the major projects on your to-do list, and everything else you've promised yourself you'd do, but haven't—and notice how tired you begin to feel just thinking about all of them. That mental list can be a subconscious drain on your energy all the time, as can the dread, guilt, overwhelm, or other feelings about those things hanging over your head.

Completing unfinished business can also enable closure, healing, and peace within you. The results of reaching closure can range from the satisfaction of returning the tool you borrowed from your neighbor last year, to the profound healing brought about by finally saying what was left unsaid to your estranged father.

The Process

The method for completing unfinished business depends on the nature of the unfinished business and the steps you feel are necessary to reach closure. In some cases you can simply complete the action you originally promised, such as sending your cousin the photos you said you'd send him, or repaying the money a friend loaned you. In other cases you can express things that were left unsaid, or write a shred letter (see "Chapter 3-24: TOOL: Writing a Shred Letter," p. 203) to apologize for a broken promise to someone who is no longer living. Another option is to visualize inwardly that you are expressing to the other person everything you still have to say to them. In some circumstances, you may feel you need to contact someone from your past, such as to renegotiate an old agreement, or to thank or apologize to someone. Some incompletions result from a situation in which someone else hasn't fulfilled an agreement with you. In that case, decide what you need in order to reach closure—such as reminding her of the agreement and giving her an opportunity to fulfill it or renegotiate it with you, or choosing to drop the matter and release any judgments of the other person.

The basic steps involved in completing unfinished business are:

1. Identify what feels incomplete from your past.

2. Identify what you need in order to reach closure and feel complete in that matter. Decide exactly what actions you will take.

3. Take the actions you chose in the previous step.

4. Release any judgments you've made of yourself or others, such as judging yourself as a bad for leaving this matter incomplete (see "Chapter 4-4: TOOL: Forgiveness," p. 224).

Examples

The following examples show how you might use this Completing Unfinished Business technique to reach closure on matters from the past:

Example A:

A junior high science teacher inspired your early interest in the sciences, which you followed into your career as an engineer. When you discover that your teacher is still teaching at that school, you realize that you never thanked her. You decide to visit her, tell her your story, and thank her for the difference she made in your life—and you follow through on that plan.

Example B:

Consider if—from the time you were a small child—your mother promised that someday she would take you to visit your family's ancestral homeland. However, she died before she could fulfill this promise. You feel sad that you never got to travel there together. You also feel angry that your mother didn't take you there sooner—that she waited too long. To complete this unfinished business, you might decide to write a shred letter addressed to your mother (see "Chapter 3-24: TOOL: Writing a Shred Letter," p. 203) or visualize a conversation with her in which you express your thoughts and feelings. Afterward, you release any judgments against her regarding the past, and you release any judgments against yourself for judging her (see "Chapter 4-4: TOOL: Forgiveness," p. 224). To help bring closure, you might also decide to visit your ancestral home on your own, if you feel that's something you'd still like to do, and find a way to honor the memory of your mother while you're there.

~~~ Chapter 4-12 ~~~
TOOL: Renegotiating Outdated Agreements

We all are constantly making agreements with others and with ourselves. Promises, plans, contracts, and vows are all kinds of agreements you make with someone else or with yourself. Wedding vows and rental contracts are both significant, official agreements. Examples of less official agreements include promising to keep a secret, agreeing to host your family for holiday dinner, or promising to help your sister move to a new home. When something changes and you can no longer follow through on an agreement, or it no longer works for you, you can ask any other people involved whether they are willing to renegotiate. They don't have to agree to renegotiate—but if they do agree, you can then update the agreement so it works for all involved, or you could all agree to cancel it.

You also make agreements with yourself, such as promising yourself you'll stick to your diet plan this week, telling yourself you'll visit Japan someday, or vowing that you'll learn to play the piano. When you make these kinds of statements to yourself (or to other people, about yourself), your consciousness treats them as if they are contracts with yourself. They stay on your mental to-do list—consciously or subconsciously—until you cancel them or renegotiate them with yourself. If you're feeling overwhelmed, unfocused, or scattered in your life, it could be because you've made too many agreements with yourself, or maybe you're bogged down with outdated agreements or with conflicting commitments you've made with yourself.

Consider how many agreements you've made with yourself that are still active in your consciousness right now. First, consider how many agreements you've made with yourself already today. They might include a plan to go to the dry cleaners, meet a friend for lunch, and balance your checkbook. Next, consider agreements you made in the last few days, such as your intention to go to bed earlier and your plan to take a workshop this month. Add to those your ongoing agreements with yourself like arriving at work on time, eating five servings of vegetables and exercising 30 minutes every weekday. Now, add to those all the outstanding agreements you've ever made in your life, including all the things you've said you'd do and haven't yet, everything you've said you'd do "someday," and all the projects you've ever started but haven't finished. Remember to include your commitments to others, such as to "love and cherish" your spouse, to pay your rent and other bills, and all of those Terms and Conditions you've agreed to on websites you've visited. Even if just you counted every agreement you've ever made that still requires action from you, that number would probably be in the hundreds, if not in the thousands. That is a huge number of uncompleted to-do list items. Even if each uncompleted item only occupies a tiny fraction of your mental energy, in those high numbers they could still be sapping quite a significant amount of your energy (as described in "Chapter 4-11: TOOL: Completing Unfinished Business," p. 249).

Conflicting agreements can also sap a lot of mental energy, especially if you repeatedly run up against them (perhaps because you don't recognize them as conflicting) or spend a lot of effort trying to reconcile them within yourself. An example of conflicting agreements with yourself might be a situation in which you're staying up all night to finish tomorrow's report perfectly to impress your boss, but you also promised yourself you'd sleep plenty tonight because you feel like you're getting ill. You've made an agreement with your boss to complete the report by tomorrow, an agreement with yourself to complete the report perfectly, and an agreement with yourself to sleep tonight so you don't become ill. So, you might consider how to renegotiate some or all of these agreements in support of yourself, perhaps replacing your goal of absolute perfection (which would take many hours longer) with a goal of preparing a good report that gets the job done to your boss's satisfaction, even if it doesn't meet your own lofty idea of perfection. Because you can now finish the report in a shorter time, you can still keep the other two agreements of finishing by tomorrow and getting some sleep.

Benefits

Agreements can really pile up and clutter your consciousness. Each agreement you make requires ongoing mental energy to hold that agreement in your consciousness until you've fulfilled, renegotiated, or cancelled it. By the time you become an adult, you may have thousands of agreements floating around in your head, many of which you have forgotten about—

such as telling your grandmother when you were 13 that you'd help her finish the family scrapbook, or promising yourself when you were 17 that you're going to learn kick-boxing. These agreements can weigh on you without your awareness, sapping little bits of mental energy and cluttering your consciousness while you're trying to focus on other things. So, renegotiating agreements can free up the mental energy they previously required to maintain, as well as the energy being sapped by stress, guilt, expectations or other associated mental and emotional factors.

Also, each agreement that you do not fulfill eats away at your personal integrity—the part of that who keeps tabs on your promises and makes sure you fulfill them—thereby eroding your trust in yourself to fulfill commitments. You may begin to not trust yourself to follow through on any agreements you make. Rebuilding trust in yourself can be a long process, just as is rebuilding trust in other people who have let you down. So, renegotiating outdated agreements can maintain healthy personal integrity and self trust, provide more mental energy, and clear the way for you to focus on what's important to you in your life right now.

Another important benefit of renegotiating agreements is that it helps you honor agreements you've made with others, which can contribute to good relationships built on mutual trust. Honoring agreements with friends and family helps maintain healthy relationships, honoring your agreements at work can perpetuate job security and career success, and honoring your financial agreements (such as paying bills) enables you to maintain the type of lifestyle you desire.

The Process

To use the technique for Renegotiating Outdated Agreements, identify an agreement with yourself or someone else that is no longer working for you—one that you would like to renegotiate. Then follow one of the two sets of instructions below, depending on whether you made the agreement with yourself or with someone else.

For each outdated agreement with yourself:

1. Decide how you would like to change the agreement you made with yourself. You might choose to redefine, postpone, or cancel it. Alternatively, you might decide to redefine it as something other than an agreement—for example, as a possibility or an idea.
2. Release yourself from the old agreement by saying to yourself or out loud, "I release myself from the agreement to (*state the old agreement*)."
3. (Optional) Replace the agreement with a new agreement by saying to yourself or out loud, "I agree to (*state the new agreement*)." Alternatively, you can replace the agreement with something other than an

agreement, such as a possibility or idea (neither of which is an agreement), and then make a mental note of it or add it to your list of things you might like to revisit sometime.

For each outdated agreement with someone else:

1. Determine how you would like to renegotiate the agreement you made with the other person. Clarify within yourself the updated terms that would work well for you, or whether you want to ask the other person if they would agree to cancel the agreement or replace it with a new agreement.
2. If you feel clear to do so, ask the person if she would be willing to re-negotiate the agreement. If appropriate, let her know what has changed for you and why you would like to renegotiate. Note that you cannot force someone to renegotiate. If you made a commit-ment, it remains a commitment until both parties agree to change or cancel it.
3. If the person agrees to renegotiate, do so until you arrive at an updated agreement that works for both of you (or until you both agree to cancel it).

Examples

Here are some examples that apply the Renegotiating Outdated Agree-ments technique in the context of dream interpretation:

Example A:

Consider a dream in which a swarm of flies surrounded you. When you awaken you explore the dream and determine that it portrays your feeling of overwhelm due to an overabundance of real-life commitments you've made, represented in the dream by the swarm of flies. You've stretched yourself too thin by promising too many things to too many people. You might decide to ask others whether they are willing to renegotiate the agreements with you, such as by getting help from another person instead or by postponing until you have more time. You might also decide to set an intention to think carefully before making future commitments (see "Chapter 4-7: TOOL: Setting Intentions," p. 234).

Example B:

Imagine a dream in which a friend knocked on your door, interrupting your dinner with your parents to collect on a pledge you had made to support her in a charity marathon. You realize upon awakening that this dream represents the real-life situation in which you promised to help a friend move into a new house. However, in the meantime, your father has developed a health issue and you've promised your parents you'll stay with them that day instead of helping your friend move. In this case, you might choose to ask your friend if you can renegotiate your commitment with her—perhaps help her unpack boxes after she has moved, or maybe even help her with the cost of hiring a moving company. Another alternative would be renegotiating your agreement with your parents, perhaps by asking them if it would be okay if one of your sisters spends that day with them instead.

Chapter 4-13
TOOL: Decision Making

Y ou make decisions all day long, every day: what to do next, how to do it, and when to work, rest, eat, exercise. Even when you're engaged in an activity, you're deciding in each moment to continue it, until you decide to stop doing it. Sometimes you make decisions that you know will have significant consequences, such as which college to attend, whether to change jobs, which people to choose as friends, and which paths to take in your life. The consequences of a single decision can range from whether you'll enjoy lunch today to what course the whole rest of your life will take. Even something as innocuous as deciding to take a later plane flight could change your whole life, for example, if on that later flight you met the person who would end up being your life partner.

When you have a decision to make, information is your friend. The more information you have about the various options, the better decision you're equipped to make. Information includes facts, but it also includes other decision factors such as pros and cons, what you really want, your intuitive sense about the various options, the likely consequences of each option, and how you would deal with those consequences.

In many cases, there's no great benefit in making a decision earlier than you have to. In fact, making a decision later rather than sooner can actually provide an advantage: you may have more information later. You can't have less information later than you have now, and you could very well gain more information by decision time—such as new options you hadn't considered, a better idea of what you want, clearer intuition, additional input from other people, and so on. Also, conditions and options may change between now and decision time. For example, consider if you decided to go on a cruise to a certain tropical island, and you booked your trip for 14 months from now. Well, maybe eight months from now the cruise line goes out of business or a hurricane destroys the island. You would have benefitted by delaying your decision to book your cruise.

Here's another way that delaying a decision can work in your favor: it allows your subconscious mind time to mull your choices and gives your intuition a chance to come forward clearly. In fact, you can open the door for intuition to come forward by engaging in activities that you find tend to trigger intuitive insights, such as by taking a break and putting your mind into neutral, going for a walk, spending time in or around water, or centering yourself spiritually through prayer or spiritual meditation.

When you're making a big decision, you may find it helpful to "lean into" one or more options beforehand—kind of like creating a preview or a practice run. For example, if you think you might want to change your career to firefighting, you might decide to lean into that idea by local fire-fighters to get a better idea of what the job is like. Another example might be when you're trying to decide whether to write a book, you might lean into the idea by writing a daily blog, talking to successful authors about their experiences, or taking a creative writing class.

Remember that information is only as credible as its source, so be wise about where your information comes from and how much weight you give each piece. Always consider the source—the person, website, group, company, or network—before allowing information to influence your decisions. In some cases, you'll need to find out more about the source by researching it in order to evaluate and validate it.

Beware of self-defeating beliefs and negative self-talk that can lead to decisions that work against your best interests. For example, you may have bought into the self-defeating belief that "since I've already eaten something unhealthy today, I might as well just eat whatever I want today and start my healthy diet tomorrow." Other examples include "All I've done is watch TV all morning, so I might as well just blow off the whole afternoon, too" and "That person walked away from me at the party last night, and so since nobody likes me, I'm not going to any more parties." (For more about transforming beliefs and negative self-talk, see "Chapter 4-6: TOOL: Transforming Beliefs," p. 231, and "Chapter 4-8: TOOL: Transforming Negative Self-Talk," p. 238.)

Also, keep in mind that indecision is actually a decision in and of itself. When you are being indecisive or avoiding a decision, you are *deciding not to decide*—which results in its own consequences. If the time for the decision comes and goes and you still have not decided, you've actually *decided* to do nothing. So, consider ahead of time the consequences of non-decision compared to the consequences of making the decision and following through.

Benefits

Making well-informed, mindful decisions—for which you've considered the various options, consequences, and contingencies—can lead to better decisions and outcomes with fewer problems and regrettable surprises down the road. Completing a decision that you feel good about can immediately reduce your stress level, bring peace of mind, and reduce second-guessing yourself. When you make a decision to take a certain action, the decision promptly directs your energy in that direction and rallies your inner resources to follow through. Great decisions can also end up taking you down rewarding life paths and through experiences that bring you joy, meaning, and a sense of purpose.

The Process

The following Decision Making technique collects information upfront and allows the maximum amount of time to gain clarity about the decision:

1. Gather information—including facts, your best educated guesses, your intuitive sense, wisdom from others you trust, and anything else to support a good decision. This gathering phase might also include processes for getting clear within yourself—such as analyzing pros and cons, visualizing possible outcomes and your feelings about them, devising contingencies or backup plans, and creating space within which your intuition can come forward clearly. Allow plenty of time in your decision-making process for this important step, which may mean you need to start considering your options early.
2. Wait until the latest time when the decision needs to be made, unless you see more benefit in making the decision early.
3. Make your decision, based on everything in Step 1 and any new information that has come to light since. Ideally, choose a time when you're feeling calm, relaxed, and clear-headed, and you're in an environment conducive to good decision making.

Examples

Here are some examples showing how you might use the Decision Making technique:

Example A:

You're trying to decide what to have for lunch. You've been craving pizza all week, but you're also trying to eat a healthier diet. You consider what it is about the experience of eating pizza that sounds good to you, and you realize that you're craving food that's fun and that you can eat with your hands. You decide to opt for a healthier kind of fun food than pizza. You end up eating a chicken wrap with yummy dipping sauce, and one of your favorite finger foods: grapes. You also decide to make a deal with yourself:

if you're still craving pizza by the weekend, you'll have some then, after your week of healthy eating.

Example B:

You're considering attending an expensive business seminar, but you're not sure if it would be worthwhile to you. You gather information on the seminar's content and instructors, read past reviews, talk with people who have attended in the past, consider the benefits you expect to receive—such as knowledge, skills, certification, and new business contacts. You check with your supervisor to see if your company will help cover the costs, and then consider what it would cost you within the context of your current financial situation. You explore the idea of attending the seminar by imagining the experience you'd have there and how you would apply its benefits afterward. You make a list of pros and cons of attending. The seminar has plenty of space, so you wait to decide until just before registration closes. After you've gathered all the information you can, you weigh all the facts, the cost and expected benefits, and your intuitive sense, and you decide to attend the seminar.

Chapter 4-14
TOOL: Leaning into Your Strengths

Y ou can probably come up with a short list of your strengths pretty easily—things you're good at or that you like about yourself. However, you may forget some of the things you excel at—or you may have gifts that you underestimate, take for granted, or don't value. You might also have hidden strengths you don't realize you have, or potential ones that you haven't fully developed yet. Once you're aware of your strengths, you can lean into them by finding ways to incorporate them more fully into your daily life, and by choosing which to develop even further. Leaning into your strengths can carry you forward into rewarding areas and opportunities you might never have thought possible. Your strengths give you a chance to shine, to bring more of yourself to life.

One way to become more familiar with your strengths is by considering what you've excelled at in the past. Maybe you did well in geometry, maybe you stood up for kids who were being bullied, or maybe you were really good at making up stories. Another way to discover strengths is to consider pursuits that you enjoy or have enjoyed in the past. Often we often enjoy things that we do well—and whether you do something well or not, your enjoyment of it can motivate you to learn to do it well. To look for more clues from your past, you might choose to review your life—decade by decade, or even year by year—considering what kinds of activities or projects you did well at that time.

Another source of information about your strengths is other people. Consider the feedback others have given you about what you do well, or what they like or admire about you. Maybe you've heard people talk about how intelligent you are or how comfortable they feel with you, or maybe you've noticed that people really respond to your sense of humor. You can review written feedback you've received in the past, such as on report cards, in performance reviews, and even in things people wrote in your school yearbook. You can also ask people directly what they consider your strengths to be, which can provide some interesting answers. Keep in mind that other people are sharing their own perspectives, and they may not see you as you really are or the same way you see yourself. They also may not be aware of all your strengths—including hidden strengths you have yet to develop—so be sure to do a reality check within yourself regarding their feedback.

Your strengths can also show up in dreams. In your dreams, you may find yourself doing well at things you're also good at in real life—or things for which you have a natural talent or ability. For example, if you dream that you're in a meeting at work in which team members are floundering due to lack of organized thinking, and you find yourself jumping in and organizing their work process, then perhaps process design comes naturally to you and you might decide to further explore that area in real life.

Remember that a strength in one context can translate into a strength in another context. For example, if you were great at strategy when playing games as a kid, you might also excel at strategy in corporate marketing or nonprofit fundraising. If you got into trouble for always making up stories as a kid, maybe that wild imagination can pay off in a career as a novelist, video game developer, or artist. If you were great at your high school job as a tour guide in your hometown, that strength of engaging people's interest may come in handy elsewhere in your life, such as in teaching, writing books about history, or managing community outreach for a museum.

Benefits

Your strengths are part of what makes you unique. There may be no one else in the world who has the exact set of strengths you have. Your strengths represent potential ways you can provide value in the world and ways you can experience the rewards of providing that value—including the satisfaction of doing good work and doing it well.

Understanding your strengths gives you personal power. Becoming aware of your personal strengths can help you in every area of your life as you make decisions, choose life pursuits, and foster friendships. For example, being familiar with your unique strengths can help you choose an ideal career that allows you to fully demonstrate your excellence in a way that other people greatly value. Understanding your strong relationship skills can help you strengthen and maintain successful relationships with a partner, family, and others.

A familiarity with your strengths and gifts can help you decide where to focus your personal development efforts. Understanding areas in which you have the potential to do well can help you decide which areas to develop further. For example, you may have a knack for engineering that you're not yet aware of, and therefore that you're not using in your life, but that you could develop further if you knew about it. In other examples, perhaps you're a natural public speaker but still a diamond-in-the-rough who's in need of practice, or perhaps you have within you the seed of incredible artistic talent waiting to be developed.

Many characteristics that you might initially consider as having no value—or even as negative—can be translated into strengths. For example, maybe you think you talk too much. Well, that tendency could come in handy in a job that demands a good talker, such as sales or politics. Perhaps you always tend to find flaws, criticize, and pick things apart. Those abilities could translate as strengths for a job in quality control, product testing, or other pursuit in which critical thinking is important. Maybe you're great at coming up with ideas but not following them through to completion, leading you to think of yourself as a quitter. You could put those "idea skills" to use in a job where all you do is come up with ideas, such as advertising, new product idea consulting, or product naming.

The Process

The following steps show the process for Leaning Into Your Strengths:

1. Make a list of your strengths and gifts of which you're already aware. Include talents, skills, abilities, areas of knowledge and expertise, and character strengths such as boldness or sensitivity. Also include interpersonal strengths, such as encouraging or motivating others, seeing both sides of an argument, empathy, patience, good listening skills, unconditional acceptance of others, or explaining complicated things in a way that people can easily understand.

2. Review your past for clues about more strengths you've forgotten or undervalued, or tendencies that could become strengths if you developed them. Write everything you can think of that you were good at, whether or not it seems valuable to you now.

3. Ask others whose feedback you value what they consider to be your strengths. Write what they tell you without interrupting them to make comments, and then thank them for their feedback. Review their lists of strengths, and then add to your own list the ones that resonate with you.

4. After each strength you've written, make notes about contexts or situations in which it would be valuable. In other words, think about

how you could apply that strength in various situations, settings, jobs, disciplines, and so on.

5. Choose how to use your strengths from your list. You might choose one or two you'd like to put into use right away or perhaps to develop further. At work, perhaps you'd like to bring some of your unrecognized strengths to the attention of your supervisor and suggest ways you can incorporate them into your job or develop them further. You might decide to incorporate strengths from your list into your resume or college application. Perhaps you have an underutilized strength to which you're so drawn that you decide to explore a career based on that strength. How you use your list is completely up to you.

6. Maintain your list of strengths, adding new ones as you discover them. Review your list periodically—not only to bolster your self-esteem—but also to remind yourself of strengths you could be using more in your life or applying in new ways in your life.

Examples

The following examples show how you might use this technique for Leaning Into Your Strengths:

Example A:

As part of creating your list of strengths, you carefully review each year of your childhood. You consider what you did well, what you enjoyed spending your time doing, what games you played well, and what you tended to enjoy doing when you were alone. One thing you remember hearing a lot from others is that you were "very bossy," and you always had your own ideas of how things should be done. At first, these seemed like negative characteristics, but then you realized that they could translate into strengths. You are a natural leader. You have strong ideas, vision, and imagination. You are also great at getting others to see your vision and join in supporting it. These strengths could translate well into a number of careers, including film making, politics, or managing a company. You've always felt drawn to politics and have enjoyed participating as an active member of your community. After some consideration, you decide to lean into these newly-realized strengths by running for city council in your small town.

Example B:

You create a list of strengths that includes those you remember from your past and those you're currently using in your job as a math teacher. You ask several co-workers, friends, and family who know you well to describe what they see as your strengths. Among the strengths you hear from several people are your resourcefulness and your ability to come up with creative solutions to problems. You hadn't realized that you excelled in those areas, and that others considered them so valuable. Those strengths resonate with you so strongly that you decide to consider a different career in which those strengths can shine. After exploring various potential careers for several months, you decide to pursue a career in mechanical engineering, which you begin by enrolling in college engineering classes at night.

⟪⟫ Chapter 4-15 ⟪⟫
TOOL: Creating More of What You Want

Creating more of what you want in life means, in essence, fostering the conditions that provide more of the kinds of experiences you want and fewer of the ones you don't want. When you decide you want something in life, it's really the *experience* of that thing that you want, rather than the thing itself. Here's an extreme scenario that demonstrates this point: imagine that you decided you wanted a house next to the ocean, and so you bought one, but then you accidentally bumped your head and went into a coma. In this case, you would *have* the house, but you wouldn't be enjoying it because you wouldn't be able to *experience* it.

You can't enjoy anything in life without experiencing it. An experience consists of thoughts, feelings, physical sensations, and everything else in your consciousness—which together form the overall experience. When you decide you want something, what you're really wanting is the experience you think you'll have with it—which you anticipate will affect you in certain ways.

So, if what you desire is not the actual thing or situation, but instead the experience that you expect it to trigger within you, then here's where the real power comes in: *you have the power to create any experience within yourself at any time.* You don't have to rely on external factors to create enjoyable experiences within your consciousness.

When you start realizing that you can create your own experiences, rather than believing that the external things are what create those experiences—you'll realize that you are the one with the power to create your experiences, and there are many ways you can create a particular experience for yourself. For example, if you decide you want a job that you love, what you really want is the *experience* of loving your job, of enjoying your work and your relationships with co-workers. So, if you open your mind you may realize that there are many ways you could love your job and

266

enjoy your work, including changing the ways you think about your current job and relate to your co-workers, or looking for a new job. In another example, if you decide you want a new car, what you really want is the experience that you expect you'll have if you get a new car—perhaps feeling happy about having given yourself a gift, enjoying other people's positive reactions, and feeling inspired by the beauty of the car. So, if what you really crave is receiving something wonderful, positive reactions from others, and inspiration from your surroundings—then there are many ways you can create those experiences without buying a new car. The lesson here is that you can ask yourself when you find yourself wanting something, "What is the *experience* I want, at the most basic level?" and then get creative about all the different ways you could create that basic experience for yourself.

Keep in mind that being creative about how to provide yourself with experiences does not mean cheating yourself out of the experience you really want. Instead, it's about determining what you really want at the most basic level—the experience level, rather than the thing, person, or situation think you want—and then exploring the different ways you can create that desired experience in your life to deliver an experience that works for you.

In some cases, a desire for something can point to an underlying issue to be resolved. In an example, maybe you saw a fantastic $500 pair of pants that you feel you absolutely must buy. You stop and consider what basic experience you're seeking, and you conclude that you want that satisfaction of feeling good about yourself when you look in the mirror, and you enjoy the looks you receive from others when wearing something interesting or different. Then you realize that spending a large amount of money on yourself also seems to confirm your value to yourself, and leads to you feel more worthwhile. Once you recognize your issue of needing to feel more valuable—of not feeling valuable enough—you decide to work through that issue (read how in "How to Work Through an Issue," p. 97). After you've released underlying judgments of yourself regarding your self-worth, you revisit the idea of buying these pants and notice that the "charge" has faded from that desire.

You may be thinking that what you really want is to get rid of a certain horrible situation your life. So, what's really happening in that case is that you're experiencing that situation in a way you don't like. (Of course, if the undesired situation is a harmful one, then you must use common sense, remove yourself from it and seek help, as appropriate.) Once you start considering how you can change your *experience* of that situation, you are suddenly in a more powerful position because *you* are the one who's in charge of how you experience things. *You* are in charge of your own consciousness. So, you can choose to shift the way you relate to the situation so that your experience is a more positive one. For example, if you are bored out of your mind in Economics class, you could set an intention to find interesting things about the class topics, perhaps enhancing your interest through extracurricular reading or watching economics videos on the internet. Alternatively, you could decide to play a game of figuring out how each topic could relate to you in your life at some point, how it could affect the world you live in, or find some other way to become engaged with the material. Another idea is that you could *imagine* you're interested in Economics and see if eventually it does begin to peak your interest.

You get more of what you focus on, so focus on what you want. Don't fall into the trap of focusing on what you don't want, which does the opposite of what you really want—it places that unwanted situation at the front-and-center of your mind and focuses your energy on it. Focusing on what you don't want is kind of like continually pressing the button on the car radio for the station you dislike, rather than the one you like. The more you dwell on what you don't want or what you dislike, the more energy you give it. Dwelling on negativity is like building a mansion in your mind and allowing negative thoughts to take up space there, rent-free. Your mental energy would be much better used to focus on creating experiences that you *do* want.

Benefits

Creating what you want puts you in the driver's seat in own your life. Rather than relying on others or on external circumstances, hoping they'll deliver what you want, you are taking responsibility for creating the experiences you desire. By taking responsibility for your own happiness, you shift the way you experience the world around you by changing the ways you think about it and react to it: the world does not exist to make you happy—instead, you are in charge of your own happiness. If you don't like a certain experience you're having in your life, you can change the situation—or change the way you relate to the situation in order to change your inner experience of it (read more about how to change your frame of mind in "Chapter 4-5: TOOL: Reframing," p. 228).

When you find yourself wanting something in life—an object, relationship, activity, and so on—if you can understand the actual experience you are craving (excitement, entertainment, security, and so on), you may find that there are many different ways to bring yourself that essential experience. Once you understand that your desire to go camping is really about experiencing peace through nature, you realize that you can also fulfill that desire a number of different ways—by camping, hiking, visiting a lake, or even visiting a park during your lunch break. If your desire to go camping is more about wanting some alone time, you could create that experience by going for a drive or to a movie by yourself.

Understanding the essential experience that you seek makes it easier to find ways to fulfill that experience for yourself, often with less dependence on other people and external circumstances. Being creative with how you fulfill your desired experiences also makes it more likely that you *will* fulfill them somehow, and it may even save you time and money. For example, consider that perhaps a trip to the nearest big city will satisfy your weekend wanderlust just as well as a trip to the other side of the world—and you can do it now rather than waiting for vacation time from work. Again, distilling a "want" down into its most basic desired experience is not about denying yourself what you really want. Instead, it's about understanding yourself more deeply and providing more options to choose from to create the experience you're really after.

The Process

Here are the steps in the technique for Creating More of What You Want:

1. Identify the experience you would like to create, at the most basic level—what specific mental, emotional, physical, spiritual experience you're seeking. Keep driving down to a more basic level of experience until you reach the essential experience you're after. For example, if you want a new pair of boots, you may really be wanting to fulfill a need to feel pampered or loved, or perhaps to meet the physical need to keep your feet warm and dry.

2. Consider all the various ways you can create that kind of experience within your own consciousness or out in the world (or both), and choose a way to create that experience. For example, if the essential experience you want is to feel pampered, you may be able to identify many different experiences that will fulfill that want (not all of which involve spending money).

3. Focus on the experience you want to create, and give it energy in your mind. There are many ways to do this, including setting an intention for what you want (see "Chapter 4-7: TOOL: Setting Intentions," p. 234), creating an affirmation, and imagining in great detail how the experience will feel. The point is to focus your energy in a way that spurs your enthusiasm about the experience you want. In the example of wanting to feel pampered, you might decide to create a collage of pictures showing various ways you would feel pampered,

such as a new pair of boots, bubble bath, pedicure, cup of tea, or an indulgent coffee-table book.

4. Take at least one action step out in the world that begins the process of creating the experience you want. Then take another step, and so on, until you have created the experience you desire. It's okay if you don't know all the steps ahead of time. You can make them up as you go. If something doesn't work, try something else. In the example of wanting to feel pampered, you might plan to take a bubble bath when you get home from work, ask your spouse to pick up dinner on the way home, and schedule a pedicure for the weekend.

Examples

The following examples illustrate how you might use this technique for Creating More of What You Want:

Example A:

Imagine that you are single and you decide you want to be in a relationship. When you consider the essence of the experience you're really wanting, you realize that you mostly want companionship and to feel needed by someone else. You consider the various ways you could create that experience, such as finding a new relationship partner, mentoring a child, adopting a puppy, or volunteering with a group who assists homeless people. You feel drawn to the idea of helping homeless people, and you decide to pursue that option. To focus your energy on this pursuit, you set the following intention: "I intend to serve and uplift people who are in need." You also envision the kind of experience you would like, including how many hours a week and how far you're willing to travel. You take action by visiting the websites of homeless assistance programs in your area, and you follow up by calling several of them and discussing how your involvement could best benefit people through their programs.

Example B:

Consider a scenario in which you decide you're tired of being surrounded by people who tend to express negativity. You identify the specific experience you'd like to create as "feeling more support and encouragement from people around you, " and then a more basic desire to "feel more positivity and encouragement within yourself." You consider various ways you could arrange this experience for yourself, such as releasing friendships with people who express excessive negativity, being more supportive and encouraging of friends and seeing if perhaps they begin to relate to you more positively, releasing judgments and updating your beliefs about your friends to change the way you experience them, and providing yourself with the support and encouragement you crave. You decide to first try creating your own support and encouragement rather than relying on others for it. To focus your energy on this, you create the following intention: "I intend to love and support myself unconditionally at all times." You also take further action within your own consciousness by practicing positive self-talk (see "Chapter 4-8: TOOL: Transforming Negative Self-Talk," p. 238), self-forgiveness (see "Chapter 4-4: TOOL: Forgiveness," p. 224), and deepening your spiritual experience to center yourself in that source of love that is always within you (see "Chapter 4-16: TOOL: Deepening Your Spirituality," p. 272). You may also notice others becoming more supportive of you as you shift into a more fulfilled existence because you've been providing yourself with the support and encouragement you've been desiring.

Chapter 4-16
TOOL: Deepening Your Spirituality

(Note: In this section, I use the words "the Divine" to refer to the highest power—which you might choose to think of as the holiest of holies, creator, source of pure love, or some other name. As you read, you can substitute whatever name with which you feel comfortable, according to your personal preference.)

Strengthening your connection with the Divine is all about spending time attuning to that higher power in your daily life, and endeavoring within yourself to create a deeper spiritual connection. If you feel you don't have a strong connection with the Divine the reason is most likely on your side of the relationship, since the Divine is always present and always available to you in the deepest way possible. The Divine is a constant, so if you want to change your relationship with the Divine, you must take action or make changes on your side of the relationship.

Sometimes you may get in your own way when trying to connect with the Divine. More specifically, certain dynamics within your consciousness can act as blocks that interfere with your ability to experience the Divine's presence. These dynamics that can block your experience include judgments, beliefs, intentions, past decisions, negative self-talk, and distractions. It might help to think of your connection with the Divine as being like a phone connection, where the Divine is always on the other end of the line, and all you need to do to connect at any time is pick up the phone on your end of the line. However, sometimes there can be static on your end of the line—such as "static" created by your judgment that you are not worthy of the Divine's attention. Another possibility is that perhaps you refuse to pick up the phone because of a belief or decision—such as the belief that the Divine does not support you based on the fact that you didn't receive something you prayed for. You can take steps within yourself to release or transform the dynamics that interfere with your direct

272

experience of the Divine, as described in the detailed process of this technique.

Benefits

Of all the techniques listed in this section, this one has the potential to affect your life experience in the most significant way. Opening to and connecting with the Divine can lead to the life experiences to which you've aspired—and beyond anything you've even imagined. Opening yourself fully to the presence of the Divine can result in healing, a greater capacity for love within yourself, profound peace, joy, a sense of well-being, a stronger center within yourself from which to relate to others, spiritual assistance, finding meaning in life, among many other benefits. The results of a deeper ongoing connection with the Divine reach far beyond feelings of inspiration, into profound transformation, enactment of your life purpose, clear inner vision, and exquisite peace.

The unique benefits you experience due to a deeper spiritual connection will depend on how you maintain and participate in your relationship with the Divine. Because the Divine is already present with you, your benefits will result from improving your side of that relationship so that you can experience the Divine more of the time, in a more direct and personal way. This means taking steps to enable an open connection with the Divine in all areas of your being—including physical, emotional, mental, and spiritual levels. Divine presence is healing, uplifting, transformative, peaceful, and fulfilling. So, the greater the connection you maintain—the more often and more deeply you touch into the Divine, and the more you integrate the Divine into your way of thinking and being—the more benefit you're likely to experience.

The Process

The following process can help you in Deepening Your Spirituality:

1. Release or transform the dynamics within you and other factors that interfere with your direct experience of the Divine, such as:

   Judgments—Such as "I'm not worthy of the Divine" or "The Divine is horrible for allowing bad things to happen" (see "Chapter 4-4: TOOL: Forgiveness," p. 224).

   Beliefs—Such as "The Divine has nothing to offer me" or "I'm completely on my own in life" (see "Chapter 4-6: TOOL: Transforming Beliefs," p. 231).

   Intentions—Such as an intention to connect with the Divine only on a certain day of the week, or an intention to connect with the Divine "later"—where later never comes (see "Chapter 4-7: TOOL: Setting Intentions," p. 234).

Outdated Agreements—Such as a "deal" you made in the past with the Divine, or a promise to yourself like "I'll never to speak to the Divine again if I don't get what I prayed for" (see "Chapter 4-12: TOOL: Renegotiating Outdated Agreements," p. 252).

Past Decisions—Such as a decision not to be a "spiritual person," or a decision to not accept help from anyone else (see "Chapter 4-10: TOOL: Revisiting Past Decisions," p. 247).

Emotions—Such as anger at the Divine, or fear of the Divine (see "Chapter 4-3: TOOL: Processing Emotions," p. 222).

Negative Self-Talk—Such as telling yourself that "My mother was right, I'm just not the spiritual type" or "I'm not the kind of person that the Divine wants to be involved with" (see "Chapter 4-8: TOOL: Transforming Negative Self-Talk," p. 238, as well as "Chapter 4-4: TOOL: Forgiveness," p. 224, and "Chapter 4-6: TOOL: Transforming Beliefs," p. 231).

Projections—Such as projecting your own judgmental or punishing tendencies onto the Divine (see "Chapter 4-9: TOOL: Exploring Projections," p. 241).

Distractions—Such as allowing internal chatter in your mind or external noises intrude on your conscious connection with the Divine. When you "get distracted," what's happening is you're allowing yourself to be distracted. You are in control of whether you choose to be distracted or choose to stay focused. When a distraction intrudes, you can choose to let it go. You can strengthen your ability to focus through mindfulness or concentration exercises. You can also reduce your susceptibility to distractions through practicing meditation.

Consciousness-Altering Substances—Many people notice that certain substances tend to interfere with their ability to sense the presence of the Divine. To help raise your consciousness level and increase your sensitivity to the presence of the Divine, avoid things like sweets, toxins, and psychoactive substances.

2. Connect with the Divine. At the most basic level, all you need to experience a connection with the Divine is to direct your inner focus to the Divine. You can use a phrase such as "I open to the Divine" or

a keyword such as the specific name you use for the Divine. But even that is not necessary, because as soon as you create the intention to connect with the Divine, you've already opened your end of the connection, so the connection has been made (like picking up a phone on which the operator is always on the line).

3. Stay connected with the Divine, such as through intention, focus, prayer, or meditation with the Divine. You may notice that the longer your consciousness remains in a state that is open to the Divine, the deeper your experience and more profound the effects. You can also consciously attune to the Divine as many times as you choose throughout the day, or set an intention to remain attuned to the Divine ongoing.

Examples

Here are some examples of ways you might go about Deepening Your Spirituality:

Example A:

You might decide to connect with the Divine every morning as soon as you wake up. Before opening your eyes, you say inwardly, "I open to the Divine in all ways and in all areas of my being." For the next 15 minutes you inwardly repeat the words "Divine Love" and focus your awareness on the Divine's presence within you that is filling and uplifting you, and on your gratitude for that presence. Whenever a distracting thought enters your mind, you let it go. After you finish your meditation, you renew your intention to maintain your connection with the Divine throughout the day.

Example B:

Imagine a scenario in which you have a strong intention to center yourself in the Divine as you go about your daily life. However, sometimes you feel like you pull away from that idea as you focus on various projects during the day. So, you get creative about ways to remind yourself to renew your connection with the Divine. You choose "Peace" as a quick keyword to redirect your focus back to the Divine. You put sticky notes saying "Peace" in key spots around your house, such as next to your bed and on your bathroom mirror. You find a wallpaper graphic for your smartphone that says "Peace" so you'll be reminded every time you look at your phone. You also create an affirmation of "I am one with the Divine," which you repeat throughout the day whenever you think of it. At bedtime, you spend "quality time" connecting with the Divine.

PART V

DREAMS INTERPRETED

Chapter 5-1
About These Interpretations

The examples in this part of the book illustrate how analysis and intuition can be applied to interpret dreams. Each example shows how particular techniques in "Part III: Dream Analysis Toolkit" (p. 101) are chosen to examine the dream and suggest possible dream meanings, according to the particular content of the dream.

The dreams interpreted in this part of the book are real dreams submitted to me in the course of my professional dream interpretation work. The meaning of each of these dreams—like all dreams—is individual and personal to the particular the dreamer. Therefore, for each dream I chose interpretation approaches that were particularly suited to that dream's content, the feelings the client described experiencing during the dream, and other comments the client included in the request. Because I'm not familiar with all the details of each client's life, my approach is to provide enough clues and suggested meanings to assist the client in identifying the meaning that resonates intuitively and feels accurate for her or him. As the dreamer, the client is in the best position to recognize the aspects of waking life or self the dream is representing.

Each example in this part of the book includes:

- The dream information that the client provided, including dream description, feelings during the dream, elements that stood out, and any real-life events or situation the client felt might be related.
- My interpretation of the dream with suggestions about possible meanings, including significant symbols, themes, and messages.
- The client's feedback about my interpretation.
- Relevant dream analysis techniques.

The clients who submitted these dreams for interpretation have graciously given permission for their dream information to be published. A few details have been edited to protect client privacy.

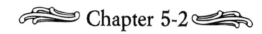

Chapter 5-2
The Bear Sculpture Gift

In This Chapter:

I received this first dream example from a woman in her forties. She provided the following information on the dream interpretation request form, which prompted her to describe her dream, her feelings during the dream, elements that stood out, and possible related situations.

The Dream

Describe your dream.

I dreamed someone gave me a carved wooden sculpture of a bear about the size of my palm. It was a blonde/light colored wood, a very light brown. The bear was very round, as were all its features, rounder than a direct replica of a real bear. I knew it represented a dark brown bear despite it being beige. The figure was welcoming and I was happy to get it. Then two Japanese young women took the bear away from me, although I did not mind since I knew they just wanted to look at it. They quickly gave it back, and it was then I saw the back of the wooden bear had a pouch carved in, and there were two live white worms crawling out of the pocket. I was grossed out but not scared. Intuitively, I knew the bear was now mine.

For some reason, during the dream, I thought the bear represented wisdom. When I awoke, I kept reminding myself to investigate if bears have any correlation with wisdom.

Describe what you were feeling during the dream and when you awoke after the dream. Include emotions as well as any physical sensations.

When I awoke, I knew something was trying to be communicated to me, as I have had meaningful dreams many times. Usually, I can figure them out, but this one

has me baffled. The dream was seven hours ago, and after researching the bears'
meaning in dreams, I am nervous and upset.

Describe any objects or other elements in the dream that seemed important or stood out.
I am a born again Christian, but not judgmental (as I have enough faults to worry about my own instead of trying to point my finger at others).

Do you think the dream is related to events or situations in your life? If so, describe how.
Possible life situations influencing dream:

- *I have a very sick elderly dog.*
- *I am going to a big conference soon, on which I think my career is riding.*
- *I am very unhappy at my job of many years.*
- *My elderly parents are deteriorating mentally and physically.*
- *I've battled chronic health issues.*

The Interpretation

I prepared the following interpretation for the client, suggesting possible ways of translating the dream's symbolism:

Overall Interpretation

The bear being given to you in the dream seems to represent wisdom or inner resources being given to you, perhaps by Spirit or perhaps through your life experience up to this point. The Japanese women borrowing the bear to look at it may represent someone in your life "borrowing" your wisdom—needing your help or advice, perhaps. Your discovery of the worms may represent something specific you've discovered about your inner wisdom, or it could represent a challenge that has shown up in your life (perhaps your parents' health problems). The overall theme of the dream seems to be about you being given something that is now yours, something that others need or want or will benefit from.

In the next section we'll look in greater detail for more clues to dream meaning.

Significant Symbols, Themes, and Messages

First of all, when reading dream dictionary definitions of bears (or any dream symbols), keep in mind that the most important key to meaning is the context of the bear in the dream. The bear's characteristics and how it fits into the dream story are the most important things to consider, along with what's going on in the dreamer's real life and mind around the time of the dream.

You mentioned that you had the sense that the bear represented wisdom. We'll take that into consideration as we examine other clues to its meaning.

Let's look at the context of the bear sculpture in the story. Someone gave it to you, and you were happy to have it. You said it felt welcoming. And then two Japanese women took it away temporarily to look at it, and then they gave it back to you. And then you noticed the two white worms crawling out of the pocket carved into its back. You weren't grossed out or scared, probably because you already knew what the worms represented—and it wasn't something gross or scary. And then at that point you intuitively knew the bear was yours.

So, this dream likely represents a series of events in your real life that parallels the events in the dream. Consider what in your real life you gained, then someone else examined it, then you discovered something new or interesting about it, and then you "owned it" or internalized it as your own.

This scenario could fit in with any of the possible real-life situations you mentioned, but because there were two worms, I wonder if the worms might possibly represent your parents' health problems. Worms often represent things that show up uninvited, that dig themselves in without permission or awareness, which is consistent with how health problems can show up in the elderly—gradually and often unbeknownst to others until the problems have developed far enough to be obvious. Worms are especially known for living and doing their thing underground or unseen, which also reflects the idea of previously unknown problems showing up. So, for that matter, I suppose they could also represent your dog's health problems—or both of the above. But the fact that you weren't grossed out by discovering the worms and you just took them in stride suggests that they represent something you already know about in your life—your subconscious mind already knew what they represented because it's the one who created them, and the whole dream.

Let's take a closer look at the bear. You said it was very rounded, more rounded than a real bear, and that it was welcoming. You also said that it was light colored wood, but you knew that it represented a dark brown bear. This doesn't sound like a grizzly bear or other aggressive bear. So, this bear probably represents some bear-like characteristics other than aggression. When thinking about bears, consider what comes to mind for you in particular. Since your subconscious mind created this bear, it apparently had something in mind that it was representing by this bear. One primary characteristic of a bear is her protectiveness of her cubs. So, this combined with the feeling that the bear represented wisdom suggests perhaps the idea of you taking the role of wise caretaker. This symbolism could simply be an acknowledgment that you have been taking more of that type of role in your life lately (for your parents, your dog, yourself, etc.), or perhaps a realization that you are being called to become more of a wise caretaker.

I get the sense that this bear being given to you represents some sort of rite of passage in your life, perhaps the beginning of a new phase, even if it is temporary—almost like being handed a responsibility or set of responsibilities. The intuitive sense I get about the bear being given to you is like, "Okay, you've come this far—now here's what you need for what is coming in the next phase." In other words, perhaps the bear represents the wisdom you are being given (and/or you have gained through life experiences) to help you to deal with the situations in your life. So, the dream may be sending the message that you have all the resources you need to deal with the upcoming challenges in your life. And the wisdom it represents may not be limited just to your own wisdom, but it may also refer to Divine wisdom that is being made available to you, within you, for the challenges ahead. In any case, this feels like a very reassuring dream.

I'm still curious about what the two Japanese women represent. If the bear represents wisdom, as you thought, then the women would have been borrowing your wisdom to "examine it." This would suggest a situation where people whom you feel are different from you in some way or maybe come from a different way of thinking (represented by Japanese) asked for your advice (represented by them taking the bear to look at it). Could this perhaps represent a situation where your parents asked for your advice or perspective on something? Or maybe someone else in your life? If this doesn't sound familiar, then it may represent something your subconscious mind is imagining may happen in the future—perhaps that your parents or someone else will benefit from your wisdom (represented by the bear).

It's also possible that the dream events don't refer to any specific situation in your life, but to your life in general. In other words, the dream may have been delivering the message that you have the (Divine and/or other) wisdom you need to deal with whatever challenges show up, and that when they do show up (as the worms did), they aren't necessarily things to fear, but things that could even be positive (since white can represent positive or even sacred) or at least a normal and healthy part of life.

I hope I've provided enough clues here to help you discover a meaning that resonates with you and feels accurate for you. Since I don't know all the details and dynamics of your life events, you as the dreamer are in the best position to recognize what in your real life the dream is referring to.

Feedback From Client

After receiving my dream interpretation, the client sent me the following message:

Dear Nancy,

I wept as I read your very accurate interpretation. You are indeed blessed with a great gift. I absolutely will come to you again. Thank you very, very much.

Relevant Dream Analysis Techniques

In this case, the client provided a good amount of information about possible related situations in her real life, which allowed me to spot some parallels between the dream and her real life. I also suggested particular ways of exploring the dream for deeper meaning based on her own personal life experience. My interpretation of this dream was based on the following approaches included in "Part III: Dream Analysis Toolkit" (p. 101):

- Chapter 3-2: TOOL: Parallels Between Symbols and Real Life (p. 105)—Suddenly noticing the two worms emerging from the bear seemed to carry possible symbolism of something in the client's life suddenly "emerging" into her awareness. The symbolism of the worms emerging from an animal specifically suggests a possible reference to the health issues the client mentioned. The fact that there were two worms could mean they represent something involving the client's two parents, such as their deteriorating health she mentioned.
- Chapter 3-3: TOOL: Generalization Analysis (p. 110)—The bear can be generalized to something received by someone, borrowed by someone else, and then returned; the Japanese women can be generalized to someone the client may consider different or foreign, who "borrowed" something; and the worms can be generalized to something emerging and coming into awareness, whose existence was previously primarily beyond awareness.
- Chapter 3-6: TOOL: Character Analysis (p. 121)—The client already had the sense that the bear represented wisdom (a characteristic or concept). What stood out about the Japanese women according to the dreamer was that they were young and were Japanese, suggesting possible (characteristic) symbolism of someone young—or associated traits such as inexperienced, eager to learn, curious about new things,

and so on—and "coming from a different place," either literally or figuratively. These clues provided guidance to help the client explore what the women might represent in her real life. The actions of the worms portrayed "emerging" into the client's real life or awareness (an action), possibly showing up in the form of a pair (a characteristic)—since there were two worms. I left it to the client to confirm intuitively whether the worms might represent her parents' emerging health issues.

- **Chapter 3-7: TOOL: Levels of Existence (p. 126)**—The dreamer already had the sense that the (physical) bear represented (mental) wisdom, and the specific symbolism of the (physical) worms suggested that they might represent her (physical) parents or her (mental) perception of their health issues.
- **Chapter 3-12: TOOL: Timeline Analysis (p. 147)**—The dream contained a series of distinct events that seemed like they might reflect a series of events in the client's life: receiving the bear, the women borrowing the bear temporarily, noticing the worms, feeling the bear was hers to keep.

Chapter 5-3
The Hiding Cat

In This Chapter:

A woman in her fifties submitted this dream for interpretation. She provided the following information about the dream, her feelings during the dream, elements that stood out, and possible related situations.

The Dream

Describe your dream.

I was at a friend's weekend house and everyone was upstairs in the attic looking for one of her cats that was hiding. My friend said the cat was pregnant. The cat came to me and I took it into another part of the house. I was holding the cat and the cat appeared to be in discomfort. As I held the cat, it was apparently ready to give birth to a kitten. I held the cat while she had the kitten. The kitten came out, and was adorable and was running around. The cat was okay. The mother cat was a tan color and the kitten was gray like one of my cats. I have two cats, but I can't remember the last time I dreamt of cats!

Describe what you were feeling during the dream and when you awoke after the dream. Include emotions as well as any physical sensations.

I felt happy to be able to help the cat. I also felt very calm. Everyone was running around like crazy looking for the cat. I just knew the cat would come to me. When I woke up, it just seemed like such an odd thing to dream about.

Describe any objects or other elements in the dream that seemed important or stood out.

Initially I was in an attic, even though my friend's house doesn't have an attic. When I left the attic, the place where I was not familiar.

Do you think the dream is related to events or situations in your life? If so, describe how.

I have been in my career for more than 30 years and I am now wanting to sell my business and start something else. Not sure what the next adventure will be yet.

The Interpretation

I wrote the following interpretation for the client, suggesting possible meanings for her dream:

Overall Interpretation

This dream may have been created by your subconscious mind to express and perhaps explore your thoughts and feelings relating to your "next adventure" in your life. Birth in a dream can represent the beginning of a new phase or project, especially one involving responsibility on the part of the dreamer—which would be consistent with starting a new phase of your career and taking on new responsibilities.

Significant Symbols, Themes, and Messages

A weekend may represent a break in a process, or a break between phases of something in real life—just as a weekend is a break from the work week, a break in the work cycle. It's possible that the "weekend" setting in the dream represents the "in between" phase you are entering in your career. Although you haven't sold your business yet, it sounds like you have mentally moved beyond it and are starting to explore (at least subconsciously) what the "next adventure" might feel like (represented by helping the cat give birth, and feeling calm during it and happy about it).

Next, you mentioned that everyone was upstairs in the attic at this friend's house. An attic in a dream can represent something "higher" (perspective, wisdom, etc.) or more advanced (think about "climbing the ladder" in one's career, having years of experience, etc.). An attic can also represent the spiritual level of a person's experience, such as spiritual connection, inner wisdom or guidance, Higher Self, etc. So, consider which of these (or something else) you would use to characterize "everyone" who was up in the attic. For example, are many of your friends well advanced in their careers, or experts—or perhaps well-tuned to inner wisdom or intuition—or perhaps spiritual or on spiritual journeys? Hopefully, something here will resonate with you—and if not, consider what about those around you seems higher, more advanced, more toward higher wisdom or perspective, etc. It could just represent the wisdom that comes with many years of experience on this planet (age).

Next, your friend said the cat was pregnant, and when it came to you (which you said you knew it would), you took it to another part of the house. So, all the people were running around and looking for something that you just knew would come to you. Again, this would be consistent with "everyone" looking for the "right" career, a good life experience, happiness, fulfillment, etc.—and you just knowing that it will come to you. And perhaps you are anticipating it coming soon, before it comes to some others you know who are searching—since the cat came to you before/instead of seeking out someone else.

Pregnancy in a dream can represent expectation of and preparation for something new (as it involves in real life), and birth can represent a new phase or project or responsibility, as I mentioned previously. So, the mother cat in the dream may represent the opportunity or potential for your new career, your expectation of and or (mental and emotional?) preparation for a new phase in your life. The cat coming to you could even represent the idea "coming to you" to sell your business and start something new—a harbinger of change and new beginnings. Another possibility is that the mother cat represents you (which may be why you knew it would come to you in the dream), "giving birth" to the next great thing in your life—your new project, your new responsibility, your new "baby." This last possibility seems most likely to me, but you are the expert since you were the dreamer of the dream, so consider which meaning resonates with you.

So, along the same lines, the kitten would represent your "new adventure"—your new phase or project in your life/career. The fact that the kitten was running around, thriving, may represent the idea of your new business effort thriving—your expecting or imagining or maybe even knowing that it will.

You said that when the cat came to you, you took it to another part of the house. This may represent some aspect of your process change in your career area. Going to another part of the house—presumably a quiet place away from the others—may represent the same in real life. Maybe you have given yourself space in real life to explore new business possibilities away from others, or maybe you feel the need to do more of that—to get things clearer in your head, maybe to tune into your inner wisdom or intuition.

It's interesting that this cat only had one kitten, since so many have multiple births. The single birth may be another confirmation that the kitten refers to one new project/phase in your life (as opposed to many changes or new responsibilities at once). This would be consistent with your saying that you want to start "something else" (not several new things).

Now, the fact that you dreamed of a cat specifically—not a human or a dog, etc.—may provide some more clues. Consider what salient characteristics come to mind when you think of cats, how you feel when you are around them—and this may be how you feel (or expect to feel) about your new adventure. Based on the feelings you described during the dream, it sounds like you may feel or hope that it will be fun, light, enjoyable— feelings like you experienced about the kitten in the dream.

As for the colors of the cats, I'm wondering what clues to meaning they can provide. You said the mother was tan, and I'm wondering if that's a color you associate with yourself (perhaps you're blonde, or wear tans or beiges a lot, or have those colors in your house or office, or you associate tan with your current business somehow?). If so, that could confirm the idea of the cat representing an aspect of you. The kitten being gray may be a nod to the gray cat you already have, which is an ongoing presence and responsibility that (presumably) also brings you fun, light, enjoyment, etc.—perhaps feelings you'd like your "new adventure" to bring more of. I suppose that the cats in the dream could symbolize that your new business could have something to do with cats, play, or something else you associate with cats—but that's not as likely, since dreams often aren't that literal.

So, in summary, this dream may be portraying your current thoughts, feelings, expectations, imaginings, etc. about something new coming up in your life. Keep in mind that the feelings you had during the dream—during the preparation part when you found the cat, during the change part when the kitten was born, and after the change had taken place (after the kitten arrived)—most likely are the same feelings you feel (or hope to feel in the future) about the change that the kitten birth represents in your real life.

Feedback from Client

After receiving my dream interpretation, the client sent me this message:

Thank you so much for your incredible interpretation. It has been very helpful. I will use you for sure in the future if more stuff comes up in my dreams. Thank you!

Relevant Dream Analysis Techniques

The dreamer already had the sense that the dream was related to her plan for a career change, as she mentioned in her request. The strong symbolism of a new beginning seemed to confirm that idea, although I left that to the client to confirm through her own intuition. I also made specific suggestions to guide the client in the further exploration of this dream meaning based on her own life and perceptions. My interpretation of this dream was based on the following approaches included in "Part III: Dream Analysis Toolkit" (p. 101):

- **Chapter 3-2: TOOL: Parallels Between Symbols and Real Life (p. 105)**— The birth in the dream is a new beginning that may refer to a new beginning somewhere in the client's life, and the client specifically suggested that she is ready to make a new start in her career. The mother cat coming to the client before giving birth also may represent something with new potential showing up in her in real life. I provided some specific suggestions for exploring what personal symbolism the cats and their particular colors might hold for the client in real life, since only she would know that.
- **Chapter 3-3: TOOL: Generalization Analysis (p. 110)**—The pregnant cat can be generalized to something in the client's life that's full of potential, since the cat was full of potential new life. The cat giving birth can be generalized to a new beginning or something new coming to exist in the world. Relocating the cat before it gave birth can be generalized to a change consciously made before a new beginning occurs.
- **Chapter 3-4: TOOL: Emotion Analysis (p. 114)**—The client feeling calm during the kitten's birth and glad to help provides clues about the real-life new beginning represented by the birth, since the client likely feels the same way about the real-life situation symbolized in this dream.
- **Chapter 3-6: TOOL: Character Analysis (p. 121)**—The pregnant cat may represent potential or anticipation (concepts)—especially since the client didn't mention knowing anyone in real life who is pregnant or recently gave birth. The pregnant cat could also represent the client (a person), who is ready to "give birth to" a new career adventure. The newborn kitten may represent the beginning of a process (an activity).
- **Chapter 3-7: TOOL: Levels of Existence (p. 126)**—The (physical) presence of friends in the dream may represent the (mental/emotional) presence of friends in real life. The (physical) cat giving birth may represent the client (self) ready to "give birth to" a new career, with

the (physical) distress of the birth perhaps representing the (physical, mental, emotional) ordeal of starting on a new career path.

- Chapter 3-12: TOOL: Timeline Analysis (p. 147)—The dream contained a series of distinct events that seemed like they might reflect a series of events in the client's life: being with friends, going off on her own, the cat coming to her, helping with the birth, and the new kitten thriving.

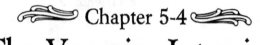

Chapter 5-4
The Vampire Intrusion

In This Chapter:
The Dream 292
The Interpretation 294
Feedback from Client 296
Relevant Dream Analysis Techniques 297

T his dream example was submitted by a woman in her fifties, who provided the following account of her dream, her feelings during the dream, elements that stood out, and possible related situations.

The Dream

Describe your dream.
It is the Sabbath and I am following Jewish tradition, even though I am not Jewish. I live in this large two-story house with many others. So it's Saturday and we are getting ready to turn the lights off, but there is also a vampire who is in the area of our town and I think he will be coming to our house. So I also say, "Let's make sure all the windows are locked before we turn off the lights." I get two others to go upstairs to help me and we are armed with sharp objects just in case. As we go to go up the stairs, the stairs are not where they should be. Like in the Harry Potter movie, the stairs moved. So we had to push them back to get them to be where we needed to go up. We go up and all the lights are on and we start searching rooms. I walk into a bedroom and I hear noises and I can see in the bathroom mirror the vampire, either sucking someone's blood or maybe an animal's, but it was busy doing its thing. He was an ugly one—you know how sometimes they turn into something that looks like the devil in a way, just ugly and evil. So we run. He doesn't see us, but we run to go back downstairs to warn everyone he is here in the house. Two of us run down the stairs but when the third one starts to come down, the stairs are moved again and she has to run around through a door to get to the stairs. But before she does, she stands there looking at me like a deer in the headlights, but I am yelling/whispering, "Go around." So she does and she makes it

292

down the stairs. Everyone is running around the house, not really looking for a place to hide like I was, but just running all over. All the lights are still on, and it's very bright in the house. We hear him upstairs, and my image is that he is walking towards the stairs and he is talking in this old language, almost like he is telling us a story or putting a curse on us. He just keeps talking or reciting in this strange language. I am still searching for a place to hide and I realize my weapon is no longer in my hand, so I look around for another one and find three small, pointy objects on a table. They are all different but sharp, so I put them in my hand and continue to look for a place to hide. Then someone says, "He is gone."

During the dream I was feeling very confident. I had the weapons and was arming others, yelling out orders to do this or that, to prepare for the Sabbath, but also for a vampire. I was in charge, it seems. The third girl who came upstairs with me didn't really want to go, but I convinced her to come. She was also the one who got stuck and had to go around to get to the stairs. Even when I was trying to hide, I still felt confident, although afraid—I wasn't going to let him kill me, and if he did, I was going to do some damage to him. I thought as I was going upstairs to lock windows how some of them gave me trouble locking and I was a little worried how I was going to get them to lock. I am not sure why I thought a locked window would keep a vampire out. When I saw his reflection in the mirror—I think I did, or maybe I saw him and also his reflection—I was surprised it was one of "those" kind of vampires—the ugly, evil looking ones. And I thought to myself, "Oh, no! One of those." I was not really afraid. I mean, I was to some degree, but more so, I was brave and determined. There was something with the stairs, how they kept moving and why. I remember coming down them and they were not like regular stairs. When I came down I didn't just walk down them, I had to jump over the railing. They were weird, almost like a long bed or something strange. But I got down them.

When someone said he was gone, I knew he would be back and we needed to be better prepared for the next time.

Describe what you were feeling during the dream and when you awoke after the dream. Include emotions as well as any physical sensations.

Feeling confident, afraid but confident. The whole time, feeling in charge.

Describe any objects or other elements in the dream that seemed important or stood out.

The stairs, the weapons, the third girl, the windows and locks on them, the evil vampire and not a "handsome" one. All the people in the house that were not family, and the Sabbath. Perhaps the lights that were on all over the house.

Do you think the dream is related to events or situations in your life? If so, describe how.

Can't really think of anything.

The Interpretation

I completed the following dream interpretation for the client, suggesting possible ways its meaning could be translated:

Overall Interpretation

This dream tells the story of you helping a group of people prepare for an event (represented in the dream by preparing for the Sabbath), while at the same time fending off a perceived threat or intrusion—and succeeding at both. Your subconscious mind is most likely using this dream to portray its version of your thoughts and feelings about a real-life situation with the theme of helping a group with a project and dealing successfully with a challenge. In the next section we'll take a closer look at the symbolism in the dream and look for deeper clues to meaning.

Significant Symbols, Themes, and Messages

A house in a dream often represents the dreamer or the dreamer's current life. Since you said you lived in this house in the dream, the house may represent your life right now (or perhaps recently)—or possibly something you imagine in your life. More clues to come later.

Since there were lots of people in the house, the house may represent a shared experience in your life. Since everyone there seemed to be celebrating the Sabbath, consider what real-life group of people you are part of—perhaps even providing leadership for—that shares something in common: a cause, a belief system, an interest, etc. (represented in the dream by the Jewish religion, which has a huge shared set of beliefs and traditions). The group could be people at work, in your church, a hobby group, an internet discussion group, etc. They could be an official group or just a number of individuals you know who share something in common (again, represented in the dream by the Jewish religion). Look for a real-life group in which you feel like a leader or perhaps more capable than some of the others, and/or perhaps in which you sometimes take the role of helping or guiding others. It's also a group where everyone knows what they're there for and all have a similar purpose to be there (represented in the dream by everyone working together on the shared goal of preparing for the Sabbath). This could end up represent something like a recent project at work (or elsewhere) where you ended up providing encouragement and helping others play their roles to accomplish the overall team goal.

Next, let's consider the fact that you were getting ready to turn the lights off to prepare for the Sabbath (in real life, your shared group effort), but you were all also aware that a vampire (in real life, an expected threat of ill will) was in the area. So you were on the lookout for something that could challenge your group. The fact that that challenge showed up in the dream as a vampire (known for sucking blood from its victims) could mean that in real life it represents someone or something that takes from people—that it "sucks" energy, time, emotions, or something else from them. So, this threat could represent a real-life person who is a taker or a troublemaker, or it could represent something more general like obstacles that intrude on the group's ability to meet their goal—perhaps requiring them to spend more time and energy, or tiring them out (since the symbol of a person having her blood sucked out by a vampire might suggest feeling like her energy or life-force had been sucked out in real life). Is there something you've experienced lately, probably along with other people, that threatened to wear you out or "suck out" your life force, your morale, your happiness, etc.?

So, consider where in your real life there was a challenge that you suspected would show up, and it did, in a worse form than you expected (you were surprised the dream vampire was the ugly, evil type)—but you dealt with it and then noted that you needed to be better prepared for next time.

Now let's look for more clues about what the process of preparations could represent in your real life. You started off at the beginning of the dream in a lower level of the house, and then went upstairs, where you came across the vampire. In dreams, the lower floors of a house often represent lower levels of the dreamer's consciousness, and higher floors represent higher levels of consciousness (for example, basement = subconscious; ground floor = self; upper floor = Higher Self or spirituality). The upstairs could also represent greater awareness and/or accomplishment, such as the greater awareness or understanding of a project once you get into it and start accomplishing the necessary tasks. The fact that the stairs were moving and were strange in ways that made them difficult to navigate may represent a real-life challenge of "getting to the next level" or "moving between levels" somehow in life. This could suggest challenges in moving into a higher awareness, spirituality, etc. and then back to everyday life. Or it could represent challenges in moving into the more advanced aspects (upstairs level) of your project or whatever the Sabbath preparations represent in real life. For more clues to meaning, consider what kind of rooms were on the second floor and what they may represent in real life (for example, bedrooms = personal life, office = work life, etc.).

295

Now consider that you all started out on a project of turning off the lights, as part of your preparations. But then you (the dreamer) added in the precaution of also closing the windows and locking them before turning out the lights. Consider where in real life you suggested an additional precaution or step in a process you were working on with others—in order to avoid a threat or intrusion into the integrity of your group—a precaution that turned out to be difficult (in the dream you had trouble locking some of the windows) and ended up not avoiding the threat (the vampire was already in the house)—but you dealt with the threat best you could and it eventually subsided (you found a weapon, then the sharp objects as protection, and eventually the vampire left).

Another clue is how die-hard vigilant you were against the vampire, not afraid of it and not afraid to die trying to take it down. This likely means that the vampire represents something in real life that you feel strongly against, not afraid of, and willing to go all-out to defend against. So consider what "sucking"-type threat you have encountered that turned out worse than you expected (evil vampire), that you capably dealt with the best you could, and it eventually went away, for now.

Now, if you are not finding anything in your real life that parallels the events and symbolism in the dream, consider these possible alternative meanings:

- The dream could represent something you fear or imagine or expect could happen (consider what "evil" you have been defending against in your mind lately).
- The dream could have been triggered by something in a movie or the media, and your subconscious mind took it and ran, creating its own adventure as a variation on a theme. The dream could even represent something like the wrong candidate threatening to win an election, and you working with others to keep that from happening.

Hopefully I have provided enough clues that you can identify what real life situation your subconscious mind was portraying so vividly in this dream. Also, keep in mind that whatever the vampire represents, the dream may be reminding you that you intend to be more prepared for it next time it shows up in your life.

Feedback from Client

After receiving my dream interpretation, the client sent me the following feedback:

Wow!!! You're really good!

Ok, I will have to sit with this and think about it. The group thing throws me because I live alone and I am pretty much a loner, but I do live two seconds from family. This could be a number of things. Working on my spirituality, yet, family always taking me back down in daily life—which is why I stay alone a lot of the time. I have one female relative who is always negative and is the one I gravitate to—mostly because she is very accepting, too. But it's very difficult to be around her and be positive.

The first thing that comes to mind—and it's probably because it was the last thing I read last night—was this sink hole I heard about. It started small and now it's huge. The fear-mongers are saying it could be really bad if it gets to the oil and natural gas in the ground. I think of this and of moving. Or if I stay, perhaps I would have to help groups of people.

Then I thought of the "many me's" and having to gather them all up and fight against this addiction I have and had for years, that I control—but still, it's there.

Or the doomsday scenario where, when the going gets rough, I always felt I would be in control and would be able to help.

Other than those things, I just don't know. But as you said, it could be the others you mentioned. But I was thrilled at your perception and how you broke it all down. I have other dreams and I will for sure write you again. I truly loved reading and exploring what you said.

Thank you!! It was all very interesting. Plus, I will digest it, and more will come to me.

Relevant Dream Analysis Techniques

As in every case, this client was in a much better position than I to understand which aspects of her real life this dream represents since she is more familiar with the details of her life than I am. Therefore, I translated the dream symbolism language into several possible meanings for the client to consider. My goal was to provide enough clues and guidance to enable the client to recognize the dream meaning that resonated with her, since her subconscious mind is the one who actually created the dream. My interpretation of the dream was based on the following approaches included in "Part III: Dream Analysis Toolkit" (p. 101):

- **Chapter 3-2: TOOL: Parallels Between Symbols and Real Life (p. 105)**— Because the dreamer didn't give any information about possible related situations in her life, or any other information about herself, my approach was to provide clues to help her explore what the various elements of the dream represent in her real life. For example, the group of Jewish people living together in the dream probably represents some group with a shared belief system, philosophy, or cause (or something else shared) in the client's life or imagination. The evil vampire likely represents a threat to the group, as perceived by the client's subconscious mind.

- **Chapter 3-3: TOOL: Generalization Analysis (p. 110)**—The group of Jewish people in the dream can be generalized to some group of people (formal or informal) with something in common, such as beliefs, philosophy, or a particular cause. The vampire can be generalized to someone or something perceived as a threat. The idea of a vampire taking blood can be generalized as taking something from victims, which in real life could represent depleting physical well-being, happiness, morale, money, security, peace of mind, or something else. The vampire's sudden intrusion into the group can be generalized to something that shows up unexpectedly and creates loss, such as a real-life disaster or an opposing organization that threatens the group's integrity or beliefs.
- **Chapter 3-4: TOOL: Emotion Analysis (p. 114)**—The client feeling confident and comfortable with her leadership role may echo a real-life confidence and comfort with leadership roles, and these feelings may be the real-life feelings she has experienced in the past while leading others.
- **Chapter 3-6: TOOL: Character Analysis (p. 121)**—The group of Jewish housemates may represent an actual group in the client's life (a group), or something else that binds people together, such as a way of thinking or a shared cause (a concept or activity). The vampire most likely represents a perceived harmful force (a concept, person, or group). However, without more information about the client's real life, there's not much indication of what the group and the vampire represent in her life—or whether what they represent is real or imagined. Therefore, I provided guidance to help the client explore further the characters' relation to her real life or mind.

Quick Reference

You can use the following summary of "Part II: How to Interpret Dreams" (p. 69) as a quick reference during your dream interpretation process.

1. Review Your Dream (p. 74)

a. Before opening your eyes, review your dream from beginning to end as an observer.
b. Assign a keyword to each key scene (Driving, Falling, Swimming) (p. 74).

2. Record Your Dream Description (p. 75)

Write the following about your dream without analyzing it yet:

a. Keywords from Step 1-b (p. 75).
b. Date you had the dream (p. 76).
c. Description of your dream with as much detail as you remember (p. 76), including emotions (p. 76), symbols, characters, actions, words, time frame, setting, setting characteristics, mood, colors, weather, sensory information, reactions, and anything else that stood out (p. 77).
d. A dream title (p. 78).
e. Note if this is a recurring dream or if it contains a theme or element you've dreamed about before (p. 78).

3. Analyze Your Dream (p. 78)

a. Create a quiet space (p. 79).
b. Write your first hunch about meaning and set it aside (p. 79).
c. Open your mind: let go of preconceptions, set an intention to view your dream from a neutral perspective (p. 79).
d. Identify the theme of your dream (p. 80).
e. Connect with your intuition: "I call forward my highest inner wisdom" (p. 81).
f. Notice what stands out in the dream and any associated emotion (p. 81).
g. Analyze your dream until your intuition recognizes the true meaning (p. 81). Use the following order of analysis:

"Consider Common Dream Symbolism First" (p. 82)

The first six techniques in "Part III: Dream Analysis Toolkit" (p. 101):

Other techniques in "Part III: Dream Analysis Toolkit" (p. 101):

4. Act on Your Dream (p. 87)

a. Work through any issues that came up in your dream (p. 97):

Express your current emotions (p. 97).
Make inner adjustments (p. 98).
Take external action (p. 99).

b. Choose from the techniques in "Part IV: Dream Action Toolkit" (p. 215) to shift underlying dynamics and take further action:

Glossary

This glossary contains definitions of terms as they are used in this book:

Acceptance
Admitting to yourself that something is the way it is right now, or was the way it was in the past—regardless of whether it is the way you want it to be, was the way you wanted it to be, or whether it might be different in the future.

Archetype
A particular type of symbol that is an iconic image or idealized version of a person, object, or concept. A generic version or stereotype of a certain type of character. Examples include The Hero, The Mother Figure, The Rebel, and The Trickster.

Belief
An idea that you take as fact, whether or not it is accurate or has been verified in any way. A belief may have formed when you chose it for yourself, were convinced by someone else, or it slipped into your subconscious mind from an outside source without your awareness.

Clarification Dream
A type of dream that clarifies something about yourself or your life, usually providing insight into your experience of a current or past situation in your waking life.

Conscious Mind
The part of your consciousness (your nonphysical self) of which you are aware. Refers to all the aspects of your nonphysical being of which you are conscious.

Consciousness
The collective aspects of your nonphysical existence, including mental, emotional, and subconscious levels. The total of your inner experience, including both your conscious and subconscious experience.

The Divine
The highest power that exists, sometimes referred to as the holiest of holies, creator, or source of pure love (substitute whatever name with which you feel comfortable, according to your personal preference).

Dream Analysis

In this book, refers to an active mental process with the aim of under-standing or exploring a dream—a systematic examination of a dream, such as a logical assessment of its symbolism and structure. A mental approach used as part of the overall dream interpretation process that applies the mind to examine a dream.

Dream Character

A character is anyone or anything in your dream who had the capability of consciousness or who took action—such as a person, animal, other being, or animated object.

Dream Description

A written account of the story of a dream. A narrative that tells the story of a dream from beginning to end—including dream events, characters, actions, settings, and other details about the dream.

Dream Dialoging

A technique to assist in dream interpretation, in which you create an im-aginary conversation with one or more elements from your dream to gain greater insight into the dream's meaning.

Dream Dictionary

A collection of dream symbols with suggested meanings for each.

Dream Interpretation

Assigning meaning to a dream or its parts, translating dream symbolism in a way that's significant to you (the dreamer), attempting to discover mean-ing or purpose that is relevant to you. Usually involves intuition, and can also include an active mental process of dream analysis, as well as an exploration of emotions.

Dream Intuition

Intuitive recognition of dream meaning. An intuitive realization—or a series of intuitive realizations—during dream interpretation.

Dream Journaling

The process of writing descriptions of your dreams, notes during your interpretation and follow-up process, and other dream-related writings such as personal insights and intentions. A tool to organize and facilitate the dream interpretation process, usually in a paper format, such as in a blank journal or notebook.

Dream Recall

Remembering all or part of a dream you've had, thereby transferring it from your subconscious mind into the conscious mind. Not everyone remembers dreams well, but it is possible to improve dream recall.

Dream Symbol

A unique element of a dream that correlates to something outside the dream, providing clues about the meaning of the dream. Dream symbolism is the language through which a dream tells its story. Examples of dream symbols include characters, objects, settings, events, and actions.

Dream Theme

The main subject matter or topic of a dream. The most basic description of what the dream was about, the essence of the dream's story, the overarching nature of the story. Examples include abandonment, betrayal, or invasion of boundaries.

Dream Type

A category of dream, according to dream content and structure.

Dynamic

Something that changes, or is capable of changing, shifting, or transforming. Examples include a belief (which can be transformed into an updated belief) or a judgment (which can be released).

Forgiveness

Releasing one or more judgments of yourself, another person, or something else—such as society, the environment, or the world. Often, a judgment is "locked in" by its associated emotions, such as anger or guilt—which must be processed through before the judgment can be released.

Free-Form Writing

A technique that involves a stream-of-consciousness expression through written words, with no rules or limitations.

Hierarchy of Meaning

Various levels of meaning that a dream symbol can have, from very specific to very general. For example, a barking dog in a dream could represent something very specific in your life (your dog's barking that awakened you this morning), something less specific (your dog), something even less specific (pets you've had), something general (someone for whom you're responsible), or something more general (the general idea of responsibility).

Hypnagogic Dream

A dream that occurs just after you have fallen asleep, often including experiences such as vivid impressions, visions, voices, or tactile sensations. Often contains no useful or significant meaning for interpretation.

Implanted Belief

A belief you hold but did not create yourself. A belief that was not originally your own, but that you adopted by picking it up from another person, group, the media, or another source outside yourself—perhaps without your awareness, and in some cases through no conscious intention on the part of the source.

Inner Block

An inner obstacle to your progress. Also, one or more inner dynamics causing a certain aspect of your consciousness—such as a memory or a repressed emotion—to be inaccessible to you.

Intention

A commitment you make within yourself that begins with "I intend...." A determination toward a certain action or result—such as determining to be or act a certain way, arrive at a certain result, create a particular experience or quality of inner life, or begin a new way of being, thinking, or acting.

Interaction Dream

A type of dream in which you make contact with another actual individual.

Intuition

Direct knowing, independent of rational thought or sensory cues. An inner channel through which truth flows. A powerful tool for recognizing the true meaning of your own dreams.

Issue

A matter within your consciousness or life that is not at peace and needs your attention, usually requiring you to take action in order to resolve it, or in order for healing to take place.

Judgment

A mental criticism in which you label someone or something as "bad" or "wrong" in your own mind. A judgment includes two aspects: the value statement, and the object to which you're applying that value statement—meaning the person or thing you're judging. A judgment can be made against anything—including yourself or an aspect of yourself, another person, people in general, the environment, or the world. Often, a judgment is "locked in" by its associated emotions, such as anger or guilt—which must be processed through before the judgment can be released.

Levels of Existence
The levels in which consciousness operates—including physical, emotional, mental, and spiritual.

Life Purpose
One or more reasons for your existence in your lifetime, a role to play, something to accomplish, an experience to have, or lessons to learn—according to your conscious choice, your inner wisdom, or your calling by a higher power (or more than one of these). One or more things meant for you to fulfill during your lifetime as determined by your inner wisdom or a higher power.

Limiting Belief
A belief that has an effect you consider to be an undesired one, usually a belief that is untrue, irrational, or based on faulty evidence. Limiting beliefs can be outdated, irrational, or implanted, and they can limit you by impeding your personal progress or interfering with your personal growth process. Examples include "I'm not worthy of friendship" and "I can't keep a job."

Message Dream
A type of dream that contains information from an outside source, often with an indication that you or someone else needs to know something or that some action may be needed.

Nightmare
A frightening or unpleasant dream, often vivid. Nightmares can be triggered by your subconscious mind exploring your fears or reliving a past traumatic or scary event (even an imaginary one, such as from a movie); by physical, environmental, mental, or emotional stress, or compromising your responsibility for your own well-being (such as drinking alcohol, taking drugs, or eating too many sweets); or by something else.

Parallel
In dream interpretation, a correlation between a dream and your waking life in which your waking life is symbolized within your dream through subject, action, form, or some other way.

Personal Dream Dictionary
A dream dictionary you create for yourself that includes dream symbols and the meanings you tend to associate with those symbols.

Personal Symbolism

The meaning of a dream symbol that is particular to you, based on your experience, your perceptions, and the associations you've made with the symbol in the past.

Premonition Dream

A dream that predicts the future, in which case one or more events portrayed or symbolized in the dream happen in real life after the dream has taken place.

Pre-Sleep Intention

An intention you set just before you go to sleep, often with the aim of affecting the dream or sleep process in some desired way. Examples include "I intend to remember the dreams that are beneficial for me to remember" and "I intend to sleep well and awaken refreshed in the morning."

Projection

A mental dynamic wherein you subconsciously deny something about yourself—such as your own thought, feeling, characteristic, or tendency—and instead attribute it to someone else.

Psychoactive Substances

Substances that alter your consciousness, such as your perceptions, thoughts, feelings, mood, or general state of consciousness. They include common substances such as caffeine, tobacco, alcohol, as well as some prescription medications and illegal drugs.

Real Life

In this book, refers to your waking life—although technically the dream state is also part of your real life, in that it is one aspect of your personal experience.

Recurring Dream

A dream that occurs on more than one occasion, each time repeating the same or similar content.

Reframing

Consciously changing your internal frame of reference through which you view something (often a situation or event), thus changing your inner experience of it.

Rehearsal Dream

A type of dream that involves a run-through of an actual event you are expecting in the future.

Resonate

Something resonates with you when it "strikes a chord" within you—perhaps because you recognize the same thing within yourself, it has special meaning or significance for you, or it aligns with something within you (even if you don't know why)—often creating an inner awakening or a sense of inner knowing. When "like finds like," or when one idea or emotion meets its "kindred spirit" elsewhere. In dream interpretation, when you come across the true meaning of your dream, it may resonate with you such that you feel, "Aha! This is what my dream means." Based on the phenomenon in physics called resonance, which is when vibrations of a certain frequency from one active object (such as singer singing a note) cause another object with a predisposition for that same frequency (such as a piano string tuned to the singer's note) to respond with its own vibration. To the observer, it may seem like the singer reached in and touched on a similarity within the piano, which then responded in kind.

Self-Talk

Self-talk is the way you relate to yourself within your own mind, the inner conversation you have with yourself as you go about your daily life. Sometimes referred to as the "tapes you play in your head," meaning the things you tend to say to yourself.

Shred Letter

A technique that involves writing a letter that you never send, in order to express what you're thinking and feeling, and to give the aspects of yourself who need to be heard a chance to express themselves. After you write the letter, you shred it instead of sending it.

Story Arc

The narrative, line of progression, or sequence of events in a story.

Subconscious Mind

The part of your consciousness (your nonphysical self) of which you are not directly aware. Refers to all the aspects of your nonphysical being of which you aren't conscious.

Symbolism Dream

A type of dream prominently featuring one or more key symbols which you experience as having great significance.

Timeline Dream

A type of dream that portrays a sequence of events or other time-related aspects of your real life, beginning at a certain point in your life and ending at a later point.

Toxic Dream

A type of dream triggered by a toxic state during which you are physically, mentally, or emotionally overloaded during sleep. Often a very realistic, upsetting dream that simply indicates you were in a toxic state at the time of the dream, more than providing any useful meaning to interpret.

Transformative Dream

A type of dream during which actual transformation took place within you in the dream state—such as a judgment or self-defeating pattern being released, or some other shift into a healthier, more peaceful, or more integrated inner state. A dream during which inner healing took place.

Vision

An image seen inwardly (in your mind's eye), often during a dream or other altered state of consciousness. A thought, concept, or scenario you create within your mind or imagination. A situation you would like to see realized in the future.

What Did You Think of This Book?

Tell the author what you liked about this book and what you would like to see more of in future books. Nancy welcomes your comments, which you can share by posting them on the website of the book purveyor where you purchased this book, or by visiting TheCuriousDreamer.com and clicking the **Contact Us** link at the bottom of the page.

Keep Exploring

To learn more about dreams and access interpretation tools, explore these additional resources from the author of this book:

Free Bonus Download

For a limited time, get a free bonus download as a thank-you for purchasing this book: *Ten Dream Interpretation Pitfalls and How to Avoid Them.* You'll learn:

- Which dreams you shouldn't waste your time interpreting.
- Whether your dream is likely to come true.
- How long before your dream loses its value.
- How your morning routine can enhance dream recall.

When you sign up you'll be among the first to receive updates on new dream resources and books by Nancy Wagaman.

Bonus link:
http://eepurl.com/cFmp2j

TheCuriousDreamer.com

TheCuriousDreamer.com is a free online dream dictionary website with more than 15,000 dream symbols defined for personal growth by Nancy Wagaman. Try the convenient dream analyzer tool by typing a short description of your dream and then seeing a list of possible dream symbol meanings. Explore DIY dream resources, including meanings of common dreams, top dream symbol categories, and how to program your dreams using focused dreaming.

MyDreamVisions.com

MyDreamVisions.com is Nancy Wagaman's professional dream services website dedicated to understanding dreams and their meanings. Get a professional dream interpretation from Nancy, and read how her interpretations are helping dreamers. Take advantage of dream interpretation tools, sample dream interpretations, tips for improving dream intuition and recall, and educational dream quizzes.

Social Media

Discover more dream information and inspiration by following Nancy's social media accounts:

Twitter: @CuriousDreamers
Facebook: facebook.com/thecuriousdreamer
Pinterest: pinterest.com/dreammeanings
Instagram: @TheCuriousDreamerOfficial

Submit a Dream for Interpretation

You can submit a dream to be interpreted by Nancy Wagaman by visiting her professional dream services site, MyDreamVisions.com, and clicking **Buy an Interpretation.** Type in your dream information, and Nancy will email you a custom dream interpretation exploring dream meaning. Choose the In-Depth Dream Interpretation and Nancy will also include an analysis of dream messages, subconscious thoughts and feelings, any dream indicators about life direction, and any follow-up actions that may be appropriate, such as steps to resolve issues that came up in the dream.

Clients tend to rate Nancy's dream interpretation services very highly and report that they're extremely satisfied after receiving their interpretation. Feedback has been overwhelmingly positive, including comments such as:

Wow. I hardly know what to say. Your analysis was incredible!

Your knowledge and interpretations are very inspiring!!

Incredibly insightful in-depth interpretation.

Bravo, Ms. Wagaman!...Thank you for having this service.

WOW!!!!!! All I can say is WOW!!!!!

I have been working with someone...but your work goes to another level.

Great analysis! Right on target!

Thank you so very much...my mind can rest now.

Such an in-depth and fascinating look at my dream.

About The Author

Nancy Wagaman is a human technologies innovator specializing in personal growth and transformation. Her practical techniques enable people to transform self-limitations and improve their lives. Rooted in science and intuition, Nancy's transformative techniques are practical and easy to use. Nancy began developing human technologies during her early career at Bell Laboratories, and she has also consulted and conducted research for corporate, university, and private clients. Her work has been featured in magazines, radio, and television. Nancy holds advanced degrees in applied psychology and communications, and bachelor's degrees in psychology and biology. She is the creator of *The Curious Dreamer's Dream Dictionary* (TheCuriousDreamer.com) and has written extensively on applied psychology, intuition, and other personal growth topics.

Index